GW00360056

Majes

SPIRITUAL GUIDANCE THROUGH THE MENOPAUSAL GATEWAY

Melanie Santorini

*From bad-ass vicar to bare-breasted priestess in seven years
via a horse, a motorhome and a boat*

BALBOA.
PRESS
A DIVISION OF HAY HOUSE

Balboa Press books may be ordered through booksellers or by contacting:

Balboa Press
A Division of Hay House
1663 Liberty Drive
Bloomington, IN 47403
www.balboapress.co.uk
1 (877) 407-4847

Print information available on the last page.

ISBN: 978-1-9822-8049-9 (sc)
ISBN: 978-1-9822-8051-2 (hc)
ISBN: 978-1-9822-8050-5 (e)

Balboa Press rev. date: 02/15/2019

Contents

Preface

Going through the menopausal 'Change of Life' was like riding on a rollercoaster – there were moments of intense pleasure and moments of sheer terror. Writing this book was for the most part in the pleasurable category; putting it out there in the world has definitely been in the terrifying category. Self-doubt still reigns supreme inside me and it isn't going to be allowed to have the last word.

I wanted to write something confident without being arrogant; proud of my achievements without being boastful; heartfelt without being sentimental; hopeful without being self-satisfied; positive without being smug; and impassioned without being preachy. I'm not sure I've managed it. It's been like trying to dance on a high-wire and – you've guessed it – at times I've fallen off.

The purpose in writing this book, however, isn't about whether or not I succeed in getting the balance right on that particular high-wire. It's about daring to get my voice out there as a mid-life woman, in spite of the self-doubt and the fear. I care too much about the global mess we're in to stay silent and to stay safe. My hope is that this story will help you to step out onto whatever particular high-wire confronts you and dare to fall. Then, rise up and share your voice too.

Introduction

The story of my menopausal journey begins at the beginning of the end – as it does for so many of us - the end of my first marriage and the end of my life as a vicar in the Church of England. I didn't recognise it for what it was at the time – few of us do. That is part of the reason for writing this book: so that more of us will understand what is happening – what is really happening and why. The more we understand menopause, the more we can anticipate its onset with enthusiasm and negotiate its challenges with confidence. The truth of menopause is not what we've been led to believe. It is far more exciting, empowering and downright incredible than we've been told.

It is, or can be, the beginning of the most powerful and effective phase in a woman's life. When you're in it, it rarely feels or looks like that. Yet underneath the losses - deeper than the negative cultural messages, wilder than your wildest imaginings - something profound and mysterious is taking place. And it's taking place within every cell and fibre of your physical, emotional and spiritual being. Take your seat and buckle up, for we are in for a roller-coaster ride. Be warned, this ride is rightly called 'The Change of Life'. The woman who gets off this roller-coaster, legs wobbling, disoriented and slightly nauseous, will not be the same woman. Menopause will have changed her forever.

This is certainly true for me. I look back at the various Melanies who existed at different stages in my life: the convent schoolgirl; the young Oxford academic; the wife; the mother of two sons and two daughters; the vicar and Church of England priest; the banker; the mental-health worker; the women's retreat facilitator - and I know that all those former Melanies are still here with me. And yet, the deeper truth is that I am no longer she. I am freer, wilder, more passionate and creative, less restrained and less afraid than she was. I am more in love with the life of this planet, and more at peace with myself, than ever before.

When I look in the mirror at the Melanie I am now – the woman in her mid-fifties who has just become a grandmother and is reluctantly embracing her greying hair – most of the time these days, I'm content with what I see. I like the woman who is vibrantly in love with her husband. I'm comfortable in the company of the woman who spent a year so-called 'freedom-camping' across Scotland in a motorhome. We wild-camped, parking up each night on roadside lay-bys, quiet farm or forestry tracks. It was a gypsy-style adventure. Most of the time we kept ourselves as far away as possible from the hustle and bustle of busy, modern life. Well, I want to take my hat off to her. I am proud of her – that she made it this far, firstly. And, secondly, that she made it this far with her sense of humour still intact, and her heart still aching with love for so much and for so many. This is her story: the story of the seven years of my menopausal journey.

The story begins with me leaving behind my life as a vicar and fleeing to a new life in Wales. It follows me as I file for divorce and struggle to pay the mortgage. It unfolds as I find a new life-purpose and then as I fall in love with a quiet Welshman. The story closes as I prepare to move into a new home in Scotland. What an utterly unexpected adventure began to unfold the day I left England and left the church. It took me across stunning Celtic landscapes, in which wild-swimming and horse-riding and mountain-walking turned out to be a twenty-first century version of an ancient Celtic-style initiation. I needed to learn how to become a shape-shifter of sorts: I morphed from bad-ass vicar to bare-breasted priestess to feisty Autumn Queen. My menopausal years were the holding space for a profound transformation. It was like being thrown into a magical cauldron and stirred around vigorously until something tasty and sustaining was properly cooked – the new me.

This is a story of loss and of seeming-failure; of heartbreak and breakdown; of learning how to fish for salmon and of re-learning how to ride horses; of leaving much behind and of much letting go; of falling in love and of finding my G-spot; of seeking sisterhood and discovering inner sovereignty. The Change of Life proved to be exactly that – a complete transformation. When my periods began to become irregular it was the sign – the sign that, unbeknownst to me, I was embarking on a Quest. The Holy Grail I sought (and which was seeking me) was me – a happier, healthier, wilder and freer me.

I'm through 'the Change'. I love that it's commonly called that. It makes me think of a woman who howls with the wolves. The traditional marker that 'the Change' is complete is the thirteenth full moon after your last bleed. I passed through that portal in November 2017 – coincidentally (or not) it was the same month I became a grandmother. Finally, I can look back – back across the dry bones and debris of those seven years and reflect upon what happened. This book is part of that reflection and it is my gift to you.

Wherever you are on your menopausal journey, this book is for you. You might be still regularly menstruating, or in so-called perimenopause. Maybe, like me, you're postmenopausal. Or perhaps you're one of the millions of women who've had a sudden menopause as a result of an hysterectomy. You'll probably have experienced a very different journey from mine. But, whoever you are, I hope you'll find in these pages something to inspire and support you to re-frame menopause in a more positive light. My story is offered in the hope that it'll encourage you to embrace who you truly are both more fully and more kindly. I hope it'll inspire you to bring forth your own mid-life gifts with confidence and courage in service to a world that desperately needs women – all women - to stand up and make positive global change happen.

I call the journey of menopause 'entering the Majesteria'. I've deliberately capitalised the word Majesteria because – to me – it's a proper noun. It's a quality, like courage or steadfastness or integrity, for sure. But it's also a *place* (like Scotland) that you come to inhabit. And, perhaps most importantly, it's a process. It's a process that calls us to let go of the guilt, the shame and the fear which keep us bound to a small, edited version of ourselves. What the world needs now are BIG, brave and bold women – this is our true beauty. This book is my call to you to become the bravest, biggest version of yourself – all you dreamed you could be. Your gateway into this new you is menopause. I am grateful to have lived this long and to have lived this life so abundantly with so many people and places to love. My hope is that in reading my menopausal story you will be reminded of the riches, the blessings and the achievements of your own herstory.

Before I dive in further, however, I'd like to explain why I call menopause entering the Majesteria. Why write an entire book about the process of entering into something? Well, because that is precisely what menopause is: a *process* of entering into a new phase of life. The menopausal years are the initiatory years for all that follows. They are hugely important, incredibly precious and rarely talked about. They are the subject of this book for those reasons. We often hear about the importance of the formative years 0-7 in laying down the foundations for a happy, healthy first-half of life. We rarely hear about the importance of the 7-10 years of menopause in laying down the foundations for a woman's happy, healthy second-half of life. This book seeks to redress that silence.

The menopausal years are a pause in our life cycle. We are neither one thing nor the other. Most of us aren't even sure where we are at any given point: am I menopausal, premenopausal, perimenopausal or postmenopausal? And what do all those terms mean anyway? We stop bleeding. Then we start again. Then we stop. Then we start. It's all very confusing. On top of this, we're led to believe that being menopausal is somehow a cause for shame. So most of us keep quiet about it, and treat it like a miserable secret which we seek to hide even from our lover or life-partner. I couldn't disagree with this attitude more. The years when our periods start becoming irregular and we experience some or none of the effects that we're led to expect – this is the moment not to panic, but to pause. The *pause* is what menopause is all about. The pause is sacred space – neither this nor that – the pause invites you to look closer, dig deeper and learn how to make the choices that will serve you best for the rest of your life.

The menopausal years offer the opportunity to sift through things. They are the chance to sift through carefully and conscientiously to see whether there's something (or someone) you no longer need in your life and which now must be left behind. We cannot take it all with us – it's simply too heavy. I'll repeat that, even at the risk of sounding preachy, because I know how hard this is for women to hear. We cannot take it all with us – it's simply too heavy for older bones to carry. Some of what you've carried in your bundle thus far needs to be let go of and left behind. So, look around you and *choose*. Don't wait, like I did, until it's taken from you. That might sound harsh but it's the only way. It's the only way, if you're to be free to travel into a future of your own creating – to become the woman you really want to be: happy, vibrant, and fulfilled. Menopause is the time, writ large, to shift some baggage. It's an invitation to sift through the many pieces of your life, like sifting through a basket of patchwork materials to decide which to keep and which to let go.

Sometimes this experience of sifting is not so kind. It feels more that we're being sifted than that we're doing the sifting. It can arrive with the severity of something precious being severed: job loss, marriage ending, mental breakdown, betrayal, or medical diagnosis. However fierce the face she wears, menopause is there to show us the way towards a greater freedom. In menopause we are squeezed and pushed through a birth canal as strong and unrelenting as that which gives birth to a newborn baby. Only, this time, what is being birthed is a new you. The experience is painful, messy and wonderful beyond belief.

I created the word 'Majesteria'. I created it because I dislike the term postmenopausal, the term which is most often used to describe the status of women in the years following the cessation of menses. Are we simply postmenopausal from the ending of our periods until the day we die? That seems to me to be a very limiting way to look at the decades that may yet unfold. Menopause is a threshold – a rite of passage, an initiation. One which lasts for many of us between five and ten years. It comes to an end nevertheless.

Once we've crossed the threshold, completed the rite of passage, and fulfilled the demands of the initiation, a new phase of life opens up. I like the old descriptor: She Who Holds Her Blood (i.e. her power) Within Herself. But I wanted an expression to capture the *process* of transformation required to become her. Nowhere could I find a satisfactory name for this life-changing journey, this radical process of becoming someone new in the world. I wanted a word that would express my understanding that the cessation of menses marks a new beginning, potent, radical and hard won. I wanted a word which would subvert the notion that after bleeding ceases, women simply fade away. I wanted to replace it with the encouragement to become *more* visible and substantial. I wanted an expression that was strong, positive and uplifting; and that would counter the relentless negative messages surrounding menopause: hot flushes, vaginal dryness, and weight-gain; the loss of libido, mental battiness, and so-called senior moments.

What the media portrayed was not what I was experiencing. As the menopausal years unfolded I felt strong, sexy and sassy. I was beginning to stand in the world braver than ever before, and I was buzzing with fresh purpose. I wanted a word that could express my deepening realisation that menopause is a creative process as profound, life-changing, bloody and worthy of celebration, as is child birth. Though I looked, I found no adequate word or phrase to describe either what I'd experienced during menopause, or what I felt like as I completed it. Nothing was expansive enough. Nothing was inspiring enough. Nothing thrummed with the vibrancy of the energy that now coursed through me. So, I created one. I began calling the years following menopause, 'the Majesteria years', and I began calling the experience of menopause, the entire seven years of it (for me) – 'entering the Majesteria'. I began calling postmenopausal women 'majesterial women'. Whenever I did, women loved it.

Let's take a moment to explore the different phases of a woman's life arc so we can place menopause accurately within it. In some traditions women are described as having three phases of life: Maiden, Mother (aka Matrona or Creatress), and Crone. This has often been linked to the three phases of the moon: waxing, waning, and full. It's also been linked to the ancient Triple Goddess who was worshipped in many places B.C.E. (Before the Common Era). Nowadays, however, many women are recognising an additional phase; a third phase that exists after the second phase of Mother/Matrona, and before the final phase of Crone. This new awareness more accurately reflects the four lunar phases: the waxing, full, waning and dark moon; as well as the four phases to the solar cycle: spring, summer, autumn, winter.

The rich, juicy, and productive autumn phase of a woman's life isn't to be confused with her winter phase – which has its own gifts. Women told me: "I've stopped menstruating but I don't feel old. So, who am I?". This third, autumn phase in a woman's life-cycle is, for the most part, simply ignored by the dominant culture and the media. It's unnamed, undocumented and, quite definitely, uncelebrated. Yet this is the phase of life in which I, and millions of mid-life women around the globe, now find ourselves. No wonder we struggle to find our feet, to raise our heads and to speak out. In story and song, in fashion and advertising we are at worst derided and at best ignored. That's not the whole story, of course, and it's beginning to change. But it's still the predominant one.

So, what to call it? How should we name this ripe autumn phase when our periods have ceased, our hair (left to itself) begins to turn grey, and our tastes and interests change? In spite of the availability and popularity of implants, uplifts and botox treatments, our maiden-springtime years are way behind us. Our mothering-summertime years, during which we took care of young children or households or careers (or all three) are, for the most part, done. Children are grown up; careers are established or about to be launched afresh. And, for many of us, our first marriages are over. Despite the appearance of wrinkles, ripples and softening breasts, we are not yet old and in our wintertime. Elders, yes, we're that, for sure. But we're elders who know that we haven't yet earned the right to call ourselves Crones. So, who are we if we're no longer Maiden, no longer Mother (though many get stuck here) and not yet Crone? I've seen us called Baby Crones, but that doesn't do it for me. It fails to affirm the validity and importance of the fully grown-up phase of life I am in right now. Increasingly, women are naming this mid-life, postmenopausal autumn phase, as that of the high priestess or the Autumn Queen. Now, that is more like it.

When we're in menopause we're in transitional, liminal space. It's neither one thing nor the other. It's a threshold from an outworn and outdated phase of life into a new phase – admittedly a threshold that can last years. Transitions are often tricky, uncomfortable places to be. Transitions lasting several years are especially difficult to negotiate well. Messages, fired at us from all directions in British and U.S. culture, teach us that to be comfortable is our right. Menopause, by contrast, seeks to teach us to stay with discomfort and to dig deep. The temptation can be to retreat back into the familiar Mother/Matrona phase, especially if the mothering role is strong in us (as it was for me). Disoriented and feeling slightly lost, we're easy targets for the lure of trying to retreat even further back, into the youthful Maiden-springtime phase. A lure offered in the seductive appeal of facial botox treatments and breast implants.

Those of us who are literal mothers will always feel the tidal pull of our youngsters - that's a given. In menopause, however, we learn to renegotiate that pull. Something new is calling to us - something unknown and, for most of us, unimagined. It is the call of the future you – the YOU whom you suspect you have it inside you to be. This is the woman who has learned how to be at peace with herself (the good, the bad and the ugly), and who has thereby earned her right to sit in the Elderwomen's circle. There are very few spiritual guides for this initiatory process through menopause. *Majesteria* is my offering into the circle.

So, what is menopause in a nutshell? Well, it's a rite of passage from one phase of life into another. This rite of passage, as my story attests, usually takes five to ten years to complete. Much as we'd like to rush it - and who doesn't want to be a high priestess or an Autumn Queen? - menopause takes as long as it takes. And, like all the truest initiations, I predict that you'll probably want it over well before it's done and finished with you. For those of you who've undergone an earlier than usual menopause, or if you've experienced a sudden menopause caused by an hysterectomy, the message of *Majesteria* still applies. The process of reflection, for all of us, is both during the events which mark 'the Change', and in looking back over what happened. In whatever way menopause occurs on a physical level, I believe that the energetic of the process remains the same.

If you allow menopause to work her magic in you – which I hope my story will help you to do – and if you choose to embrace this new phase of life that is calling to you, my suspicion is that you, like me, will step across the threshold as the sovereign Autumn Queen. You'll be a self-authenticating, self-authorising, self-willed WILD woman. You'll be a woman in her full power – a woman who no longer needs to look to an external authority for validation or permission. You'll have entered your Majesteria years. You'll know when it happens - and I can't wait to meet you there.

Just a quick word, before we go too much further, about my use of the terms 'feminine' and 'masculine'. I use them as a short-hand. For me these terms signify different and complementary states of being. They are synonymous with every binary duality imaginable - yin/yang, dark/light, inner/outer, below/above, soft/hard, negative/positive, passive/active, death/life, horizontal/vertical – to name but a few. Both 'feminine' and 'masculine' are therefore qualities or aspects which are present in every human being. I believe that at a soul-level we each hold these polarities in balance, and the balance shifts and changes throughout our lives. A traditional (and easily stereotypical and thereby potentially limiting) view is to link all 'yin' qualities with females, and all 'yang' qualities with males. I'm very aware of the risks of doing that. I respect those who choose no longer to use gendered terms. However, I find them useful and, as I say, a quick and easy short-hand. I hope that my usage isn't a stumbling block for you in hearing the subtler understandings of selfhood which I'm seeking to convey.

When we become women who are self-authoring and self-authorising, claiming and creating our lives from deep within ourselves – which is my definition of wild - we then have gifts to share with the younger women around us. You don't need me to tell you that young women today face enormous pressure from every direction imaginable. As women entering our Majesteria years - if we've done the soul-work - we have wisdom to share. A wise, wild older woman can offer a holding space while a younger woman negotiates, in her own way and in her own style, issues around the menstrual cycle, pregnancy and childbirth, infertility, termination, or miscarriage – to name but a few of the possible events that can derive simply from having a womb.

One of the most surprising and delightful discoveries for me during the years of menopause was the increase in my sexual pleasure. It wasn't until my late forties that my G-spot woke up. I fell in love and, as many older women entering second marriages and life-partnerships find, my libido re-ignited. Mid-life women always grin from ear to ear when I say that. Younger women look slightly surprised and then grin too. It's got to be a relief to hear that it's not all downhill and dryness after we turn forty or fifty or sixty.

That having been said, when you step into your power as an Autumn Queen, you need a very particular kind of strength and presence in your lover. You need someone who's also standing in their sovereign power. If you're heterosexual, you might like to think of him as King Stag to your Autumn Queen. Our culture produces a lot of princelings (and, admittedly, some very cute Crown Princes and young bucks), but very few fully-grown kings. As for a King Stag, I suspect that, sadly, he's a pretty rare breed these days. For the heterosexual menopausal woman who is stepping into her power, no-one less than a king will do. Not surprisingly, many mid-life women consequently feel frustrated and dissatisfied with their sexual partners and appear to 'go off' sex. Menopausal women tell me that rather than pretend pleasure or endure unsatisfactory sex, as they sometimes did in their younger years, they now simply say "no". The good news is that when you claim your birthright to become a sassy, sexy Autumn Queen, you challenge and entice your lover into his or her full sexual glory too.

However, before we go too far into the exciting world of mid-life sexuality, let me cool things down a little, and take a moment to explain my new word 'Majesteria' in detail. Words matter. Moreover, the words we use to describe ourselves matter hugely. Before I was a vicar I was a budding academic. I completed my doctoral thesis in English Literature at the University of Oxford, with Latin as my subsidiary subject. Later, I studied New Testament Greek at Theological College. It's not surprising therefore that there are Latin and Greek roots to my newly created word. In Latin, *magister* means teacher, in the sense of someone with authority and knowledge. In English we derive the word 'magistrate' from it. The word 'Majesteria', therefore, includes the idea that women in our mid-life years hold much-needed knowledge and that we have something important to teach the world. We have wisdom to share – all of us – whatever our life circumstances.

I also wanted an echo of the energy of 'hysteria' to be included in my newly created word. The word 'hysteria' stems from the Greek word for the uterus or womb, *hystera*. I wanted to redeem and radicalise its long-held negative associations. For centuries 'hysteria' was defined medically as madness of the womb. As recently as the 1950s, it was used to diagnose women as suffering from a variety of so-called mental disorders. These ranged from 'nervous disorders', to promiscuity, to giving birth to an illegitimate child, to disobedience to a husband or a father, and to general wilfulness. The cure for lack of submission or obedience in so-called 'difficult' patients was commonly a clitoredectomy. This is where a woman's clitoris is surgically removed. Perhaps the horror of the procedure – which struck at a woman's intimate, joyous, pleasurable sense of herself, cured the 'disobedience'. I imagine it did. As a former mental-health worker, let alone as a woman, this knowledge appals me. Reading about the uses to which the word 'hysteria' has been put makes my skin crawl and my stomach churn. I have a similar physical response when reading the accounts of the sixteenth- and seventeenth-century witch trials. It's pretty clear to me where real madness lies.

Part of the initiatory process of menopause is that it teaches women about our anger. It's not an easy lesson. Most of us are afraid of our anger. Many of us are wary of it. We feel that if we unleash it, it might change us – and not for the better. But be reassured - I've never met a woman who hopes that she'll go through the menopausal gateway and come out the other side as a destructive harpy. We all want to be transformed into better, kinder, wiser people. Menopause offers this transformation, but, interestingly, it's often through the doorway of our anger that we get there. In my experience, when we take a look at our anger as women – when we take a long, honest look at it - the size and depth of it absolutely terrifies us. Most men are afraid of our anger too. They're afraid because they sense we are powerful. And we are afraid for the very same reason. Potentially, we can all be ball-breakers, emasculating men by verbally tearing to shreds their self-esteem. I know. I've done it. Again, this isn't where most women want to end up in the long term.

Finding safe places and safe ways to work with our rage - what I've come to call 'wrathing' - can be profoundly healing. I was initially surprised to hear from the women, with whom I've done wrathing work that their primary relationships calmed. They became kinder, more pleasant to be around, more loving – not less - as a result of allowing their anger full flow. After a while though, it made total sense. Suppressed anger doesn't serve us, and it doesn't serve our beloveds. In fact, it can make us ill, or depressed, or both. We hold our suppressed and repressed anger in so many places of the body. The commonest, I've found, in the women with whom I've worked, is in the womb - *hystera*. Feeling, releasing, and creatively riding our rage is, I believe, an essential element in menopause. It is part of the profound healing that is her gift. So I wanted an echo of 'hysteria' to sound within the word Majesteria. I hope you can hear it.

I love the naming of the autumn phase of a woman's life as her Autumn Queen or high priestess phase. I deliberately spelt the word to include the notion of 'majesty'. This is about women standing in our power. It's about us being sovereign over our own lives and bodies. It's, perhaps especially, about us ruling our inner realms, i.e. what we think and feel and believe about ourselves. This is not about power over – our world has seen enough of that sort of power. I also wanted within the word a resonance with 'mage' and magic. I wanted there to be a hint of that wild mysterious energy which erupts within a woman (of any age) when she's standing her ground and standing in her power. Then she's a force to be reckoned with.

The soul-work which I've been privileged to share in with women, during the thirty-five years of my professional life, has shown me again and again that when a woman "works her own shit" (as one woman so beautifully expressed it), she transforms not only her own life but also the lives of those around her. We women are immeasurably influential through the myriads of connections we make – in our homes, in our communities, in our gardens, in our workplaces. We are powerful. When we wake up to that, and take responsibility for it, we step into the world as game-changers. We helped make the mess we're in – every last one of us – so, as far as I can tell, we each have a responsibility to help clear it up. An integral element in taking responsibility for the mess the world is in, is to "work our own shit" or, in my language, to do our own soul-work.

I have a red spiral tattooed inside my right ankle. It was my fortieth birthday gift to myself. The design is inspired by a First

Nations Native American carving I saw on a massive redwood tree hidden deep in a forest on Vancouver Island in British Columbia, Canada. I lived there in my twenties. It changed me. The carving on the tree showed the medicine path – the soul's path - as a spiral. It's an ancient motif echoed across the world in many spiritual traditions. My tattoo reminds me that our life paths and our spiritual paths are not linear, they are circular. In spite of our youthful resistance to the idea, by mid-life we know that we need to go over the same ground many, many times. Like menopause, wisdom grows in us and changes us at her own pace.

If you're anything like me, well-organised and goal-oriented with a strong 'masculine' side, on occasion you'll wish things could go a bit faster and in a somewhat tidier fashion. But the truth is, menopause, like spiritual growth, is fundamentally a 'feminine' process – most of what it involves takes place in a dark, womb-like space, in the silence beyond words and in the depths well below conscious knowing. We grow like the rings of a tree, from the inside outwards.

Reflecting upon the experience of my own menopausal years – the complexity, the richness, as well as the cost – meant I needed a term that had depth and resonance on many levels. I hope that the term 'Majesteria' provides that. Originally the term was 'magisterium', i.e. the masculine form. I liked the ring of it: 'entering the Magisterium' sounded like something exciting and fantastical from a Harry Potter story. It took some work to loosen my own cultural conditioning (where it's always the masculine form in Latin and Greek which are learned first). I had to dig deeper until I found a term that truly said all I wanted it to say. When I read Philip Pullman's *His Dark Materials* novels, and discovered his use of the term 'the Magisterium' to describe an oppressive church authority, I had to smile. It was perfect. My new word points precisely to the equal and opposite force, which Pullman's fictional Magisterium would undoubtedly seek to destroy.

Someone in their Majesteria years is recognisable by the way in which their life acts as a counter-balance or a counter-flow to oppressive cultural norms. The majesterial women (and men) whom I'm privileged to know, exert a subtle but insistently powerful and subversive influence. They offer a low-key alternative to the almost-irresistible magnetic attraction of male-dominated modes of 'authority' (of which the church is but one example). These majesterials make me think of rivers influencing and shaping rock. Water is a very particular kind of power. I think of the influence of wild, flowing water as an expression of authority that is very distinctive. When I see it in people, I admire it. However, it's a form of authority that is, as yet, still unfamiliar to most and undervalued by most. Majesterial women evidence it in many, many ways. Some are community and grass-roots activists, quiet revolutionaries, artists or writers; or some, like me, are somewhat-embarrassed-to-find-myself-here visionaries. Universally, however, we seek a more just and equitable future for our planet.

And yes, the rollercoaster ride nicknamed 'the Change' will definitely have some moments of excitement. It can certainly be fantastic. Finding your sexy soul-mate in your late forties is difficult to beat. But it's not about a fantasy – Hollywood-style or otherwise. *Majesteria* is about reality – the nitty-gritty reality of real life – my life and yours.

Thank you for reading this long preamble. We're now almost ready to begin. A caveat, however, before we start the story proper … I've functioned as a priest, and more recently as a priestess, for over thirty years. I've officiated at countless ceremonies, rites of passage and life transitions both within and beyond the Christian church. These days I no longer choose to label myself as a Christian, both because the label feels excluding and limiting, and also because I no longer feel connected to the institutional church. I do, however, still dance with, and deeply value, elements within the Christian spiritual lineage. I tell several stories derived from that lineage within this book. I still love those stories and believe they hold much wisdom for us.

I'm no longer officially associated with the church though I remain (at the time of writing) a Clerk in Holy Orders – which is the legal status of a Church of England priest. To relinquish this legal status requires a lengthy and expensive process delineated in English Law by The Clerical Disabilities Act of 1870. I'm as yet unsure whether or not I have the wherewithal to choose to step into that particular process, which will require me to re-engage with the church at an institutional level. At the moment I have no wish to do so.

As you see, the separate threads of our lives weave together and, often as not, refuse to be tidily untangled. Though I stand upon very different ground these days from the one I stood upon as a Church of England vicar, I've no wish to dishonour or to disparage the many disparate elements which have gone into creating the warp and weft of my life. This book is, however, an honest book. It takes a forthright and strong stance on many issues – including the church. I recognise that some of what I say may offend or upset. My intention, always, is not to do harm but to help us to heal. I know, however, that the process of healing sometimes hurts. Such is the menopausal way.

I will finish by saying that this book is an unreservedly positive book. I'm happier and healthier now than I've ever been – and this has been consistent enough over enough years for me to feel that this is now my 'normal', default state. Being around an unreservedly positive person, if you're going through life-challenges and trials of your own, can be inspiring and encouraging, or it can be draining and downright irritating. I know the latter because friends have told me so. I very much hope that my happiness hasn't made me smug, self-righteous or arrogant, but I suspect that on occasion it may have. So, whilst I will not apologise for my happiness – I do apologise if my exuberance sometimes feels a little insensitive or bruising. I don't intend for that to be the case. The deepest, best part of me is simply overflowing with gratitude and joy that I've landed where I am now. What you'll find in these pages is Melanie – the good, the bad and the ugly – a woman of contradictions and flaws, with a big heart and on fire with purpose. I like her and I'm proud of her. I very, very much hope that you'll enjoy travelling with her through her menopausal years. Welcome to *Majesteria*.

PART I

Chapter One

IN MY END IS MY BEGINNING

I sat in the bishop's office, an empty box of tissues on my lap as tears ran down my face. I blew my nose noisily into the soggy bundle in my fist, staring him down and trying to catch my breath. I trembled from head to toe as my heart thumped in my chest. I was furious. What I had anticipated as a supportive chat about my reference for the new job I'd been offered in another diocese had, unexpectedly, turned into a rant about my recent supposedly unacceptable behaviour.

"Are you accusing me of professional misconduct?" I asked. "Is this a disciplinary? If so, I should've been warned and I wouldn't be sitting here without a Union rep at my side."

"No, no. It's nothing like that, Melanie. You're one of the best priests we have and I've nothing but praise for your work. It's just that I'm confused. You don't seem to know what you want. One minute you're flying off to Los Angeles to take up a post there, and the next you're applying for jobs in the Diocese of Oxford. I thought you wanted me to find you a suitable post here?"

I reminded him that it was through no fault of my own that the job offer in Los Angeles had been withdrawn. I had subsequently begun looking for a post in the Diocese of Oxford because I wanted to be closer to my parents, but I was also open to the possibility of continuing my ministry within the current diocese. I didn't deny that there was more than a hint of panic in the way I was going about it. But, after all I'd been through in the past year, what did he expect? The license for my current post, which had been granted a second term of seven years, was about to run out. A third term wouldn't be good for me or for the parish. It needed new blood, and I needed out. The man who sat in front of me was the gatekeeper. Without his support, I could go nowhere. I knew it and he knew it.

"Speaking as your 'Father in God'," he continued, "you should have told me that you're in difficulty with your marriage. It was embarrassing to find out about it from a brother bishop."

Ah, there was the rub.

"In the circumstances," he concluded, "I don't feel able to release you to take up your new post."

This was the red rag I needed to vent my pent-up rage. Words poured out.

"I cannot believe you just called yourself my 'Father in God'," I exploded. "How long have we known each other? Apart from the fact that I'm a feminist theologian – a fact about me which I thought you respected - I'm about the same age as you, *and* as qualified, if not more so. The only reason you are sitting there with the power to make or break my career is that you have a dick and I don't."

The bishop raised his eyebrows; perhaps surprised into silence by my rudeness. So, I continued.

"It's one of the many injustices still perpetrated by the church, that women cannot be ordained into its ruling body – the House of Bishops. I'm sick of the pretence that women are regarded as equals in the church. We are not."

He went to make a comment, but I kept on going.

"Moreover, I've been arguing for some kind of a clear boundary around the role of a bishop for years. As it stands, you think you've a right to know about my personal problems. Yet at the same time, it's you who has the power to veto my job prospects. The role of confidential pastor and employment boss are mutually exclusive. You know all this just as well as I do."

By now, I was fully in my stride.

"And, how dare you ask me about the intimate details of my marriage when I've come to you for a job reference. I'm a professional woman and I expect to be treated as such. I've served the church faithfully for over twenty years – twenty bloody years. It's not always been easy. I've struggled to be as creative and loving as I could be in an institution which – to be blunt – I find patriarchal, misogynistic, homophobic, and profoundly disempowering of most people. We behave exactly opposite to what we're called to proclaim. In fact, most days when I listen to the news about the church on BBC radio, I'm ashamed to call myself a Christian!"

At this, he looked stunned and opened his mouth once again to speak. But there was no silencing me – the words that I'd held back, on so many occasions, for so many years, wanted to be heard.

"I've thought about leaving the church on and off for years – ask your predecessor - but I hung on because I thought there was something here, something so profound, so mysterious, and so beautiful, I wouldn't be able to find it anywhere else. I've clung on through thick-and-thin. Now, when I'm going through a rough patch and I need your support, you betray me."

"Melanie, I hardly see this as a betrayal."

5

But I did. I got to my feet.

"I am done with it. This conversation is over," I announced as I headed for the door, clutching the empty box and pile of tissues. Just before exiting, I turned back to face him.

"You shouldn't have spoken to me like this," I said. "It was unprofessional and unfair."

I walked out past the bishop's startled P.A., a woman whom I'd known for ten years and who, having clearly heard our upraised angry voices, stood mouth agape. I handed her the pile of soggy tissues.

"Goodbye," I said.

And I meant it. I never went back.

I got into my car, drove a couple of hundred yards down the road into a small cul-de-sac, pulled up, put my head in my hands, and broke down. And when I say broke down, I mean really broke – hook, line and sinker. I sobbed as if my heart was shattered. You see, for all my difficulties with the church, the central core of my being was woven from the fact that I loved God. I had loved God since I was eight years old, and it was over. The house of cards which was my life in the church - the very public expression of my love of God - had unexpectedly and suddenly come crashing down. I stood now in a house of dust and ashes. There was no going back and I knew it.

Once I could breathe properly, I phoned a couple of friends who calmed me sufficiently so that I was safe to drive the ninety miles to our holiday cottage in west Wales. I remained there. I took sick leave and was eventually diagnosed with Situational PTSD (Post Traumatic Stress Disorder or Syndrome). It would be almost two years before I recovered sufficiently to hold down even a part-time job as straightforward as a cashier in a bank. It was four years before I was able to enter a church without having a panic attack. It was five years before I was able to return to my former parish, for the briefest of visits, in order to attend the funeral of our youngest son's much-loved godfather.

In fairness to the bishop, he did regret our conversation. It was uncharacteristic of him and he later wrote to me and apologised for it. It would, moreover, be wrong to lay my breakdown and the PTSD at his feet. The conversation with him was body blow number five. It was the proverbial straw which broke the camel's back – and this camel had been carrying an overly heavy load for a good long while. In the year running up to that fateful conversation, I'd suffered a series of blows. The fiasco surrounding the job offer in the diocese of Los Angeles was one of them. Let me tell you about the 'series of unfortunate events' that led me to drop *everything* and 'flee for my life' to a tiny village in rural Wales.

After a ten-day all expenses paid trip to L.A. for me, my husband and our four children, I'd been offered a plum job setting up a new Godly Play church in Pasadena. Godly Play is a Christian practise based upon the teachings of Jerome Berryman. It offers to children (and increasingly to adults) an imaginative, open-response engagement with Scripture. I was deeply immersed in the practise of Godly Play, and I was passionate about it. I was an international trainer for Godly Play U.K. and had initiated a Godly Play project in the church where I was the vicar. We had converted a side-chapel into a Godly Play classroom which was used by neighbourhood schools and hundreds of children. At the time of writing, the project still thrives ten years on.

Back to my story, though. On returning from L.A., I tendered my resignation. I prepared my final service at the church where I'd been vicar for thirteen years. I then packed up the contents of our large Edwardian Vicarage ready for shipping. I had our two excited youngest children measured up for their uniforms at the private school they'd be attending in California. I then waited for the visas to come through. They didn't. Out of the blue, on the morning of my forty-fifth birthday, I opened a letter from the bishop of Los Angeles stating that the job offer now needed to be withdrawn as the funding for the post was no longer available. I was stunned and hugely disappointed. As were my children. Body blow number one.

Fortunately, my resignation hadn't yet been processed and I was able to stay on in my current post. The news that I was staying as their vicar was welcomed with typical generosity and warmth by the majority of the congregation in our church family. Not by everyone though. Not by the couple of people in the church who hated me. Or, at least, they hated what I represented as a woman-priest, or what they thought they saw in me. On several occasions during that final year I was subjected to extreme verbal abuse. There were only a couple of perpetrators but one of them was relentless. She had hated me from the moment I'd arrived in the parish thirteen years before. After I failed to land the L.A. post, her vitriol became severe. In order to protect me from being shouted at during church services, she was required by the bishop to be accompanied by a Warden when on church premises. Under English church law, no-one can be disbarred from a Church of England church service except in very specific circumstances. Verbally abusing the vicar in public during worship didn't count. It was a horrible and embarrassing position to be in. Body blow number two.

Then we were burgled. Our large Edwardian Vicarage, set in its own grounds amidst streets of tiny terraced houses, naturally drew attention. For the most part it was friendly. Children on their way to school would stop at the gates and chat to me as I fed our hens and ducks. Local people knew me. I'd conducted countless funerals, weddings and christenings for them, doing my best to be alongside people as they faced the ups-and-downs of life. I like to think they trusted me. Inevitably, however, living in such a large prestigious-looking house meant we also attracted envy. People thought we were rich, not understanding that the privilege of living in the Vicarage was part of my stipend (my wages). We didn't own the house. Over the years we'd had minor stuff stolen from the grounds. One night, the garden was used to hide in by a criminal fugitive, which resulted in a helicopter hovering over us, illuminating the Vicarage, while officers rushed through the house. The children found the whole thing very exciting.

In spite of these few episodes, however, I felt safe. It felt a friendly, welcoming, if economically challenged, neighbourhood. Then we were burgled. My husband, always an early riser, surprised the intruder downstairs and tackled him to the ground, getting severely kicked and bruised in the process. The man was about to make off with three laptops – probably our most valuable possessions, if the truth be told. The kids clapped and cheered at their heroic Dad, and life settled down again. You never forget though. Body blow number three.

During all this, I put on a brave face. The vulnerable, confused, angry, hurting, frightened Melanie was kept well hidden, except to a few close friends and to my family. Understandably so, as in any other professional role, there needed to be some distance between my personal, private life and my public life. The difficulty in being a parish priest living in a Vicarage, however, was that there was nowhere properly private. The role didn't have clear boundaries. A burglary breaks down the boundary of safety around the home for anyone. In a Vicarage, however, safe boundaries are an especially live and potentially sharp issue. Let me explain.

Living on the job, in a house owned by my employer and counted as part of my stipend, it was hard to see where my professional and private life began and ended. This is particularly the case when the job means as much to you as it does to most clergy – including me. Moreover, it's a job which many people think gives them a right to access you 24/7 when you're 'at home' in the Vicarage. Hence there was the need for our little holiday cottage in Wales. Partly, though, I kept the close-to-breaking-Melanie well hidden because I was ashamed of her.

It's worth pointing out at this juncture how lonely the life of a vicar can be. The role makes it hard to have friends in the parish – real friends with whom you can kick off your shoes, make un-PC jokes, get drunk or be unashamedly silly. On Sunday morning, every week, you stand behind an altar and offer up all the secrets which have been shared, all the suffering which has been witnessed, and all the hopes-and-dreams expressed by those now kneeling in front of you. It's a huge privilege and a weighty responsibility. The role brings with it others' expectations, which I wouldn't have wanted to betray through shabby or unprofessional behaviour. Friends, therefore, tended to be other clergy or people outside the parish. As a busy parish priest and mother of four young children, how to find the time and energy to stay in touch with old friends? It can be lonely – but not just personally, professionally as well.

During the fifteen years of my ministry, my professional role as vicar was almost completely unsupervised. On a daily, weekly or monthly basis, I was accountable to no-one. I attended a weekly staff meeting, but it was a meeting of colleagues, of peers. None of them sat in a regular supervisory capacity in relation to my work. Every three years I had a ministerial review. That was it. Off my own back I met with the Diocesan Pastoral Advisor once a month. But those meetings (kind and supportive as they were) had no direct relevance or impact upon how I handled my job on a daily basis. This lack of accountability, and the lack of regular, objective professional support, added to the weight of responsibility which came with the role. The Church of England was aware of the problem at an institutional level but, at the time of my leaving, had failed to address it effectively. Slowly I was becoming worn down and worn out.

And, of course, underneath the professional isolation was the simple fact that I was lonely because I was afraid. I was afraid that if people got too close, they'd see the 'real' me – the woman who struggled a lot of the time with a lot of things. So I projected a super-happy, super-competent façade – the all-singing-all-dancing vicar, the ever-loving wife and super-mum. It did what I (perhaps unconsciously) wanted it to do. It kept people at a distance. I've very few real regrets in my life. One of them is that I missed out on the opportunity to cleave to some seriously amazing women within the parish. I could have trusted them with the real me – I know that now because I'm still in touch with several of them. But I couldn't do it then. I wasn't ready. I remained quietly lonely and secretly struggling.

Don't get me wrong. I loved my parish and I loved the life of a parish priest. I struggled with the Church of England as an institution, for sure. At times I found it almost unbearably reactionary, old-fashioned, insular, patronising and hierarchical. However, the role of a vicar, rooted and grounded in a particular place and in a particular community of people, I enjoyed. And my love for God, my deep knowing that the mystery at the heart of existence is Love, never faltered.

The parish where I was vicar was an inner-city parish in a multicultural and multi-faith town in the middle of England. I'd often say that what we didn't have in material wealth and resources, we made up for with the richness of the variety of people who lived there. Our four young children were as comfortable in the local temples belonging to other faiths: the Sikh Gurudwara, the Buddhist Vihara or the Hindu Mandir, as they were in church. However, as the years wore on, more and more diverse groups of people, from ever more different cultural backgrounds came to live there. As a result, community tensions increased. Gangs of young men began to form and to pit themselves against each other out on the streets, with increasing levels of violence. There was a shooting at the pub just a few doors away from the Vicarage.

So, onto body-blow number four. One warm evening in late spring, a few months after the Los Angeles debacle, I was outside in the Vicarage garden. The garden backed onto the church and was separated from it by a wrought iron fence. I was feeding our hens and ducks at the rear of the garden when I heard voices coming from the community centre which adjoined the church. Nothing unusual, I thought, until I realised that the voices were in fact coming from up on the church roof. There were three young men up there, one seated and two standing. I recognised one of them. I'd taught him Religious Education for several years in the neighbouring primary school when he was younger.

They were smashing glass bottles against the slate tiles. I asked them to come down off the roof. We've just celebrated our centenary, I told them; and I want this church still standing in another hundred years. I don't imagine they had a clue what I was talking about, and they turned away laughing. I climbed up onto the concrete fence post so that I was closer to them, and again told them to come down and to stop damaging the building. This time they rattled off a litany of abuse. I stood my ground. The man who was seated with his back to me, turned round to face me. He was quite a bit older than the others. He smiled, drained his bottle of beer and lobbed it at me. I felt it skim my hair. It had only just missed my head.

"Fuck off, bitch," he shouted. "Fuck off before you get hurt."

My legs turned to jelly, but I wasn't going to yield the space. This was sacred ground. I loved this space. Graffiti-covered and sometimes littered with used needles, but sacred space nonetheless. I warned them that if they didn't come down, I'd report them to the police. The younger two looked uneasily across at their leader. He got to his feet and held a bottle out ready to throw. He clearly expected me to back down. When I didn't, he lobbed another bottle at me. This one didn't miss. It was full and hit my shoulder with a dull thud before shattering on the ground.

The older man hunkered down and picked up another bottle. He held it by the neck and smashed it against the roof. He then stood up and held the shard of glass out to show me.

"See this?" he shouted. "See this? I'm gonna climb down and slash your face with it, you fucking cunt. I'm gonna cut your face until even your own children won't know you. Do you hear me, you bitch? I'm gonna do it over and over just 'cos I want to. I know where you live and every time you turn around, I'll be there waiting."

I stepped backwards in the face of this verbal onslaught and fell onto the ground before scrambling to my feet and running into the house. I was alone in the house with my eldest daughter, so I called her to me as I ran to phone the police. While I waited for the police to arrive, I shut and locked the several entrances to the Vicarage and all the windows. I was terrified. Body blow number four.

The diocese offered to 'airlift out' me and my family to a safe house away from the parish, but I refused. I'd been there too long, and I loved the place too much, to yield the space to those bullying blokes. I didn't want my ministry there to end like that. It would've felt as if those violent men had won. I picked myself up, pulled myself together and carried on, hoping to land a satisfactory new post quickly that would allow me to leave with dignity.

Two of the three men took to sitting on the wall opposite the Vicarage where they could see me in my kitchen. On several occasions they followed me as I walked the short distance from the Vicarage round the corner to the church. Once they followed me right into the church vestry. To this day, I'm convinced that if someone hadn't come into the empty church at that moment, they would've beaten and raped me. I was absolutely terrified. I reported them again to the local police, but was again told that unless they physically assaulted me, there was nothing the police could do. I lived in a state of almost constant high alert.

So, why didn't I leave? I wanted out, but I wanted out on my terms. Hence the unseemly scrabble for a new post - hence the frustrated and angry conversation with my authorising bishop. I didn't want to leave with my tail between my legs. I'd done a good job in the parish and I wanted to leave well with my head held high. I smile wryly as I write. That fateful conversation with the bishop – which constituted body blow number five – ensured that I didn't leave the parish with my head held high, trailing clouds of glory. Far from it; I crawled out on my hands and knees, as it were, in the dead of night. After body blow number five, the conversation with which I opened this chapter, I fled. No-one saw me go. I simply fled. It felt as if I was running for my life and I never went back.

Chapter Two

BREAK OUT AND BREAK FREE

When I left the church and hid myself in our little cottage in Wales, I was in pieces. I was afraid. I was ashamed. I was exhausted. I was incapable of doing anything more than feeding our two youngest children and walking our dog. Fortunately, I had an excellent doctor back in the West Midlands who knew me well, and whose Practise Surgery had recently moved outside the parish. I was therefore able to attend appointments, as well as get the support I needed. Over the ensuing months while I was on sick leave, I would drive the ninety miles to my G.P. appointments without the fear of running into parishioners. What could I say to them? Eventually, I was diagnosed with Situational PTSD and advised to take early retirement from the Church of England on the grounds of mental ill-health.

The following year I began divorce proceedings. Within a twelve month period, my career, my ministry, my home, and my marriage, had all gone. Even my faith – the faith that had journeyed with me like a beacon of light all my life - that too, was gone. My life was unrecognisable. Unbeknownst to me, I'd stepped onto the roller-coaster ride called 'The Change of Life'. It would turn my entire life upside down and inside out.

The first phase of this transformational journey was pretty ghastly. The ground underneath my feet had given way and nothing solid and reliable seemed to remain. I had exited my former life and entered a darkness which was almost unbearable. Sometimes I even thought of suicide. Without my four children to give meaning and purpose to my life, I would undoubtedly have given those thoughts more house room. As it was, the need to care for my youngsters kept me moving forward, one faltering step at a time.

Then, on top of everything else, I discovered a lump in my right breast. The mammogram at a private hospital in Cardiff showed it was nothing more than a knotty contusion – but it gave me a horrible scare. Back in my cottage when I looked in the mirror, I felt old. Old, ugly, unloved and unlovable. I knew I needed to do something drastic to yank myself up and out of this slough of self-loathing. I phoned my Gay Best Friend – also a vicar - and told him what I planned. He roared with laughter.

"Good for you!" he said. "I love it that you still have the ability to surprise me, even after we've known each other for almost twenty years".

To be honest, I surprised myself.

Sometimes, during menopause – I've heard women say this again and again - we look into the mirror and wonder who the hell is that strange woman looking back at us? I believe she's our future self. She's the one egging us one - daring us to break out and break free in order to find a deeper, truer happiness. Oftentimes, it needs saying, this breaking out wears the face of break down. Staring at *her* face each morning in the bathroom mirror definitely isn't easy.

Feeling like I was breaking all the rules, I cashed in an insurance policy and booked an appointment in London at Harley Street for a consultation. The procedure I was enquiring about was a 'boob job'. After breast-feeding four babies over a total period of eight years, my breasts looked unattractive to me and I wanted to do something about it. I told no-one apart from my GBF and my eldest daughter. I was embarrassed *and* I was also energised by the prospect. The procedure was by liposuction – taking fat from my belly and injecting it into my breasts. I didn't want a massive or noticeable change – just enough to look beautiful in my eyes. The consultant told me that my breasts would age naturally. She said they'd soften along with the rest of me as I grew older. I liked that idea. Afterwards I convalesced for a week in London while my eldest daughter lovingly and discreetly looked after me, and then I returned to Wales. I felt stronger, more beautiful and more myself afterwards, and I've never regretted the decision.

I took yet another radical step towards a new relationship with myself when I legally changed my surname. I gifted myself a name that had belonged to no-one else in my immediate family – and certainly not father or husband. However much I might love them, as an independent mid-life woman, I wanted to have my very own name. It had some loose Romany gypsy ancestral association, but mostly I chose it simply because I liked it, and I was free to do so. I became Melanie *Santorini*. A new woman was starting to shape up. The process of entering the Majesteria had well and truly begun.

In the fecund darkness and silence of my soul a change was underway. I had absolutely no idea that this is what was happening, of course. I certainly didn't think these experiences had anything to do with menopause. In fact, the one occasion a woman-friend suggested to me that I was possibly menopausal, I was indignant and defensive. I felt quite offended. My periods were still regular, after all. There was no way I was *that* old surely? It's only with hindsight, knowing what I now know about the process of entering the Majesteria – what it does to us, what it costs us, how it changes us – that I recognise the episodes I've just described as being the beginning of the initiatory journey which was to take me seven years to complete.

Not all women begin the menopausal journey with quite such a radical break as I did - but many do. Something is calling to us and if we don't heed her, she will become increasingly insistent until we do. I knew I needed to leave the church. I'd been toying with the idea for a long time, but I'd absolutely no idea how to do it. Well, what I couldn't do for myself was done for me. Fierce grace I call it. It was messy, it was bloody, and it was necessary. I know it was necessary because underneath the grief, the fury, and the despair, was something else. It was a sense of relief. I had let go. Finally. I had failed. Finally. All the years, the decades, of trying to be something, to be someone: the good little girl, loved by her father and mother, and admired by her two older sisters; the clever student and academic; the loyal and understanding wife; the wise and loving priest; the ever-present presence of 'Mum' – it all crashed to the ground and shattered as irrevocably as my assailants' beer bottles. When I had told the bishop, "I am done with this," I had absolutely no idea how true those words were to prove.

Let's be clear here at the outset of my story that entering the Majesteria is not about a 'right' way of being over a 'wrong' way of being. It's not a clear-cut path that you can follow from A-Z. That sort of thinking derives from the mind-set of the old paradigm, the old world order where 'right' and 'wrong' are sticks with which to beat people who are different from the 'norm' (and whose 'norm' is it anyway?). Entering the Majesteria is more like a three-legged dance across a boggy wasteland shrouded in fog. We come to dead-ends, take the wrong turns, get stuck, get lost, fall-over, get the giggles, lose our shoes and fuck-it-up – and it's all exactly as it needs to be. We're shedding skins. And this process inevitably leaves mess behind.

A not uncommon cultural perception is that we women are inconsistent and contradictory. Traditionally, one of the reasons given for fathers and husbands feeling obliged to 'look after their women' economically and socially, was that we don't know our own minds. Moreover, even when we did, we changed them. It is, of course, what my dear bishop angrily accused me of doing. This cultural perception is even sharper when we're in our menopausal years. And it's not just what the dominant culture tells us, it's often what we're experiencing for ourselves. Inconsistency and contradiction become familiar companions. We think we've grasped it, and then it's gone. We think we've understood it and it turns our understanding inside-out. We think we've arrived, and we discover that we're just setting out. The Trickster, Fool or Joker becomes our closest ally, our secret best buddy. And we'll need all the allies and buddies we can get, because along the way our inconsistencies and contradictions are likely to lose us some friends.

The relief I felt in those first months after I'd left the church, moved to Wales and filed for divorce, would've been difficult to admit at the time, to myself or to anyone else. It would've felt like such a betrayal of all that I had loved the most: my ministry, my husband, our children, and the family life we'd shared together for almost twenty years. It's important to name now because it's such a significant piece of evidence that attests to the fact that, in spite of the outward bloodied reality I was nearly drowning in, something good was going on. Yes, the grief, the fury, the despair were there too, but they weren't the whole story. The easing I felt inside when, finally, I let go of all that I'd done my best to carry well for so long, was a sure sign that a positive process was underway. It was a process that would, in the end, prove to be deeply regenerative and profoundly healing – beyond anything I could have hoped for.

You see, hidden deep inside me was a raw inner truth which longed to see the light of day. This truth was crying out that it needed some serious TLC. But I was ashamed of it. I'd covered it up publicly – or, at least had tried to cover it up. I'd kept it buried deep inside me – or, at least when it didn't bubble up into a form of depression. It was a truth which I'd increasingly soothed with a couple of late-night glasses of wine after work. A truth which I'd sought to alleviate through my ministry to others. It was a simple one. I was broken. I was broken and I'd been broken for a very, very long time. Inside the Reverend Doctor Melanie was a person as fragmented as those pieces of broken glass with which my assailant had threatened to slash my face. The menopausal journey of entering the Majesteria, strange as it may sound, is what put me back together. The journey brought me home – in the end – home to Melanie.

It wasn't as if I didn't know that I was broken inside before my 'breakdown', of course. I'd been in therapy in my twenties and again in my thirties. Moreover, Anglican clergy talk a lot about 'the wounded healer'. This time, however, it was as if all the dodgy cards I'd been secretly shuffling were laid out on the table for the entire world to see. There was no longer anywhere safe left in my life to tuck them away and hide them. The inconsistencies and contradictions which had battled away inside of me all my adult life suddenly came centre-stage. My 'tidy' ordered life of loving mother, loyal wife and compassionate vicar was now a horrible mess. This Clerk in Holy Orders was in unholy disorder. So I hid. I hid in my little cottage tucked away in a tiny village in rural Wales. For the first six months, apart from my children, my G.P. and two close friends, I saw no-one and spoke to no-one.

My life certainly looked a mess when viewed from the outside. Far worse, however, was the mess unravelling inside. Hidden away, with nothing to do and no-one to be, the masks slipped off and I was face to face with the confused, frightened Melanie I'd been running away from for most of my adult life. I didn't make pleasant company in those early days. I didn't like the woman I'd become. I didn't respect the woman who'd run away and abandoned her responsibilities and the people she loved. I was ashamed of her and, to start with, was almost paralysed by the guilt produced by the belief that *I'd let everyone down.*

I disliked her, and yet it was also a kind of relief to be her. As I say, the masks were finally off - the all-singing-all-dancing, all-loving, ever-available and ever-capable mask at least. I could at last be self-centred and self-serving. I no longer had a husband, or five thousand parishioners, to take care of and to worry about. I could be a 'selfish bitch'. The selfish bitch whom I disliked intensely when I thought I saw her in others, and whom I'd worked so hard and for so long not to be. I could even go and get a boob-job if I wanted to and no-one could stop me. Fuck the lot of them!

It was a tricky moment - and one I know a lot of women encounter at some point during menopause. I was face to face with my own 'Shadow' – a deeply hidden part of me. She took the form of the woman whom I knew I didn't want to be. Basically, the kind of woman I despised – someone who doesn't give a damn about anyone else or anything else. I was aware that deep down she existed inside me. For the most part I'd managed to keep her hidden. She was secreted away in the darkest dungeon I could find within my soul's keep. She'd made her presence felt of course, over the years. But, for the most part, I had her well under control. I had her chained up tight – and the chains that bound her were guilt, shame, blame and fear.

Entering the Majesteria – at least, entering the Majesteria as a sovereign Autumn Queen – is impossible without facing our Shadow. Our Shadow is the expression of our worst imaginable self. She is the one we need to release from her bondage so that she can, at last, do what she's meant to do – which is to serve us well. She holds immense energy and we need this energy in order to ripen and fully mature into the Autumn Queen phase of life. I call my encounters with my hidden Shadow, 'Shadow-dancing'. I'll tell you more about one especially difficult piece of Shadow-dancing towards the end of my story. It's a risky, tricky business, this Shadow-dancing. It's like dancing with a scorpion. She can be mean, spiteful, violent, self-harming, and abusive in every possible way. In her most extreme form, she can lure us with thoughts of suicide.

During those early months, the most I could manage was to walk the dog and to bake biscuits on the Aga ready for when my kids got home from school. A good portion of the time, I hated myself. Unbeknownst to me, however, the process of entering the Majesteria was beginning to take root. Melanie was making her first tentative shuffle of a whole different deck of cards – a deck which would in time become something beautiful and magical. Be warned, though - menopause, as I've since discovered, hides a Joker in the pack. In a game of cards, the Joker can be whatever you want it or need it to be. It's the wild card. Its other name is divine-grace. If you consciously choose to include the Joker in your menopausal deck, you're opening yourself up to a game that's faster, wilder, more raucous, and scarier than you could ever have imagined – it's also more fun. Its only requirement is that you throw out the rule-book. The choice is yours. Play it safe, or *pause*, breathe into the stretch, buckle up and let go (gleefully to mix metaphors). Yup, we're back on that roller-coaster called 'the Change'. Enjoy the next ride.

Chapter Three

I WONDER WHEN I GREW UP

Before I go further into relating the chronological process of entering the Majesteria, I need to spiral back to my childhood years and say a little about my upbringing. It'll give you a sense of what bits of early conditioning I carry in my life-bundle. The better you know me, the better you'll get a feel for the initiatory process of menopause. Then, hopefully, you'll be able to apply whatever insights you find helpful in my story, to your own life.

A key element in my childhood experience was how aware I was of the numinous. I believe that all children are graced with a sense of the sacred. It's most evident in their natural capacity for wonder. A happy, loved child has a wide-eyed, breathless, excitement and delight in simple, ordinary things – a brightly-coloured flower, bubbles in the bath, a bed-time story told again and again. Many children begin to lose this early sense of innocent wonder at around the age of eight. At this point the neocortex or new brain is growing rapidly. The neocortex is the outer sheath which covers the older mammalian brain and the ancient reptilian brain. It's unique to humans.

As a result of this neocortical growth, humans develop self-awareness. Alongside this comes an apprehension of our own mortality, which is often accompanied by a fear of our impending death. Also, as far as we know, unique to humans. In some children, the fear of death diminishes their capacity for free, limitless, innocent wonder. In others it expands and deepens it. I was one of the latter. From eight onwards, I was acutely aware that I would one day die. This simultaneously made me acutely aware of the wondrous nature of life. I couldn't have put it in those words, of course.

However, I do clearly remember the heightened awareness and sensitivity that rendered me at times overwhelmed with sensation. The warmth of the sun on my skin, the stars at night and the smell of a flower or the taste of butter on warm toast - these were all experiences that overwhelmed me with delight. I felt transparent. I couldn't easily detect where I began and ended. The 'oceanic feeling' that mystics and meditators speak about, was a common everyday occurrence for me. Once of the most frequently used words with which people describe me – is joy. It began then.

It wasn't all about the sweet smell of the roses in my grandfather's garden, however. This sensitivity meant that I was open to, and acutely aware of, pain and suffering in the world. Often, it too was overwhelming – simply too much to bear. I cried a lot as a child – both with intense joy and sadness. I still do. I continue to feel suffering and the pain of others keenly. More often than not, I choose not to watch the daily news. It's unbearable. It gets right inside me so that my heart aches with grief. I tell you all this because it explains why I ended up pursuing a religious life in the church.

People used to ask me all the time why I'd ended up as a vicar. As one of the first women to be an ordained priest in the Church of England, I was an unusual phenomenon. I used to joke that I'd had no choice - I was born one. That's obviously not literally true, but it is true to say that I can't remember a time when I wasn't aware of a spiritual dimension to life. My earliest memory is of lying in my pram in the garden, naked, kicking my legs in the warm sunshine. It's all too easy to project emotional content onto early pre-verbal memories. However, what I can reliably say is that whenever I recall that memory, I enjoy a feeling of playful, pleasurable, peaceful aliveness. These days I might call it 'Awareness'. It's a feeling which, over the years, has become synonymous for me with the spiritual dimension of existence - if we can separate it out like that – which, of course, in reality, we can't – but more of that later.

It was at the crucial, threshold age of eight that I had my first full-blown mystical experience. I'd just moved into my own bedroom from the one I shared with my sister. She and I had been attending a Baptist Sunday School. I think our eldest sister had a ballet class, and my mother needed to leave us two younger ones somewhere. It must've been there that I first heard the word 'God' used in a religious sense. At home, the word was just a casual expletive.

Anyway, somehow I made the link between the numinous experience in my bedroom and the word 'God'. I'd woken up and I was looking out of my window at the stars. It's nigh on impossible to put the experience into words but it was something like this: I was gazing at the stars and I was overcome with a delicious sense of something GOOD. It filled me and expanded me until I felt I was actually out there in the night sky – I *was* the night sky with its billions of stars. The sense of peace and love and goodness was all there was, and *I was that*. It was a state of ecstasy in the literal meaning of the word – a standing outside of oneself – a moment of pure grace. Then I was back standing in my nightdress with tears on my cheeks. My response was straightforward and almost matter of fact:

"God is real then. In that case I have to give my life to Him," I said to myself. I can remember saying it as clear as anything.

It was my 'calling'. I danced around what that meant precisely for many years, but I never doubted it. From that night onwards, I knew that my life, first and foremost, belonged to God, and that the purpose of my life was to live for God. This sense never left me - at least not until the breakdown which heralded my menopausal journey of entering the Majesteria.

By the time I was ten years old, I'd set up an altar in my bedroom so that I could pray 'properly'. I'd sit and gaze upon a picture of Jesus. I didn't use words – I didn't need to. Young children are natural, unselfconscious contemplatives with a strong sense of 'now' and a capacity for completely focused attention. When I use the word faith, it perhaps suggests a set of beliefs, but my faith wasn't like that. It had nothing to do with intellectual ideas but was a felt experience – a glowing, wordless, imageless, embodied knowing, that felt as inevitable and natural as breathing. I took it for granted - and, as a child, actually gave it very little thought.

My faith took on a Christian garb because that was the religious culture into which I was born. I attended a Baptist Sunday School, was confirmed into the Church of England and attended a Roman Catholic convent school with my two older sisters. However, the most important key to understanding my religious faith is the fact that the 'God' I encountered in my mystical interior life as a felt presence, was a *She* – well, not a 'she' exactly, but not a 'he' either. This presence was definitely not the 'He' whom the church proclaimed and demanded that I also proclaim: God the Father, God the Son and God the Holy Spirit. It seemed perfectly natural to me to name God in female terms. It also seemed absolutely wrong to me to name God in exclusively male terms. This was to become the thorn in my side throughout my public ministry as a vicar.

My awareness of the sacred feminine was inevitable. I grew up surrounded by a throng of strong, fabulous females whom I worshipped. They filled the home I grew up in and the all-female convent where I went to school. Let me tell you about them. My two older sisters were the sun and moon around whom I moved, lived, breathed and had my being. I fought with them, lied to them - and for them - envied them and emulated them in equal measure. I wanted to be them - as tall and talented and 'together' as they looked. The longing to be seen, to be noticed and to be included, stemmed from my relationship with them. So did the jealousy, the competitiveness, the spitefulness and the betrayals. All of the above has, at times, been present in my adult relationships with women. It all began in my complex love for my two older sisters. They were like goddesses to their little sister. In my teens, I began devouring feminist literature. But I suspect that, even if I'd not done so, I would still have always expressed my experience of God in female terms. It was (and is) a female imprint of divinity I carried within me.

Recently, while I was working on this book, my youngest daughter reminded me of Alice Walker's fabulous description of what it is to be a 'womanist', i.e. a black feminist or feminist of colour. Alice says this about a womanist woman: "Loves music. Loves dance. Loves the moon. Loves the Spirit. Loves love and food and roundness. Loves struggle. Loves the Folk. Loves herself. Regardless", (*In search of our mother's gardens*). Alice says that the term stems from the use of the term "womanish", used as in, "you acting womanish", when directed at a young girl to signify that her behaviour is "outrageous, audacious, courageous or *wilful*." I can *feel* my unbreakable bond with my mother and my sisters when I read those beautiful words.

My father was also a massive influence in my life, of course. He was, and still is, a passionate, articulate, clever man, whose intelligent mind and strong opinions I still love to do battle with. Full of energy and vitality, now in his eighties, he's still the heart of our family gatherings. As a little girl I adored him – and, at times, feared him. Inevitably – as we all do in relation to our parents - I carried a tangled nexus of emotions about him into early-adulthood which took some working through. Nowadays, though, we enjoy a delightful, easy relationship which enriches my life immeasurably.

By far the strongest influence upon me as I was growing up, however, was my mother. She was, and still is, glamorous and sexy, strong-willed and independent. In her younger years, she was very beautiful – heart-stoppingly so – of the Sophia Loren variety. She was warm, voluptuous, revelling in her femininity and a head-turner if there ever was one. As a young mother, she was strict, fun, cross, loud and full of laughter. I was born in the early sixties, so on Saturday mornings, the vinyl LPs would go on the record-player in the living room, and we'd all dance wildly to loud pop music: Dionne Warwick and Burt Bacharach were amongst her favourites. We lived in a semi-detached house in a small cul-de-sac in Windsor. As a family we were pretty exuberant and noisy. I've sometimes wondered how the neighbours coped.

In the summer, after school, it was uniforms off and bikinis on - then straight into the garden to sunbathe, with the radio blaring, sipping bottles of pop from our new Sodastream machine. My mother delighted in her three daughters. She was proud of us, ambitious for us and smacked us in equal measure. She dressed us in miniskirts and hot pants, and sewed matching dresses for us. I loved those outfits at first and then grew to hate them. As the youngest of the three, and therefore the recipient of the never-ending hand-me-downs, I seemed to wear the same dress forever. She kept our hair long, and brushed it with a vigour that still makes me wince to remember. Then she'd plait it or roll it up into a bun pinned high on top of our heads. I'm still on occasion called "Topsy" by my sisters, in memory of that topknot.

My mother's was the voice I knew best, and her scent the comfort I snuggled into on our sofa. She filled me with a sense of my own beauty and instilled in me a sense of my own worth. She revelled in her own feminine body and taught me to do the same. We regularly enjoyed what she called, "girlie days". These were occasions when we three daughters would pile into our parents' bedroom to sit at the altar of Mummy's dressing table. There she'd apply Helena Rubenstein face-packs to us, paint our toe-nails and cover us in scent. Thus beautified, we'd snuggle in my parents' bed to watch an old black-and-white movie on the telly. Those "girlie days" are amongst my most delightful childhood memories. When I looked in the mirror on those days, I knew I was beautiful.

The day I ran downstairs from the bathroom to tell my mother and my sisters that my period had started, I was greeted with hugs and showered with kisses. Mummy said I was now a grown little woman. I remember feeling so proud and happy. Those experiences were precious gifts in the formation of Melanie. I'm convinced that this early positive conditioning was the raft - above all else - which carried me through the stormy waters of my menopausal journey and safely to the other side. My childhood memories are filled with the knowledge that my mother loved me. She was, and still is, my first port of call when I need uncomplicated love and comfort. She is the mirror in which I can see the best of me reflected back.

We led a comfortable and, in many ways, a privileged life. My father's Process Engineering Design Company had become very successful, and so we were sent to a private convent school. We were the only girls in our neighbourhood to do so. We enjoyed holidays abroad, and went to swimming lessons and ballet classes. We joined a water-skiing club, and went hang-gliding and para-gliding. We had cats and a dog, rabbits and guinea pigs, hens and ducks – all in our small suburban garden. I loved them all.

My mother was engaged to my father at age fifteen, and they were married when she was sixteen. She bore my eldest sister just before her eighteenth birthday, and had the three of us girls by the time she was twenty-one. It was only later, looking back, that I realised how young she was when she was raising us. In many ways, she was simply a young woman still finding her own way, and her own self, in the world. When my father's business became successful, life got very fast, very quickly for my parents – fast cars, parties, and heavy drinking became the norm. Us three girls were regularly dragged along to the pub with 'the set' after a day at the water-ski club or wherever. When their marriage got into difficulties as a result of their new, fast-paced, glamorous life-style, its ending was swift and brutal. At least as far as me and my two sisters were concerned. My mother was only thirty-six when she and my father separated, but by then they'd been married twenty years. Their divorce knocked my happy childhood off its feet.

The next bit of the story is painful to remember and part of me wishes, out of love for my mother, that I could avoid telling you.

However, it's the spindle upon which so many of the threads and fibres of my later life-struggles were spun. Without this crucial piece of information, the fabric woven from my life-story simply doesn't hold its true shape. And when asked how she felt about me including it, my mother, typically, responded that, "I trust you 100%, darling. It's your story and you tell it in the way you need to."

My father moved out to live with his new young love. Soon after, my mother also fell in love and my step-father moved into our family-home in Windsor. He was a big, strong man and he was often violent towards my mother. My older sisters had left home, so I, alone, witnessed his violence. When I came across Elaine Aron's description of an HSP (Highly Sensitive Person – see bibliography), I recognised myself in it. As an HSP child, living in a violent household was especially traumatic.

I'm aware that I've emphasised my mother's physical beauty. Whether or not she was beautiful by the cultural standards of the time - which she was – is not the point. She was beautiful to me. She was my safety. To see that beauty damaged, bruised and bleeding, rendered my entire world unsafe. Moreover, it skewed my ability to see myself as beautiful. It obliterated (or at least covered up) my earlier sense of my own beauty and worth. For many, many years, the fairy-tale that most resonated with me was the story of The Ugly Duckling – the grey, gangly cygnet who is ashamed of herself because she hasn't yet discovered that she's actually a swan. It took many years of soul-work for me to recognise myself as the glorious swan that I am. For me *to remember what I had once known and had forgotten.*

One of the by-products of this period of my life was that I began to experience shame. I felt ashamed of my mother – how could she love and stay with a man who hit her? I felt ashamed of myself for doing and saying nothing. I told no-one about what I witnessed – I didn't know how to. Deeper than the shame, and well hidden, was terror and fury – in equal measure. The teenage years, especially thirteen to fifteen, are challenging anyway. Everything feels out of sync and we're awash with strong emotional currents that we haven't yet learned how to navigate safely. My strategy was to bury the shame and terror and rage down deep, and to put on a brave face for the world. Over the years, the mask became my everyday face. But hidden behind the pretty, smiling face of Melanie was an acute sensitivity around male violence, or the threat of it, which I carry to this day. I told no-one about what was going on at home, or how frightened and unhappy it made me feel, not even my best friend at school. The smiling mask was firmly in place. A patterning was being woven deep in my soul. A patterning which it would take decades to unravel and which, in the unravelling, would - in the end - be the making of me.

Just before I turned fifteen, my father and his new bride moved back into the area. They bought a house in Ascot, Berkshire, and invited me to go and live with them. In many ways, the move into a new life worked well, and was the right decision. They loved me, and were always kind and supportive. We had a lot of fun together and I've many happy memories of my life as an older teenager with them. Not least the births of my two younger sisters. However, with that move, I bequeathed myself a whole raft of guilt. I had abandoned my beautiful mother. I had put myself first and left her behind to struggle on her own – a struggle that was leading her into heavy drinking and serious weight gain. This guilt, coupled with my intense fear of male violence, became so unbearable that in the end, for a couple of years, I stopped seeing my mother altogether – which, of course, compounded rather than alleviated the guilt.

I don't want to leave my mother's story there, however. To do so would be to do her, and my step-father's memory, dishonour. My mother remained married to my step-father for ten years. Though they divorced, they remained friends and she never stopped loving him. When he was in the final stage of cancer, just before he died, he asked to see me. I hadn't seen him in about fifteen years. As we drove to the hospice my mother told me that he wanted to see me because he knew I was a priest and he wanted forgiveness. I was furious. I got very upset and told her that I could never forgive him for what he'd done to her and for the damage that witnessing it had done to me. She said to me, "Let it go, darling. Only the love remains. Let it go." I scoffed a little and suggested that she was undoubtedly a better priest than I because I could not find it in me to forgive him. I agreed to see him but only because she wanted me to.

When we arrived at the hospice, I stayed outside his room while my mother went in and told him that I was there to visit. I stood in the corridor trembling. I wanted to run and I very nearly did. I pulled myself together and, consciously and deliberately, put on the mask of a caring priest. I went inside. I saw him and all at once everything *changed*. It was another of those moments when everything slowed right down and I was filled with a sense of expansive, all-encompassing love and peace. I held his hands as he unburdened himself to me. I gladly offered him absolution as I sought to offer him reassurance that whatever hurt and damage he'd caused in his life was now over. I said that, for Mummy and me, only love remains. I left him with my mother and went back out into the corridor where I sat on the floor and sobbed. I felt as if my heart was breaking – breaking open, but in a good way. I attended his funeral with my mother and my older sisters, and I was so glad we did. That final meeting with him didn't take away the memories, or the nightmares; nor did it miraculously wipe away the effects of those two years. What it did do was to allow me to revisit those memories with a softer, kinder heart, both towards him, towards my mother and towards myself.

I lay all this out for you at length because the manner of our rearing is important. It's hard to do the re-gathering and healing of a fragmented self if you can't remember and claim your own story – it's called re-membering for a good reason. The process of letting go which I believe is the hallmark of entering the Majesteria is only possible when we have something – or someone (indeed our own self) to let go of. We have to gather ourselves up, as it were, into a complete bundle – as far as is possible with nothing left out – in order to lay it all down and find peace. It's a process that is repeated and repeated and repeated throughout our lives, of course, but is sharply and emphatically present during menopause. This is the quintessential opportunity to complete our unfinished business with ourselves.

So, now that you have a fuller picture of the back-story to my herstory, let's hop aboard the roller-coaster once more, and see where the ride called The Change of Life wants to take us. Let's fast forward to Melanie, post-breakdown, sitting by the Aga in her little cottage in Wales, sipping a cup of tea and nibbling on a homemade biscuit.

Chapter Four

MIXED-UP, MIDDLE-AGED
AND MISERABLE

There I was, sitting in front of my Aga, wondering: what comes after being a vicar when you've lost your faith? For months I could only answer: nothing. Then one autumn morning, almost a year after I'd fled the church, I woke up knowing that it was time to get a job. For a start, the mortgage on my cottage needed paying. Although I'd now secured a works-related pension, it wasn't sufficient to meet all my financial commitments. The idea of going out and finding a job, however, was daunting.

Soon after this realisation, an acquaintance popped by and I told her about my predicament. She said that the firm she worked for needed to hire someone and if I gave her a copy of my résumé she'd show it to her boss. Bryn ran a company that was a combined estate agent, solicitors and a bank. The very next day I was invited to an interview and, within half an hour, was offered a job.

"Your résumé is pretty impressive," Bryn said. "I'd like you to start straightaway."

"Great," I replied, "what will I be doing?"

I'd assumed, since he was a solicitor, that it would be something in relation to that.

"I need a part-time cashier in the bank. You okay with that?"

I nodded. I didn't have a clue what it involved, but he seemed nice enough, the hours suited, and I needed the money. I went through the required formalities, was given a uniform, and sent to Port Talbot for training. To my surprise, I thoroughly enjoyed it. Working as a cashier in the Halifax Bank was as far from being a vicar as you could get. To begin with anyway, it was both refreshing and fun. My one banking colleague in our tiny branch in Machynlleth was friendly and pleasant company.

If you just stumbled over that beautiful Welsh name, let me give you a helping hand. I spent seventeen years living in Wales, part-time and then full-time, and I know it's not an easy language to speak. However, it's an ancient language full of poetry, story and song, so it's definitely worth having a go. Anyway, in my experience, it's always hugely appreciated when you give it your best shot. In general, the key to pronouncing Welsh correctly, or stumbling around tripping up over your own tongue, is two-fold: 'ch' and 'll'. The 'ch' in Welsh is pronounced softly, like a gentle gargle at the *back* of the palate – similar to the Scottish word 'loch'. The 'll' in Welsh is a moist sound made by placing the tip of your tongue behind your top teeth at the *front* of your palate. There isn't an equivalent sound in English. Sorry. So the name Machynlleth is pronounced (roughly) as Ma-ch-un-ll-eth. Hope that helps.

The routine of going out to work three days a week in Machynlleth felt good. I'd worked all my adult life, including when our children were small, and financial independence was important to me. To be once again earning helped me to feel better about myself. To my chagrin, however, I found I wasn't terribly good at the job. I was slow at balancing my cash-till at the end of the day and often needed help with it. In my previous professional life, I'd been the vicar of two churches and the Assistant Area Dean of thirty more. A church is a complex organisation and, as the CEO, part of my role was financial oversight. I expected to be able to fulfil the role of a banking cashier without any difficulty. It was a long time before I learned that my new-found difficulty with numbers was a not uncommon condition of the PTSD - dyslexia of a kind – and one which, even now, under stress, can resurface. In some ways, therefore, I couldn't have chosen a more challenging way of earning a living. It did me no harm though. As a successful academic high-achiever, to find myself not good at something which other people (young and less qualified people to boot) were taking in their stride, caused me to pause (that pause again) and to re-think some of my assumptions about my own status and worth. Not a comfortable process but a healthy one.

My colleague in the bank was kind and patient with me. Since, at that point, there was just the two of us, the job was manageable. I didn't share my story with anyone apart from our boss and this anonymity gave me a breathing space to begin to get back up onto my feet again. Things, however, never remain the same. Under national streamlining, the little branch of the bank where I worked was closed. I was moved to a larger branch in the busy seaside University town of Aberystwyth, where the demands were much greater.

There, we were set daily, weekly and monthly targets of how many banking products and services we could persuade our customers to sign up for. Even back then, we weren't allowed to 'sell' banking products to customers, of course. However, sometimes it seemed to me that we were coming pretty close. If we didn't meet our targets, which were written up on a whiteboard in the corridor next to the service desks where we worked, we were in trouble. We were called before a line-manager and reminded that we were well on our way to losing our bonus pay and, if we continued to fail to meet our targets, the eventual outcome was dismissal. To be fair, it was as hard on the managers as it was on us, the humble cashiers. They had their own targets to meet and were under the same pressures to perform. It's different now, I'm told. But back then, it made for a stressful working environment.

I still valued and enjoyed working with my team of colleagues, but the work itself was no longer refreshing. Apart from when we were out socialising together, it no longer felt fun. One day, during my weekly review, my line-manager, a man of about my age, thumped his fist down hard on the table in frustration with me. What Alan said went something like this:

"With your qualifications and experience, Melanie, I'd expect you to be hitting all your targets and leading the way in getting our branch to the top of the Branch League. Our telephone reps report that you've been voted the cashier with the highest 'customer care score' in the region again this month, but you're amongst the lowest scoring in delivering our products. I have to warn you that if you can't turn this around, you'll be placed under Management Review. This, as you know, is the first step along the road to dismissal. I'm sure it won't come to that, but I really need you to pick up your game."

Alan had a vague notion about my previous life as a vicar but he had no idea that I'd been diagnosed with PTSD – I hadn't been required to disclose that fact. He had no idea, therefore, how difficult and upsetting I found that conversation. I left the meeting struggling to stave off a panic attack. I felt as if I was back in the bishop's office being summarily 'told off'. With that memory thrumming through my central nervous system, I felt close to being overwhelmed and defeated. Once again, I felt the urge to run and hide.

Luckily, it was my lunch break so I headed to the seafront. I phoned a friend, one of those good friends whom I'd leaned on the year before, and our conversation steadied me. I returned to the bank and made an appointment with Alan, my line-manager, for the following day. During this meeting I shared with him my diagnosis of PTSD and asked for his support in helping me to meet my targets. It was a good conversation – a conversation between peers. I was listened to respectfully, and with sympathy and understanding. Towards the end of our conversation, I pointed out, somewhat tongue-in-cheek, that whilst my heart had been absolutely committed to promoting the Gospel of Our Lord Jesus Christ for many years - it wasn't quite as committed to promoting banking products. We both laughed.

Alan then clarified why it mattered where our branch was in the Branch League, and what this would mean to my fellow cashiers in terms of a substantial bonus payment. The managers weren't going to benefit financially, but the cashiers would. Apart from me, they were all youngsters, most with debts they'd incurred as students, struggling to make ends meet financially. A bonus of several hundred pounds at the end of the quarter would mean a lot to them. He said he valued my integrity and reassured me that he wasn't asking me to offer something to customers who didn't really need it. He then challenged me to find real need in customers' financial situations that we could genuinely help them with.

That conversation was the incentive I needed. I got off my 'high horse' of thinking that being a banking cashier was an inferior or worthless occupation for me to be doing. I knuckled down to work.

Having buckled on my determination and skills base, I smashed my targets. I began enjoying my job again. For the next several months I held one of the highest scores for promoting the bank's products and services across the region. I felt contented that in so doing, I was meeting a real need in people to make their money work for them as efficiently as possible. I got so good at it that most of the time I was moved from the front service desk and reassigned to talking with customers over the phone. My colleagues were relieved by my change in focus. I was happier, and - more importantly from their perspective - I no longer had solo responsibility for a cash-till. I still couldn't balance my till very quickly at the close of business. So, more often than not - if given the task - I'd be the person holding everyone up at the end of the day. We all got our bonus pay that quarter, though. I was thoroughly chuffed that I'd helped to make it happen.

I relate this experience in detail because it was typical of a pattern that emerged during the years I was entering the Majesteria. I encountered, over and again, a situation which stretched me to my limits and provoked the very wounds in me that needed healing. It took me ages to cotton on to this – in spite of the fact that I disported that red spiral tattoo on my ankle. In my twenties I'd read a lot of Carl Jung's writings. Among his words which stay with me are these: "when we are ready, the Universe gives us exactly what we need for our healing". I've found it a comfort to remember those words when life seems to be dealing me a difficult hand. It's not always easy to see, of course; especially at the time. I look back at my year-long banking career with fondness now. But, at the time, it was definitely hard going.

Slowly, slowly, I was beginning to heal. I'd been helping a family in the village to look after their horse, a gorgeous Shire-Dray cross. When the opportunity arose, I took a leap of faith, and bought myself my own horse. It was a dream I'd had for a long time. He was a seven year-old dark bay Welsh Cob with soft, kind eyes, a white blaze and three white socks. His pedigree name was Ding-Dong Pantperthog but we gave him the stable name 'Jackson'. He'd been a farm horse, rough-ridden, so wasn't particularly well schooled, but buying him was one of the best decisions I've ever made.

I'll go more into Jackson's story later, but suffice to say that looking after him before and after work, riding out on him with my youngest daughter and the new friends we made as a result, was immensely therapeutic. My confidence and my physical well-being increased ten-fold. I was sleeping better, laughing more, and had stopped needing to pour a glass of wine to get through an evening. I began to look around for a different job – a job better suited to my background, qualifications and interests. I found one. But before I left the banking world for good, something happened one day, as I sat behind the cashier's desk, which ended up changing my life forever.

It was a morning in June. I was sitting at my desk in the bank, wearing my navy-and-purple uniform, busy serving customers with whom I enjoyed chatting. The pastor in me loved this part of the job. People came to pay in a cheque or to withdraw some money, and by the time they left we'd chatted about all kinds of things that mattered to them. Sometimes it was their health, or a recent bereavement, their hopes and dreams, stuff that was worrying them, a possible job move, or a looming divorce. It was information that would help me assess their financial needs certainly - but, also, I just liked listening to people.

Sometimes the guys would flirt a bit and, as I grew steadier and my confidence began to return, I'd allow myself a momentary flirt in response. One persistent admirer, who would arrive in the bank every few days laden with a large bouquet of flowers for me – much to my embarrassment and the unbridled amusement of my colleagues - persuaded me out on a date. Pretty soon it was clear that we weren't suited. However, dipping my toe into that stretch of water undoubtedly softened me up for what was about to happen on that particular day in June.

A customer approached and handed me a cheque to deposit. He was roughly dressed in a checked shirt and grubby jeans. With his broad, muscular hands and strong frame, I guessed he was a Welsh-speaking farmer. I was right. He was also very cute and I won't pretend I didn't notice. While I was entering the transaction into the computer, we struck up a conversation.

"You look well tanned," he said in a strong Welsh accent. "Been somewhere on holiday?"

"Nope," I replied. "It's just spending time in the garden and being out on my horse."

"Oh, you ride do you?"

I nodded and smiled up at him. He had bright blue eyes and when he smiled back, deep dimples appeared.

"I've got horses," he volunteered.

"You haven't got one to sell have you?" I asked laughing. "I'm looking for a companion pony for my Welsh cob."

"Gelding or mare?"

"Gelding."

"Well, as it happens, I do actually. A Section A mare. Retired. Easy to handle and a good price. You could come and view her if you like? I've been wanting to sell her for a good while now. I've got too many horses and need to thin out the herd."

"Really? That'd be great," I said. "Write your number on here and I'll give you a call."

He didn't expect me to phone, of course. He was completely stunned when, a few days later, I did. Months afterwards he told me that it had taken him three visits to the bank before he'd plucked up enough courage to get into my queue so that I'd be the cashier to serve him. He very nearly lost his nerve and didn't speak a word to me at all.

Peter is indeed a man of very few words. He's first and foremost a farmer, a fisherman, and a huntsman. He's an immensely capable man who's at home in his own skin, and at home on the land, in a way which I find irresistible. He has a quiet spaciousness and a calm stillness deep in the heart of him which is balm for my soul. You'll hear more about Peter later in the story. But for now it's enough to say that while I was going through my own metamorphosis, Peter was also busy shedding skins. I can think of many titles as I watched him go through his own process of inner change: Wild Man of the Mountains, the Wastelands' Fisher-King, Keeper of the Well, Cerunnos, Druid-bard, Puck and Naga (King Cobra) are just some of them. The names don't really matter in this instance, for they can't contain the truth of who he is. What does matter is that when I was ready to step into a new life as Autumn Queen, Peter was there at my side - my sexy, mischievous King Stag.

I didn't buy the pony. I thought she was somewhat over-priced. But right from the beginning, I felt completely at ease and at home with this quiet Welshman. It was as if we'd known each other all our lives - or, in a previous life, perhaps. Anyway, five years after that first meeting, we were married.

Chapter Five

MISTRESS OF MADNESS

Soon after I met Peter and we'd begun dating, I was scanning the job pages of a local newspaper when I spotted an advertisement posted by the mental health charity Mind Cymru. It said that a new national campaign was being launched across Wales to tackle the stigma associated with having a mental health diagnosis. Mind Cymru was looking to appoint three regional co-ordinators to run the campaign. I was interested. I sent off for the job specification and an application form. The anti-stigma campaign about to be launched was called *Time to Change Wales*. It was funded jointly by the Welsh Government, the National Lottery and Mind, and was to be run by the three largest mental health charities in Wales: Mind Cymru, Gofal and Hafal, working in partnership.

Its aim was to set up twelve community-based projects across Wales led by local people which tackled mental health stigma in creative and innovative ways. The regional co-ordinator's role was to find and encourage community groups and individuals to apply for the funding to set up these anti-stigma projects; to be involved in the selection process of deciding which projects should receive the grant; and then to oversee the successful projects. The *Time to Change Wales* (TTCW) campaign was based in Mind Cymru's Cardiff offices but the regional co-ordinators would work from their own regions. One of the regions was mid-Wales covering Powys, Ceredigion, Carmarthenshire and Pembrokeshire. It was a part-time post and was for three years. In keeping with Mind's recruitment policy, one of the desired qualities of the successful candidate was that he or she would have lived experience of a mental health challenge. I applied and was short-listed. After a rigorous interview in front of a panel in Cardiff, I was appointed to the post of *Time to Change Wales* Regional Co-ordinator for Mid Wales. I was delighted. Two years after leaving the church, my professional life seemed to be getting back on track.

The first three months were a probationary period. I was employed by Mind and settled quickly into the organisation. I had – and have - nothing but respect for Mind Cymru which (unlike the church in my view) walks its talk. I was wholeheartedly committed to the aims of the TTCW campaign and (unlike the bank) believed I could use my entire skill-set in the service of its objectives. While I'd been mulling over my application form, my youngest daughter had read the job spec, and had commented that the work sounded like being a vicar but without the church. The idea couldn't have appealed to me more. After I was appointed, I spent the first weeks travelling up and down to Cardiff, meeting new colleagues and getting to grips with what TTCW was all about.

Later, out on the road travelling around mid-Wales, a stunningly beautiful part of the world, I sought to engage with various organisations to get them on board with the campaign: Mental Health organisations, Universities, NHS Trusts, Welsh Water, the Post Office, the Police, the Fire Service, to name but a few. It was much, much better than working in a bank. These organisations weren't eligible to apply for a grant, but they all reached deep into local communities and could spread the word about TTCW. Moreover, many people within the organisations themselves experienced mental health challenges and were empowered and inspired to tackle stigma by spreading the campaign message.

The statistic we touted was that one in four adults experience mental health challenges at some point in their life. More recent research actually puts the number higher. As well as engaging large organisations, we also targeted smaller community groups. The anti-stigma projects we aimed to fund needed to be independent, community-based and led by people with lived experience of mental health challenges. My remit was to meet with community groups to encourage them, either to develop an existing idea they had for an anti-stigma project, or to inspire them to develop one. By the end of my probation period I was expected to have half a dozen 'notes of interest' from a diverse range of community groups. Each 'note of interest' would potentially be eligible for a grant, and all were to be shepherded in TTCW's direction. As the three months drew to a close, I didn't have a single one.

My line-manager was based in North Wales and we met fortnightly for supervision. We got on well. I'll call her Nerys in this story. Nerys was hugely experienced in the field of mental health and seemed to know all the key players in all the key mental health organisations across Wales. She was a native Welsh speaker and part of her remit was to midwife the community projects which would be delivered in Welsh. My difficulty was that I was new to the field of mental health and new to Wales. I knew no-one in the mental health world beyond the English border. Whilst I had extensive experience of developing and supporting diverse community projects over many years, I'd done so from a context within which I was well known and trusted – as the vicar. This wasn't the case now, and I found myself struggling to make inroads.

The TTCW projects were to be led by people living with mental health challenges. People living with mental health challenges, together with the organisations which support them, are sensibly cautious around enthusiastic newcomers. Even though I was offering them the opportunity to apply for small-grant funding, they seemed to keep me at arms length. I guess it's that hopes have been raised, and then summarily dashed, too often in the mental health world. So perhaps people have become a little sceptical of the largesse of government-funded initiatives. Moreover, TTCW was a new (and therefore as yet untried) campaign with a 'Government-funded' tag.

It began to look unlikely that I'd be able to deliver on my targets. It was the bank all over again. The other regional co-ordinators seemed to have all kinds of juicy potential anti-stigma projects bubbling along nicely. I was open and honest with my line-manager about my difficulties. Nerys did her best to assist me in breaking through the impasse by signposting me in various directions. Though, as she pointed out, she did have her own heavy workload in North Wales to get through, and she wasn't going to do my work for me.

In addition to our regional work as project initiators and co-ordinators, we were part of the national TTCW campaign. We were directed to work with the many existing mental health organisations to increase awareness across Wales of the stigma which still sticks to people living with mental health issues. Alongside these many and various other mental health organisations, we were to challenge and change people's perceptions for the better. To this end the TTCW communications team created T.V. and radio adverts, billboard and bus posters, and a raft of freebies (T-shirts, mugs, pens, badges etc.) for us to give away wherever we went.

Each regional co-ordinator was responsible for organising several TTCW Days – day events to which we'd invite a broad range of stakeholders and interested parties. The aim was to present the TTCW campaign message and to encourage people-with-influence from as many spheres as possible to get involved, ready for the national launch of the campaign. We'd partner up for these days – two regional co-ordinators for each event. Nerys and I were teamed up for the north Wales TTCW day and also for my mid-Wales day which was to follow.

The north Wales event which took place in Caernarfon was well attended and deemed a success. I, on the other hand, was having difficulty getting people on board for the mid-Wales event and the number of attendees who had signed-up was low. I began to get seriously worried. I began to feel a failure and to fear that it was all slipping away from me again. Then I had an accident. I had a nasty fall off my horse and, although I wasn't seriously injured, it necessitated a trip to the hospital. I had to cancel a couple of strategic meetings I'd set up as part of my preparation for the mid-Wales Campaign Day. The fall threw me – both literally and metaphorically. My anxiety levels shot through the roof and I cancelled a couple more meetings. I feared I was sliding back into the difficulties of the early days of my diagnosis when I'd been so horribly incapacitated. I said nothing about my personal difficulties to Nerys. I hoped I could turn things around.

When it came to the mid-Wales TTCW day for which I was responsible, numbers in attendance were poor, the venue was unsuitable and the day itself was badly organised. Equipment we needed wasn't where it should have been. The rooms were tiny and hadn't been laid out ready. The refreshments and lunch orders were confused. The venue we'd been allocated was adjacent to a crowded noisy bar. It was all pretty shambolic. Nerys became increasingly disgruntled as the day wore on. At the end of the event we sat down together, as usual, to review the day. She asked me about my planning for the event. I tried to pass the buck and cover my tracks. I lied. I tried to lay the blame for the badly organised day at the door of the manager of the hotel where the event had taken place. I assumed no harm could come from it and it'd give me a breathing space. It was a foolish and a shabby thing to do.

A couple of weeks went by and I was due to have the assessment review for my probationary period. It was an uncomfortable and difficult meeting. During the meeting, a member of the TTCW team said that, based upon my recent poor performance, she wouldn't be recommending that I continue in post beyond my probationary period. I was completely devastated. I left the meeting in pieces.

In yet another serendipitous turn of events, I was heading straight from that meeting to collect an old friend from the train station in Machynlleth. She was the same friend I'd spoken with immediately after the difficult encounters with the bishop and the bank manager. A busy vicar herself, we hadn't managed to see each other in over a year, and she was coming to stay for a few days. I sat waiting for her train, struggling to believe what had taken place.

Two things were going on simultaneously inside me. Firstly, there was the feeling of panic. Inside my head, I was busy catastrophising - creating worst-case scenarios which, if my imaginary fears had been based in physical reality, would have had me burned at the stake by the mental health charity Mind Cymru. The second thing going on for me was the clear certainty that I didn't want to give up my job. There was the need to pay my mortgage. But, more than that, I loved the work and I was passionate about the TTCW campaign. This gave me the presence of mind to write down what had been said in the meeting – word for word. I'd done this habitually as a vicar following a bereavement visit. I'd sit in the car immediately afterwards and make notes, writing down word-for-word what the bereaved had said. I'd done this for more than twenty years, for almost every one of the three hundred funerals I'd conducted. I knew I could trust my notes to be an accurate record.

By the time my friend's train arrived, I'd moved into a state of collapse and was weeping. I was furious with myself. I proceeded to batter myself with self-blame and self-loathing. I wanted to quit. Quit everything. My friend, who'd known me for more than fifteen years and loved me, countered this litany of unhelpful self-flagellation. She reminded me of what I already knew: that, in spite of several errors, I'd been doing a good job, and I was capable of doing a better one. She then asked what advice I'd give to someone who came to me and described the situation I was in. I replied that I'd suggest they contact a superior officer in the organisation they worked for, lay their cards on the table, and ask for guidance in sorting it out.

So that was what I did. I sat down quietly the next day and wrote an honest account of the actions which had led to my poor performance. The CEO of Mind Cymru stepped in at this point. She phoned me at home in order to assess the situation. She did this over a number of phone calls with a professional thoroughness, a courtesy and a measured consideration that filled me with admiration and gave me a sense of being in safe hands. She advised that I take some leave while the matter was looked into. She also advised that I inform my Trade Union. She said she doubted I would need union representation, but she always advised staff that it was good practise to keep their union rep informed of a change of circumstances at work. I did so, and the *Unite* (as it was then called) union rep was supportive and helpful. The Mind Cymru CEO reassured me, repeatedly – for I asked repeatedly - that I was not on forced leave as a disciplinary measure. I was on leave as a part of the organisation's pastoral care for staff while a review of the situation took place.

After a couple of weeks, the CEO phoned to say that the enquiry was complete and she was happy with its findings. She affirmed that Mind Cymru, and TTCW in particular, did not want to lose me as I was a valued member of staff. She informed me that, if I wished to continue in post, my probationary period would be signed-off, and I could return to work. She emphasised that a note had been made in my staff file about the lie I had told. And, were I to do so again, I would be liable to disciplinary measures. I gave her my full assurance that I understood that to be the case. She suggested that I take a couple of days to catch my breath before reaching a decision about returning to work for TTCW under contract for the next three years.

It sounds strange to relate, but the entire process was surprisingly healing. It provided an opportunity for the bruising caused by the uncaring and unprofessional treatment I'd received at the hands of the senior-management staff in the Church of England to be assuaged. As the days went by on leave, I felt stronger and stronger. I knew from listening to countless 'confessions' that coming clean, as it were, takes a weight off the mind and people always feel better afterwards – more energy, clearer purpose, increased self-liking. It had been a part of my job as a vicar which I'd valued and enjoyed offering. It was more than that here, however. It was the experience of being treated as a professional within a completely different kind of organisation from the church.

Here, my professional standing did not depend upon my ability to hide my vulnerabilities, my passions, my divergent thinking, my curiosity, and my lies. Here, my professional standing required that I be honest and transparent in my dealings. If I were, appropriate support would be offered. If required, that support would be rigorous and firm. And it could, potentially, lead to dismissal. I knew where I stood - the various policies of the organisation made sure of that. The ground upon which I stood therefore felt safe ground. In the church there had been no organisational policies or contracts: grievance, disciplinary, complaints procedures were non-existent – apart from the ones I'd helped pull together as a funding requirement for various community projects. As I've already mentioned, there was no appropriate professional support – a chat in the bishop's study was the best on offer. And, as my story attests, that could be neither helpful nor professional. In the church the ethos was about exclusivity. Its tone was that of superiority. Its assumption was that everyone was striving towards 'perfection'. Here, the ethos was inclusivity. The tone was compassion. The assumption was that every member of staff would at some time or another demonstrate the universal human tendency towards frailty, flaws and failure. When they did, the organisation had in place a structure to deal with them – however serious or minor their human frailty turned out to be.

The above might seem a rather harsh or unfair assessment of the Church of England. It was, however, my experience of it over a thirty-year period. Nor am I claiming that Mind Cymru was perfect – it didn't need to be. The open and accepting attitude I experienced at Mind Cymru, and at its sister charities Gofal and Hafal (under whose joint auspices I worked), was based upon the notion that staff would bring their full professional capabilities to work. And, when that wasn't possible, for whatever personal reasons, they would seek and be given appropriate support. Moreover, the view was held that the vulnerabilities and limitations which all staff had (including those members of staff living with mental health challenges), when supported positively and proactively, made us more efficient, effective and creative workers. This wasn't about organisations wallowing in pain-bonding or allowing staff to sink into the gloom of eternal victimhood - far from it - it was about empowering and equipping staff to fulfil their roles to their highest possible potential *and* supporting them on the days when that wasn't possible.

The UK-wide national mental health charity Mind, has (at the time of writing) a track record of less than the national average for staff sick-days. This attests to the positive impact that such a working environment can have on people. This is particularly noteworthy in an organisation which employs, as a matter of policy, a much higher-than-average number of people with *declared* mental health challenges. In working for Mind Cymru my world turned upside down. There was no need any longer to hide or to pretend or to lie. I'd been liberated from having to lie, by a lie. It's hard to put into words how impactful and releasing this was. It's no exaggeration to say that it was akin to a religious conversion experience. The roller-coaster called the Change can feel a bit like a ride through the water-shoot – full body immersion, fully clothed, in cold water that's both uncomfortable and shocking, and yet leaves you laughing with exhilarated pleasure in the end. On to the next ride …

Chapter Six

STIGMA DOESN'T HAVE TO STICK

I did return to work for TTCW. The member of staff who had expressed disatisfaction with my performance moved on to new pastures. I was invited to be a member of the appointment panel for her successor. While the appointment process was underway, the difficulties with which I'd been struggling in order to fulfil my role were addressed. Colleagues in the Cardiff office were tasked to provide me with targeted key lead-contacts in mid-Wales. My appointment diary quickly filled up. Although I was still a 'remote worker' working from home, I was given office space within a local Mind organisation in Aberystwyth so that I was plugged directly into the mental health workers' network in the region. I was up-skilled through in-service training in London, Cardiff, Machynlleth and Aberystwyth: Mental Health First Aid, ASSIST (Applied Suicide Intervention) and SAFETalk (Mental Health Awareness in schools). In addition, attendance at each of these well-subscribed training programmes opened up further networks.

Finally, a new TTCW regional co-ordinator for North Wales was appointed whom I'll call Seren. Part of Seren's role was the line-management of the other regional co-ordinators, including me. With this new appointment, and with my newly restored confidence, and my new-found sense of freedom at work, a new era in my professional life unfolded. The new member of staff turned out to be my dream colleague. Seren was clever, articulate, funny, passionate about TTCW, immensely hardworking and capable. Most importantly for me, she worked from the basis that, in spite of the fact she spoke Welsh fluently and I didn't, we were peers with commensurate experience and skills. She was also someone with declared experience of living with ongoing mental health challenges. There was renewed motivation, energy and application within our team and our achieved outcomes sky-rocketed.

Within a couple of weeks of my new line-manager starting work, however, I faced my first potential stumbling block. I had booked a meeting in the Chaplaincy at the Royal Welsh Showground in Builth Wells with a gathering of church leaders. TTCW planned to staff a stall at a forthcoming Royal Welsh Country Show in order to promote the national campaign. The Chaplain had offered to assist in the organisational planning of this event. He and I had spoken briefly on the phone to arrange the initial meeting to get the ball rolling.

Part of my remit was to encourage members from the rural community to become informed about TTCW, and, hopefully, thereby inspired and involved in the campaign. The rural community across the UK has one of the highest rates of suicide amongst young men. The Welsh Government had especially tasked TTCW with targeting Welsh-speaking rural communities as a potential area where undisclosed mental health suffering and associated stigma could be an issue. The Royal Welsh Country Show attracts many thousands of visitors each year, so TTCW management agreed that our presence there could be an excellent opportunity to reach one of our target 'hard-to-reach' audiences. Moreover, as churches are still integral to much of Welsh community life, especially amongst older people and in more traditional rural villages, church leaders would be good allies in this endeavour. My new line-manager encouraged me to set up the meeting and was looking forward to hearing my report about it afterwards.

As the scheduled meeting came closer, however, I became increasingly anxious about it. One of the unexpected and unwelcome symptoms of the Situational PTSD with which I'd been diagnosed, was that I couldn't go into church buildings, or even be around dog-collared members of the clergy, without being seized by panic - hence the label 'Situational'. I disclosed my anxiety to Seren and explained what the Royal Welsh Show set-up meeting involved. She offered to fulfil the appointment on my behalf. When I said that I felt ready to try to meet this challenge, she offered to accompany me. Knowing she was busy finding her TTCW feet in north Wales, I said I thought I could go it alone. She considered this, and then said she'd support me in that decision on one condition: I was to phone her both before and after the meeting. Moreover, she gave me permission to cancel the meeting if I needed to. What a relief. With that kind of support I was even more determined to have a go at stepping into a sphere which hitherto had been off-bounds.

I arrived at the Royal Welsh Showground in plenty of time for my meeting. I was warmly greeted by the Chaplain as I drove around looking for the chapel, and, once I'd parked my car, he helped me unload my TTCW gear. We set up the room together – banners, freebies etc. I laid out the notes for the TTCW presentation, which I'd delivered on several occasions, and with which I was confident and comfortable. The room filled up. All clergy. All wearing clerical shirts – those ghastly so-called dog–collars - and one was even holding a Bible. My heart rate went up. I asked for a glass of water and was quickly provided with a cup of tea and some biscuits. I took a big gulp and began. The presentation lasted about half an hour and went smoothly.

Afterwards I prepared to open up the meeting for discussion or questions. I paused and looked around the room. What I saw was what I knew so well and had loved so very much about the Anglican Church – a bunch of ordinary, unpretentious, unglamorous, mostly-middle-class people, committed to doing their best to make the world a better place. Behind the clerical collars, and beyond the slightly stuffy 'churchiness', were warm, welcoming, friendly people wanting to learn from me about something that mattered to me hugely – the stigma associated with living with a mental health challenge. I was one of those people and I was also one of them.

"Before I open up our conversation further," I said, "I'd like to tell you a little bit about me. It'll help ground what I was saying in the presentation."

I breathed deeply. Here I go, I thought - in at the deep end to sink or swim.

"Like you," I continued, "I am a member of the clergy."

Murmured surprise rippled through the room.

"I was amongst the first women to be ordained in the Church of England in 1995. I served the church as a full-time stipendiary priest, a vicar, for thirteen years and as an Assistant Area Dean for three years. I suffered a serious physical assault and I was eventually diagnosed with Situational PTSD. I took early retirement on the grounds of mental ill-health and was pensioned off. It has taken two years to recover sufficiently enough to come and speak with you today, and to tell you the truth about myself."

The concentration in the room was palpable. You could have heard a pin drop.

"I am a living testimony to the power of stigma. Until today, in spite of working for the anti-stigma campaign *Time to Change Wales* I have never before publicly disclosed my own mental health diagnosis. I want to thank you for enabling me to do so here with you now."

The room erupted. For the next two-and-a-half hours the stories came thick and fast – of a son struggling with post-natal depression; of a wife unable to walk even down to the village shop; of the secrets hidden and now wanting to be told. There were some tears shed, and a lot of laughter, and an overwhelming sense of relief. When the Chaplain closed the meeting in prayer, several people reached out and silently held the hand of their neighbour. I sat and watched, deeply moved. As the clergy left the room, I was hugged by each of them. My courage was commended, and I was told my story was "inspirational". But the word I heard repeated again and again was, "thank you". The chaplain helped pack my TTCW gear in the car and then I drove a little way down the road and phoned my line-manager, Seren. I told her what had happened. She cheered and laughed and whooped and hollered down the phone. She knew what it meant to me. She knew what a finally liberated and fearless Melanie meant to the TTCW campaign.

From then onwards, I went from strength to strength. I loved the work and could now commit wholeheartedly to it, as someone with impressive professional credentials and abilities – but, more than that, as someone with lived-experience of continuing mental health challenges. My shame had evaporated. Within Mind Cymru I had found a 'tribe' of people who respected and valued me, both personally and professionally, from whom I no longer needed to hide parts of myself and my herstory. Over the next two-and-a-half years that I worked for TTCW, I told my story hundreds of times. I developed an increasing mentoring role to support individuals with declared experience of living with mental health challenges, so that they too could tell their own story within a variety of public contexts.

Working alongside a broad spectrum of mental health agencies, and community groups, I sought out, helped to develop and supported several superb TTCW funded community projects in mid-Wales: amongst them, a women's empowerment *Red Tent* group called *Y Babell Goch*; a series of open-mike café style events called *MadCaff*; a series of evenings of live performances called *Schizophrenic*; a film about living with multiple addictions called *Anxious About Addiction*. More detail on all of these can be found on the *Time to Change Wales* campaign website. I absolutely loved the work and at the end of the three year first-phase of the campaign, like others, I stood and wept with pride at our National Celebration event in Cardiff. I listened to person after person stand up and witness to the way in which letting go of the bonds of silence and stigma had transformed their lives, their work, their families and their communities. It was utterly inspirational.

After three years, however, the time had come for me to move on. Working for TTCW had transformed me and liberated me in so many ways professionally. I had found my 'tribe' of like-minded, socially-committed, open and aware people. And, having found them - having found a place of 'safety' - once again something more called to me. It was something deeper, more primal, and more female – both at once familiar and wholly new. *She* was calling. And, once more, I turned towards the voice of that calling.

I prepared to leave the solid ground under my feet as I sought to respond and to honour the Sacred Feminine.

Working with TTCW hadn't been the only impactful engagement that had unfolded during those three years which brought me to this threshold moment. Other events, growing out from and alongside my work with TTCW, had also wrought a profound change in me. I was ready to get onto a new roller-coaster ride - one I'd never ridden before. To this adventure, let us now turn.

Chapter Seven

TOUCHED BY FAITH

As I've outlined, there were many benefits to working for the campaign *Time to Change Wales*, both professionally and personally. One of the positive outcomes was that, through helping to support and develop the TTCW project *Y Babell Goch*, I came into contact with a group of committed, spiritually alive, awakening women. At the time, I didn't realise what an impact this would have on the direction my life would take. I simply sat there in my professional guise of TTCW Regional Co-ordinator for mid-Wales, listening to these women discuss their dream of setting up a network of Welsh *Red Tent* groups. In Wales they are known as *Y Babell Goch*. Without knowing it, I had crossed a threshold.

I was about to enter a whole new world where women were beginning to take a stand in the centre of a grassroots global revolution. Before long it would become clear to me that this 'women's movement' was about healing ourselves and, in so doing, to participate in the healing of our planet. This was to be achieved through a movement of radical female-self-empowerment. In some ways it was a world that was already familiar and dear to me, in other ways it was brand-spanking new.

I first came across the term 'patriarchy' in my mid-teens through reading Germaine Greer and Adrienne Rich. It was such an eye-opener. Patriarchy isn't a word that's much in use nowadays. I still occasionally find it a useful word though, even if it's a bit clunky. It sums up human systems (political, social, cultural, religious, and economic) in which males hold - and hold onto - more power than females. And – and this bit is important to me, as you'll be aware by now from my story – they do so by violence, including and especially, violence against females. From my reading of Greer and other feminist writers, I learned that much of the human world is dominated by men and is designed to meet the needs of men. It was a devastating realisation for a girl traumatised by witnessing male violence. Yet it made sense of so much that I observed around me about the world in general. It made such sense that I couldn't ignore or deny the existence of patriarchy in my world.

What I saw, read, and experienced through this feminist lens, angered me. Since I was, at that time, busy playing the part of the 'good girl' - the successful, shining and smiling Melanie – I hid the anger inside. The inevitable result of which were bouts of depression – a sitting on the lid of my fury. I'm utterly sure, after working with thousands of women over thirty years, that for many, many women, our experience of depression can be traced back to the simple fact that we sit on our fury. We're forced to do that, and we choose to do that. And it makes us ill. How could it be otherwise in the face of a human world which is dominated (damaged and desecrated) by men. Still, to this day, it's an unpopular viewpoint - though that doesn't make it thereby incorrect. The start of my own periodic bouts of depression, which continued until I met Peter, can be dated exactly from that awakening realisation of my place within a male-dominated world. I hated it. I hated it on behalf of myself, and on behalf of my sisters – all several billion of them.

During those tender teenage years, I also learned about earlier or alternative human systems where the female held equal sway. These were often cultures where the Great Goddess was revered. I read Merlin Stone's, *When God was a Woman*, and M. Esther Harding's *Woman's Mysteries*. I was moved by the photos of the ancient Goddess stone-carved figurines in Erich Neumann's *God the Mother.* I've let go of hundreds of books over the years - when I've moved house, had a clear-out, or down-sized - but those three volumes still sit, in a place of honour, upon my bookshelves.

When I left my mother to live with my father, after their divorce, I'd have fiery discussions about these ideas in the car with Daddy each morning on the drive from Ascot to Windsor on the way to my convent school. He was, and is, of a more right-wing conservative political bent than I am. It was good practise in sharpening my intellectual skills, as well as teaching me how to stand my ground in the face of a strong, powerful, male challenger. I still sometimes use the term 'feminist' to describe my world view – it used to froth my eldest son up into a lather, when he was himself a teenager. But, again, this helped him to hone his fierce and impressive intellect. Looking back, it's no surprise really that, in the face of a powerful woman, an authoritative priestly mother and matriarch, my feminist critique about the subordination of females, provoked a strong rebuttal from my teenage son.

I campaigned for gender inclusivity within the Church of England for a decade before they let me in through the doors as an 'equal' to my male priestly colleagues. It's easy to forget, but it was a tough, gritty battle for gender equality in the church. I marched in London with the organisation MOW (*Movement for the Ordination of Women)*, where I was shouted at and spat upon by my fellow Christians. After ordination, I promoted the message of the organisation *The Association for Inclusive Language* which sought to include female-gendered language in the sacred liturgy of the church, and to include women's experience within sacred story. I had an academic paper published with the Centre for Practical Christianity exploring the differences between female and male approaches to spirituality. I was a paid up member of WIT (*Women in Theology*) and a convenor of monthly meetings for women clergy – that new breed. I sang and praised God as 'She' in countless hymns, prayers and sermons in masculinist and male-dominated church services for over three decades.

I'd done all this, and yet I'd never encountered anything like the experience that was about to explode into my life in my forties while I was working for TTCW. Up to this point, I had stood for the most part alone in my proclamation of God as 'She'. I'd gotten into trouble over it on several occasions as a vicar. My four youngsters still reminisce (with wry amusement) about the sound of their mother singing with gusto through the church sound-system – changing every male pronoun into a female one. Years later, at the funeral of my youngest son's godfather, one of my daughters leant across to me – I was still singing with gusto and changing the pronouns - and she said to me, "I understand now, Mum." It was a precious moment.

As one of the first female priests, I'd attracted a good deal of media interest. Most of it was friendly and encouraging, though not all of it. In nearly twenty years of ministry, I experienced overwhelming support from ordinary men and women both inside and outside the church. Male clergy, on the other hand – especially in the early days - were a different matter. In some elderly parishioners as well, there was some small degree of animosity. Within ecclesiastical law (supported by parliament) individual parishes were allowed to vote not to allow a female priest to function within their church – they still can. It was humiliating. And it still makes my blood boil.

I was a walking embodiment of the sacred feminine principle. And never more so than when I stood behind the altar in church, robed in my clerical garments, while heavily pregnant. It's why, one Sunday morning, as I stood behind the altar celebrating Holy Communion, expectant with our youngest, one man spat at me and one couple shook their heads in dismay and turned away. Without meaning to be, I was a walking advert for the bodily, earthy holy communion of sex, and some traditional church-goers simply couldn't cope with it.

You have to remember that it was the 1990s. As well as being amongst the first women to be ordained priest in the Church of England, I was also the first priest to require maternity leave. The Chancellor of the diocese where I served, asked me to go and do the research *myself* to ascertain the legal requirements for maternity leave which the diocese were about to be obliged to fulfil. I even made local newspaper headlines as the first vicar to give birth in a Vicarage. That's how new it was. But that's another story – one for my forthcoming book about my life as one of the first women priests in England: the prequel to this volume which is called *Blood Sacrifice*.

Let's move forward twenty years to when I was still working for Mind Cymru. Ginny, one of the women from the TTCW project *Y Babell Goch*, invited me to join her on an all-women's retreat at a Buddhist centre near Brighton. In my previous life as a vicar, I'd been on many retreats and, indeed, had led many retreats. However, I had never participated in an all-women's retreat. Moreover, now, I'd lost my faith. As I've already explained to you, losing my faith had cracked me open and hollowed me out. It had left me in a dark, lonely and frighteningly empty, interior space.

Spiritually I had shut down. Falling in love with Peter had certainly eased that a little. Life had begun to feel sweet again and my heart's doors had begun to open. I was still very cautious though of venturing back into anything spiritual. I didn't any longer trust 'spirituality' and, to be honest, I considered the whole deal to be nothing more than hogwash.

I trusted this new friend, however. Ginny knew some of my story and she'd held my honest vulnerability with a kindness and grace that left me feeling both safe and honoured. I trusted that there was something here I was now ready for and so I said, yes. The leader of the week-long retreat was Marlies Cocheret de la Morniére. I had never heard of her. My friend told me that Marlies had been invited to teach by Adyashanti. I'd never heard of him either. The retreat was called 'The Way of Woman'. I later discovered that it's a well-known and highly-regarded female initiation into the Sacred Feminine. I was completely oblivious of this or what such an initiation might entail. This was a whole new world for me; one which I hadn't even known existed. I packed my bag, including the lovely hand-made lilac coloured silk sari which I'd been given in India, and which I planned to wear for the 'closing ceremony', and I set off with Ginny. I had no expectations and no preconceptions. In retrospect, this was probably a blessing.

The retreat was for twelve women. It opened with us sitting in circle sharing something about what we'd brought with us to place on the 'altar'. I'd brought with me a black volcanic stone from Finland. I'd been given it by Johanna at a Godly Play International Leaders' conference in Helsinki, just before I fled to Wales. It symbolised for me the sense of betrayal which I carried - many layered and ancient. Included within it was my experience of my parents' divorce, the violence of my step-father, the Church of England, the bishop of Los Angeles, the ending of my first marriage, and the weight of the frustration, the anger, and the grief which I carried in relation to my feminist perspective on a patriarchal world. The black stone was small, but what it symbolised was almost unbearably heavy. The sense of betrayal felt like a heavy tomb-stone that prevented me from opening my heart's doors into a new life and a new love. Johanna had made many of the wooden Godly Play materials and artefacts I'd used over the years in many different countries. She'd hand-carved them from a variety of carefully and deliberately chosen native trees. I still use them to tell sacred soul-stories. On giving me the piece of black volcanic rock, Johanna had said to me that when I was ready, when the grief was done, I would cast away the stone. I arrived at the retreat wondering if now was the time.

After we'd each shared the symbolism of our offering, Marlies opened up the circle and our time together with a chant and a prayer. Her words were beautiful and I began to weep. I felt myself soften and relax. Slowly, slowly I began to open. I raised my head and looked around the circle. What I saw was a group of ordinary women. No clerical robes, or gold chalices or ornate candlesticks or towering churches or resplendent cathedrals to be seen. It was simply a circle of women sitting together on the floor. And it was POTENT. I smiled.

Unexpected but absolutely right - after struggling alone in the wilderness for so long, I now had company. And it was the company of women. I felt I was back where my soul's pilgrimage had started – surrounded by beautiful, sassy women. It seemed I'd found a safe place to rest my wrung-out heart and my weary bones, even though I hadn't been consciously looking for it. Safety, as you'll have gathered by now, is important to me. Let me digress a moment and try to define what I mean by the word safe. I mean a place where nothing is asked of me except my presence - a place where nothing is demanded of me that I'm unwilling to give. A place, therefore, without violence. This, for me, is the only place where I ever feel truly safe. And it's why I feel safe with Peter.

During the retreat, Marlies wove a web of safety around us with consummate skill. She's a softly spoken woman of Dutch origin who now lives in California. In spite of the fact that oftentimes, I appear an introvert, I also have a fierce, passionate, loud, extrovert nature – although it's been frequently silenced. As an aside, I've noticed that the safer I feel - the louder and 'bigger' I seem to be getting. I've always loved and been attracted to BIG women (in all the senses of that word) though. Yet, it was within Marlies's quiet, soft and gentle holding of that circle that I found myself becoming settled. And where, finally, even though I was sitting in an ostensibly spiritual group, I felt *completely* safe.

I think the reason that I finally felt safe in that circle held by Marlies was actually very simple. It was firstly a group of only women. Secondly, the sacred was easily and authoritatively named as 'She'. In church I'd usually been the only person holding up the banner on behalf of the Sacred Feminine, in what had often felt like a gendered war-zone. Now, I was sitting at prayer, looking at a woman naming 'God' in *exactly* the terms I recognised as being my spiritual truth since I was eight years old. And, she was doing it in a way that felt so natural and low-key and 'normal'. It's hard to convey what that felt like for me. It was unexpected. It was a relief. It was also a tremendous release. It caused a grief to arise in me like a tsunami. Tears flowed down my face – quietly but seemingly unstoppable. This is what I had longed for – *for so long*. This is what my heart had ached for – the naming of the sacred feminine in recognisably female terms. This is what I'd kept faith with – even now, in what was my 'dark night of the soul'. The grief seemed bottomless. Throughout the following days, I sank deeper and deeper into the soft holding of that circle. In that circle of ordinary women I found that which I'd been fervently seeking all those years in the Christian church. I was home.

We spent a good portion of time in the circle sitting together in silence. I hesitate to describe it as meditating, because that might suggest the focus was on what was going on inside our heads. And it wasn't. Marlies' teaching is a deeply embodied spiritual practise. It encourages an acute awareness of what is happening within the body, as well as allowing a good deal of non-verbal sound and movement. Again, for me, this was a first. What awoke in me during that retreat was my body's ability to communicate deep spiritual truths. Moreover, it soon became clear that this somatic knowing was very much wiser than what I thought I knew in my head. I've tested that new-found discovery many times and in many different ways over the ensuing years. It has never betrayed me – not once.

For the first time as an adult, during the week of that retreat, I released the unedited voice of my body. And what a liberation that was. I cried, laughed, purred, sang, chanted, shouted, screamed, snarled and whooped. It was such a revelation to discover how good, holy and healthy it felt. I was not alone either. At one point, about half way through the week, the noise beginning to erupt from within the circle caused some consternation to our Buddhist hosts. Marlies negotiated for our freedom-of-expression within the retreat space with a quiet, unflustered strength. She refused to have us diminished, hushed or silenced. As she held the boundaries for each of us within the circle, so she held that boundary for us in the face of an external challenge. As I write that, I'm aware that the depth of safety I experienced wasn't shared by every woman in the circle. We each brought different degrees of vulnerability or trauma. Different bodies responded differently to the deepening levels of intimacy and spiritual awakening we were invited to embrace. I thrived in that environment.

During the retreat, I witnessed, for the first time, a woman releasing trauma while held by another woman. Just writing that sentence moves me deeply. The power of it. No shame. No explanation or justification needed. Finally, I could see that it was safe. It was okay, to let it out – unedited and untamed. And then, to be held and honoured by the entire circle of women for having experienced whatever I/we had experienced. It turned my world upside down. The roller-coaster called the Change had done a loop-the-loop, and I found myself standing back on familiar firm ground.

Witnessing Marlies doing the inner work at this soul level made me think about the stories from within the Christian tradition told about Jesus. These days I prefer to call him Yeshua ben Yosef which is his actual Aramaic name. This helps to remind me that those stories don't belong exclusively to the Christian church. It also reminds me that I'm free to continue to find in them a well-spring of wisdom, even though I no longer label myself as a Christian. According to these ancient stories, Yeshua offered a similar quiet, authoritative safety to people who were held bound by suffering. He also used an embodied approach (touch, spittle, his voice, his silent presence, expressed anger or sorrow) to enable the release of long-held, hidden, hurts – emotional baggage, trauma, wounds, 'demons', call it what you will. It was an immense privilege to witness this happening in a circle held by Marlies.

As well as being a spiritual teacher, Marlies is a trained trauma specialist. She has worked professionally with traumatised children and adults in various organisations over many years.

It's important to name that here because soul-work at this depth requires real skill. It also requires much experience, openness to grace and humility of heart. All of which is very, very rare. In my view, Marlies Cocheret demonstrates all these qualities. I value her as one of the wisest and dearest souls I've met (at least in this lifetime).

Towards the end of the week, during an encounter when I was touched gently, lovingly, intimately and reverentially by a woman called Faith (you couldn't make this stuff up!), my heart's doors were suddenly flung wide open and I was FILLED – filled with Spirit. A roar erupted from deep within my belly, my womb, my chest, and my breasts. I began to shake as the sound kept coming and coming and coming. It's the first time I'd heard my ROAR. It was the first of many times to come. Marlies came over to check out whether I, or the two women holding me, needed additional support. On seeing that we were in our element - in full beautiful FLOW – she left us to it. I began to utter those guttural sounds associated in every spiritual tradition with divine ecstasy. Then a song erupted through me. And I joined my voice to the eternal Song that, moment by moment, sings the world into being. More fully than ever before, I knew myself as LIFE: eternal, infinite, Love-filled LIFE incarnating as a human body-soul. One with the All. I AM THAT I AM.

People sometimes ask me at this point in the story, did your faith return to you then? And the answer is both yes and no. My 'Christian' faith, wrapped in its historical package of the church, once sloughed off like an outgrown skin, couldn't be re-inhabited – even if I'd wanted to. The day I fled my life in the Church of England - the day with which I began this story – is the day when I stepped onto the roller-coaster called the Change of Life. It was the beginning of the process of entering the Majesteria – a process whose hallmark is *change*. Once you're changed, you can't be unchanged. The butterfly might want to be a greedy earth-bound caterpillar again, but she can't (and I suspect she wouldn't want to either). There's simply no going back.

Once I stepped outside the employ of the church – and with it, my dependence upon it - I was free to admit some hard home-truths. I recognised that, on some level, I'd colluded with much that was anathema (blasphemous) to my soul. Or, at the very least, I'd turned a blind eye to it. In some ways, it was unavoidable and inevitable simply by virtue of the fact that I was employed by the institution. Lest you forget, the Church of England is an arm of the state. It's not merely a religious organisation – which is what I, in my innocence, thought I was signing up for when I was ordained. It's a cultural and political institution whose bishops sit in the House of Lords in Parliament. It's protected and governed through its own ecclesiastical Canon Laws which are ratified under English Law by the Parliament in whose lofty chambers those same bishops sit. It's a pretty cosy and powerful set-up. Remember too that the Head of the Church of England is the monarch – currently Her Majesty Queen Elizabeth II. The church, in which I served, is a very particular church, with a very distinctive history (and it's definitively not herstory).

If you're wondering why I'm getting my knickers in a twist over this – let me explain. As an arm of the state, the Church of England is inextricably intertwined with much that is questionable about the colonial and imperialist past of these British Isles. Moreover, it shares, with its sister churches from other Christian denominations, a degree of responsibility for some of the worst atrocities wreaked by one human upon another. Let me list a few of them for you now. Brace yourself, it doesn't make pleasant reading.

Take a big breath – though not comprehensive, it's still a long list: legalised misogyny and homophobia; paternalism (God the Father); snobbery and those very British social class distinctions; the creation of the slave trade; hidden and denied child sexual abuse; the horrors and torture of the Inquisition; the Crusades which pitted Christianity against Islam in a Holy War which continues to the present day; the cultural and spiritual impact of countless church missionaries, whose often (but not always) well-intentioned, ill-informed and short-sighted activities, sought (though failed) to exterminate so many indigenous cultures and First Nation peoples, whose ancient wisdom and ways of living in harmony with the natural world, we so desperately need to revive and learn from once more; the belief in demonology which underpinned the so-called 'witch trials', resulting in the burning and the hanging of thousands of innocent, ordinary women (including one of my foremothers); anti-Semitism with its pogroms, ghettos and ultimately the genocide of the Nazi Holocaust; the governance of lunatic asylums in which the mentally vulnerable were chained, beaten and abused; the creation of padlocked iron 'chastity belts' and 'penitent stools'; the deployment of 'scold masks' to silence a woman and make her "hold her tongue".

Well, this woman (as you'll have gathered by now), refuses to be told to hold her tongue, or to be silenced, for a single second longer. I know it's difficult to do. I know we can get unhelpfully snagged by judgement and shame – but we still have to do it. We have to turn and face our histories and our herstories – honestly and bravely. Our human world (growing out of this 'western' patriarchal paradigm which I've just outlined) threatens the very existence of so much life on this planet. If that's not incentive enough to face harsh truths, then I don't know what is.

There are, and always have been, good, honest, loving church folk at every level – from a person at prayer, to bishop, to Pope. Indeed I've been blessed by and have known many. There have always been inspired free-thinkers and socially aware activists, striving to overthrow systems of injustice and inequality, counted amongst the ranks of Christians. I've been privileged to work alongside them. There've been passionate and huge-hearted Christian mystics and visionaries in whose steps I humbly (and falteringly) follow. Yet, in spite of all this, I still maintain that the Christian church, as it stands, is irredeemable. People are usually shocked to hear me – an ex-vicar - say that.

To me, it's glaringly obvious. While Christianity continues to remain exclusively dedicated to proclaiming, 'God the *Father*' and 'God the *Son*', it remains lop-sided and half-baked. It excludes the experiences, the voices and the holiness of half the world's people – the female half. How then can it effectively help our world re-balance and restore equity for all, in these most challenging of times? Remember though that I was committed to the Church of England for over thirty years. And, for twenty of them, I worked my socks off to try and open up the institution to include 'God the Mother'. It didn't happen. It breaks my heart to say it, but I believe it never will. From where I stand, until the Christian church (each and every church) includes 'She', the Divine Feminine, at *every* level of its life – doctrinal, liturgical, ecclesial – on an equal footing with God the Father, it remains a place of profound injustice and exclusion. Disfigured and disfiguring. It takes a huge amount of courage for me, a Clerk in Holy Orders, still legally bound to the Church of England by the Oaths of Declaration and Obedience which I signed before my ordination, to say this publicly. And it is done.

A couple of weeks after the retreat with Marlies, I took that black stone given to me in Finland by Johanna, from my altar at home. You will remember that the stone symbolised my ancient and multi-faceted sense of betrayal. Accompanied by my friend Ginny, I took it to the beach at Ynyslas near Borth in mid-Wales. We sat in silence on the sand in prayer for half an hour or so, with the sound of the rolling waves holding us. Then, we swam far out into the deep sea. And, there, I let the stone go.

Chapter Eight

A CIRCLE OF SISTERS

About a month later, I stayed with one of the women I'd met during 'The Way of Woman' retreat at her home in London. I'll call her Mandy. She comfortably belonged in this vibrant, spiritual world, beyond the church, of which I was just now becoming aware. She'd been attending 'satsangs' for several years. A 'satsang' (if you, like me, didn't know), is a gathering when someone who is respected as a spiritual teacher offers their wisdom in response to questions from an audience. I'd never heard of a satsang, and I'd certainly never been to one before. However, I was looking forward to accompanying my friend, to hear Pamela Wilson one evening, and Roger Linden the following evening. Their satsangs reminded me a little of prayer meetings, only without the weighty out-of-date language and sexist/homophobic baggage of the Church of England. I enjoyed both occasions and was looking forward to then spending some time with my eldest son, and his lovely soon-to-be-wife, over the next few days.

The morning after Roger Linden's satsang, Mandy made us a smoothie for breakfast, and we sat in our pyjamas, discussing the satsangs we'd attended. Suddenly, I was outside my body – no, that's not quite it. It was as if my 'body' had expanded to encompass the room, the apartment, the trees outside, and everything beyond. The 'I' that was Melanie had 'popped'. There was no separation between my awareness of the limitless space of me 'inside', and my awareness of the limitless space of me 'outside'. All was one. Literally. 'I' was no more. There was simply Awareness: awareness free of the limitations imposed by the physical body which dwells within three-dimensional time-and-space. Duality had ceased. The edges which had once 'separated' things, one from the other, had vanished. It was a bizarre feeling. I felt HUGE, as if I filled the entire universe, and yet I remained aware of sitting on the sofa, holding my purple breakfast-smoothie. I began to laugh. I laughed and laughed and laughed. It was like being high on something – only much, much, much, much better. Mandy asked me what was happening and, I tried to tell her, but couldn't stop laughing. She instantly understood and began laughing too. I don't know how long we sat there, two middle-aged women laughing and giggling like a couple of children, but it remains one of my dearest memories.

Eventually, we got up to go and get dressed in preparation for catching the bus and carrying on with our separate plans for the day. It was absolutely hilarious to try and get dressed without a sense of where 'I' ended and my bra began. Eventually Mandy came in to help me, or we'd have been there all day. Going down the stairs of her apartment was a serious challenge – it was covered with black-and-white tiles and I couldn't work out how to walk on them. It was like being physically inside an Escher drawing; or maybe what an astronaut walking on the moon without any gravity feels like. The intensity of the experience slowly faded over the next few days and weeks. I checked in with Roger Linden, who fully understood the nature of the experience, a couple of times once I was back in Wales, just to make sure my feet finally landed safely back on firm ground.

The experience was another change. I was the same and yet not the same. I see the experience as akin to what the old-fashioned churchy word 'resurrection' hints at: a revelation of the truth of who – or more accurately, what – I am in my essential being: simple, eternal, benign, playful Awareness. I think of this as a foretaste of a fulfilment – a consummation (pun intended) after we die – that ending or completion which sometimes goes by the name Heaven, or Avalon, or Nirvana, or Bliss. Heaven isn't a place, of course - it's a state of being – most commonly a state which I experience simply as peace.

When my three years at TTCW came to an end, I decided to take the plunge and set up on my own. I created a small retreat centre offering intensive-solo residential retreats for women. I'll tell you about that in a bit. First, though, I need a break. We're a good way into the story, and it's taken some telling. It feels to me as if the first part is done. I'm going to clamber off the roller-coaster and go grab a hot-dog and some salted popcorn. Not the healthiest food out there maybe, but it's exactly what I fancy. See you in a bit …

✳ **PART II** ✳

Chapter Nine

RETREATING INTO THE DEPTHS

Setting up a retreat space for women was a delicious thing to do. I replaced the dilapidated static caravan on Peter's smallholding with a smart nearly-new one. We planted a garden at the front of it and dug out a six-foot-deep, fifty-foot-wide pond. He built an oak bridge across the pond so that we could sit and watch the fish below. It was beautiful. Overlooking the sea, with the mountain and forest at its back, the horses grazing at the front, it was the perfect place to set up my new venture.

I called it Sadhana Retreat and began to offer what I described as 'soul-medicine'. The word 'sadhana' simply means spiritual practise. It was a term I'd come across many years before when using the excellent spiritual exercises of the Jesuit priest, Anthony de Mello. Peter carved two beautiful oak signs shaped like soaring eagles to welcome guests. Following on from 'The Way of Woman' retreat and the London 'pop', I began to spend time in Sadhana Retreat alone each month at the dark moon (if possible) in a 36-hour-solo-intensive. It was transformational and I continued this practise until we left Wales. Over the next three years, a steady stream of women came to stay at Sadhana Retreat for solo-intensives, to work on whatever called to be worked upon.

I also began holding 'Sunday satsang'. To begin with, I structured this along the lines that were familiar to me from my previous Christian experience, but adapted this to echo what I had seen at various satsangs offered by different spiritual teachers with whom I was by then familiar. This meant that I sat at the front as the knowledgeable retreat-leader offering guidance and wisdom. However, the more I explored and liberated my own wilder, freer self, the more I felt uncomfortable with this model. It still felt hierarchical. The word 'hierarchy' derives from the Greek word *hieros* which means sacred or priestly. As was pointed out to me by a friend, I was simply repeating the old pattern of Melanie-in-a-pulpit, only now it was translocated to Melanie-in-a-satsang-in-a-caravan. Nothing had really changed in the practise. I was still presenting, and perceiving myself, as 'superior' in some way. It felt wrong to me and, I suspect, unconvincing to others. I soon stopped offering 'Sunday satsang'. Something good and true and Melanie-shaped was trying to work its way through me and out into the world, but I couldn't yet tell what it was. More cooking, more preparation time was still needed.

I continued to offer five-day solo-intensive retreats for women. As time went on, I began to trust the newness of what wanted to emerge through me. I began to go with whatever arose in the moment when I was working with someone. The more I felt into the truth that this was a shared venture, mutually beneficial, between retreat-guest and me-as-host, the freer I became. I began to let go more and more into the moment, and to trust life to do whatever needed to be done. My task (which is never easy), was to get my ego out of the way of life's flow and impulse and energy.

I shared the Sadhana Retreat space with some wonderful retreat-guests and I'm deeply grateful to each and every one of them. They helped 'the Change' in me to take root and to grow strong. Going with the flow of the moment, however, did make it difficult to sum up exactly what I was offering and to express it in a pithy sound-bite on my website. I dithered and dallied around how to describe what I was offering and, in the end, just stayed with the term 'soul-medicine'. I trusted that the women who needed to come would come – and they did.

Although the content of the retreats was fluid and changing, I held a clear and strong boundary for my guest. I'd seen Marlies hold that boundary gracefully and clearly in the face of external pressure. And I knew how important it was. A woman needs to feel 'safely held' if she's to feel free enough to do her soul-work with honesty and courage, good humour and tenacity. So, I recommended no electronic gadgets, or outside contact. I also suggested a period of complete silence from 9pm to 9am – what in many spiritual traditions is known as the Great Silence. This was to protect whatever fine thread or elusive scent was being followed through the day, so it wouldn't be lost. It also created a deep, dark well in which potent dreams could surface.

In that sense, it was quite a strict regime. Some found it harder than others to hold those boundaries, but it's what I recommended. My intention was to offer a space that was strong, robust and clear enough to hold *whatever* a woman brought with her to work upon. This was to ensure the best possible chance of the retreat-guest coming face-to-face with her-self - and to encounter her-self over and over again. Spiralling in, ever deeper, towards self-awareness, self-compassion and ultimately, thereby, towards self-empowerment – that self-validating, self-authorising state which I call sovereignty.

During that whole period, I continued to do my own soul-medicine work, and to deepen my own self-awareness, self-compassion and self-empowerment through encounters with women. I was invited into a circle of women to pilot a course called 'The Deepening' devised by Claire Dakin (now Dubois) the founder of *Treesisters*. *Treesisters* is an organisation set up with a dual focus: to re-forest the tropics and to empower feminine-based leadership: www.treesisters.org. We worked through the pilot course over six weeks and then continued to meet as a circle of women each month. I participated faithfully and joyfully in that circle for the next three years until I left Wales. Those of you who have sat in circle with a group of women over time, will know the deep blessings it brings. If held well, it can begin to heal what I call 'the wounds of sisterhood'.

The wounds of sisterhood are another inevitable outcome of a society where access to the dominant power structures is mostly governed by men. Let me explain. In a society like this, the dominant model is that women gain – and retain - their status largely in relation to men. Think of me in that bishop's office seeking his authorisation to take up a new post. In the Church of England, jobs are actually and legally 'in the gift of a diocesan bishop'. Whilst the church is an especially old-fashioned set-up, it's by no means unique. The same power differential is at play – though more subtle and hidden – in many, many British institutions. And, in the majority of them – even today – the person holding the reins of power is most often a man.

This dynamic forces a female to compete with other females for the attention and accolade of the dominant (historically heterosexual) male in whatever context she's seeking furtherance. It's like a female version of the stags' autumn rut. This inevitably leads to women being jealous and fearful of each other. In an environment whose hallmark (in spite of appearances) is one of lack – lack of respect, lack of freedom of movement, lack of freedom from fear, lack of parity, lack of safety – competition is the name of the game.

In such an environment, women learn early on that we're either 'too much' or 'not enough': our breasts too small, our bellies too big, our legs too short, our voices too loud, our private parts too messy, and our viewpoint too strident. In such an environment we can expect attack and 'put downs'. We learn not to trust each other. We learn to look at each other sideways out of the corner of our eyes. We learn to be alert and on-the-lookout for the stab in the back. And we learn to compare ourselves – constantly, through advertising and the media – with an idealised woman who isn't even real. We wear make-up and masks, and we hide our loneliness - our longing to be held, to be comforted, to be *seen*, to be delighted in, by our sister.

I know of no better way to heal this sister-wound than by sitting in a circle with a group of women whose intention and focus is on being deeply and honestly present - to themselves and to each other. It's what the Deepening circle did for me. I grew to love those women. We shared good food together, and laughter, and stories, and song, and some tears. Some left and some stayed. New women came and the circle held us. It simply held us. This simplicity of purpose is essential, and it's not reached without effort.

We weren't a gathering of women who met to grumble about their 'other halves'. We didn't fall into the ugly trap – which I've witnessed on so many occasions when women meet casually without men present – of making generalised unkind statements about men. Those ones that begin along the lines of, "why do men always …", or, "have you noticed how all men …". Such statements usually cause a burst of laughing recognition, because there's a grain of truth perhaps in what's being said. However, in my view, such conversations serve no-one. They merely underline the divide between males and females which already unhelpfully exists on so many levels in society. They just continue the culture of mistrust.

In the Deepening circle, we carefully agreed boundaries and purpose – and it was a high purpose, a deeply 'spiritual' (my word – we weren't explicitly spiritual) purpose. We were learning how to arrive home safely inside our own skins. Our conversations included our men-folk, inevitably. The focus, however, was on us, not our men. As we grew stronger in trusting ourselves, through listening to and expressing our own wants and needs, our sovereign freedom simply to *be* began to take root. The monthly meeting of the Deepening circle of women was the rhythm against which my life was lived – a steady, constant, quietly heard, background drumbeat.

It was these women who blessed me in preparation for my marriage to Peter. They spent a night with me in Sadhana Retreat in which we created ceremony and shared stories. They painted my breasts with incantations and song. We feasted on wild boar lasagne, and home-grown salads and vegetables (the skilled gardeners in our circle were many). We then snuggled down, sleeping alongside one another with the innocence of children. They *are* my sisters – members of an expanding circle that includes my four blood/birth sisters and ripples outwards to include all those women whose souls and hearts touch mine – online, in person, living and dead. We are one circle. One circle of women encircling the globe with our love for planet Earth and for each other. The power of this circle is immeasurable.

With a couple of women from the Deepening circle, I went to EarthHeart, a retreat centre in the Forest of Dean to participate in a four-day grief ritual for women facilitated by Jewels Wingfield. I used to carry a shed-load of grief tucked way down beneath the

Chapter Ten

WRATHING THE TIGRESS AWAKE

ch of us is different, of course, but one of the pieces that I'm led to bring forth (for myself and for you) as we enter our jesteria years, is the piece about women's anger. My own ger is HUGE. It's a volcanic fire burning deep down in my lly-womb. It's the marrow in my bones. It's the sacred red-katlo ead tied around my ankle that links my blood to my ancestral es. My ancestors are important to me – and the older I get, the ore I feel the need to pay homage to them and, somehow, to ve voice to them – especially to the voices of my foremothers.

I have strong blood lines. This blood connects me to my ench Huguenot forebears fleeing persecution. It connects me my maternal English foremother hanged in Kent as a witch. connects me to my paternal great-grandmother, Corelena – a omany Gypsy Chovihani wise-woman whose tea-leaf-reading p was bequeathed to me by my mother. It connects me to all e women in my lineage who were silenced and shamed. Or who ere forced to live lives that were less than sovereign. As I've ready said, I come from a line of strong women – strong, vibrant, ticulate, beautiful, sassy women – and I'm proud of that fact.

feelings of betrayal and abandonment - who does not? I knew from the hundreds of funerals I'd conducted that expressing grief ritualistically can be immensely cathartic. This was a very different sort of ritual expression, however, from the one with which I was familiar in crematoria or church.

This was to be the first of many visits I've made to EarthHeart. Jewels has created a really beautiful space there, in which the sacred feminine is central and honoured. A space where the sacred masculine is invited to come and stand alongside 'Her'. Two complementary energies, different and equal. I won't go into the details of the grief ritual because you really need to be there and to experience it. At the time of writing, Jewels offers it annually towards the end of the solar year. Suffice to say, it was the first time I'd experienced women sacred drumming. Wow. Two women drummed throughout the night – one carrying the rhythm sometimes, while the other rested - the sound unbroken and unceasing. The drumming held us. And we sang. We sang an ancient African women's sacred song. The drums and the song carried us as we, individually and collectively, ebbed and flowed in and out of the deep river of grief that flows through womankind.

After the grief ritual had been completed, we were invited to stay in the temple space to keep vigil and, as and when we needed, to sleep. We all bundled our duvets and pillows onto the temple floor. I've kept vigil before, in my role as a priest in church, or alongside the dying, as well as in my role as a mother sitting up with her sick child. But this was different – this time I was not on my own. This time, I was held by a community of women. Some were asleep, some awake and listening – but all of us doing our own grief work.

It was a profoundly safe space. A space in which I dared finally to let my grief rip. And, it really ripped, right through me. I began my vigil by kneeling to pray before the altar to our ancestors which Jewels had created. I'd placed upon it an old photo of my Romany forebears outside their bender tent, and a photo of my birth family. What came through though was a different sort of prayer from the one I was used to making in church. This was embodied prayer. Prayer such as Marlies had shown me, and which I now practise with the women who come to work with me in Sadhana Retreat. I fell forward onto all fours and I howled up my grief. I howled and howled. Fully spent, I crawled over to my duvet to sleep. Then, a few minutes later, I woke as another great wave of grief ripped through me. Up I lurched onto my feet, and back onto all fours before one of the altars. I've given birth four times. The grief ritual was most akin to that experience in the way that I was helpless to resist the intense waves which wracked my body unrelentingly. And, as with birthing a child, when it was done, it was done. In the morning when I finally awoke (the temple had been completely cleared and rearranged around my sleeping form), I felt emptied out, light, and joyful.

Since then, as I say, I've visited EarthHeart many times, participating both in women-only groups and in mixed-groups. It's always transformative. Each time I'm powerfully witnessed as I step ever more fully into my sovereignty as an Autumn Queen. Increasingly I name her 'Wild Woman Walking'. This woman isn't tidy. She isn't tame. She's not polite or easily pleased. She's outspoken and determined. You may not like her – I often don't. She can be uncompromising and forthright in a way that unnerves me and wrong-foots others. I'm getting to know her. Slowly. And, if I'm honest, a little warily. My conditioning from childhood, and from the years spent in the church, mean that 'goodness' is often equated with 'niceness'. And Melanie Wild Woman Walking isn't

'nice'. As I say, I'm just getting to know her. One as[however, that's instantly and unavoidably obvious, is angry – very, very angry. And so, with knees k menopausal anger let us now turn.

Being a strong woman in a world that does not, for the most part, value a woman's sovereignty, strength and sassiness, however, brings with it a price. I'd witnessed the bruising price my mother had paid for being strong-willed, sexy, outspoken, untameable and indomitable. It's a price many women, understandably, choose not to pay. Instead we choose to collude, to pay the price that keeps us protected and privileged within male-dominated structures. Most women, including me, have on occasion chosen the easier option of colluding with what we know to be wrong, because the price of standing up to challenge that wrong is simply too high a price to pay. Our anger helps us to find our much-needed courage.

Like so many of us, I'd been indoctrinated with the notion that for a woman to be angry is unacceptable. Like many women, for almost all my life, I'd kept my anger mostly hidden. It would sometimes erupt unattractively after a few glasses of wine. Or, on occasion, would come unbidden and be hurled at my husband or children. But I did my utmost to keep it under wraps. And, for the most part, I succeeded. As a woman, as a Christian, as a mother and as a priest, I considered my anger to be something negative. It was something of which I was ashamed. It was something I wished I could expunge out of me once-and-for-all, and completely eradicate.

However, as I dived deeper and deeper into the untrammelled, untamed truth of myself during my menopausal years, I discovered something startling. I discovered that I liked my anger – more than that, I relished it and delighted in it. When I allowed my anger to begin to surface, without seeking to edit, control or tidy it up, what erupted in me was an absolutely incandescent energy. It was an energy that carried within it the power of transformational healing as nothing else had. It was mind blowing. I began to practice what I later came to call 'wrathing'. I let myself express my fury through free sound and movement. I danced naked in the wind and the rain outdoors. I rattled my bone-and-feather shaker to the sky and struck the earth with the shamana staff which Peter had carved and decorated for me. It certainly helped having a retreat space which was set a good distance from its nearest neighbour!

At about this time I came across the work of Peruqois. I began to use her CD *Emotional Cleansing* both for myself and with clients. The more I danced and sounded my anger, the bigger and more beautiful it became. I began to cease to be afraid of my fury. I began to sense that here was an amazing source of untapped energy within women. I've enjoyed silent prayer sessions since my teens. But, now, I couldn't keep silent. I began to growl long and loud. I stopped sitting on my prayer stool. I needed to crouch low with my belly and breasts pressed to the earth. Then, as a result, I began to hear a sovereign, sacred, GROWL in reply. I'd sensed that my anger tapped into a life-transforming healing energy inside me. Now what revealed itself to me was the fury of Mother Earth - desecrated and demeaned. Accessing *Her* anger, was a whole different level of potency.

It's a commonplace that many women experience anger in a new way during the menopausal years. The hot flush isn't just something that happens in the middle of the night. For many of us, it rises burning in our soul, in the face of the world's cruelty. Our fuse is shorter. Our gaze is clearer. Our longing for justice is sharper and more to the point. Until I was almost through the seven years of my menopausal journey, however, I'd never had an actual hot flush – or hot flash as some call it. Then I went to Alexandra Pope's three-day workshop on menopause.

There were twenty-three women attending and that, in itself, was pretty potent. On the second evening, we were invited to mull over a question during the night. Alexandra asked us to consider what was our 'calling'? What was the high purpose that wanted to flow through us in this, the third and penultimate phase of our human life? I awoke at 3 a.m. with my entire body feeling as if it was aflame. Energy thrummed through me coming from my core. I felt that I was at the molten centre of planet Earth's heart. I reached for my journal and began to write.

At that exact same time, thirteen other women awoke. They too were experiencing a hot flush and an immense burst of creative energy. I've been familiar since my teens with my menstrual cycle synchronising with other females. I'd grown up in a household of mostly females, after all. But, until Alexandra's workshop, I'd never heard of menopausal women synchronising together in this super-charged manner. Since then, I've had occasional hot flushes at night. Each time it happens, I treat it as an incredibly potent sacred opportunity. I see it as an opportunity - while my molten core-energy is rising - to fuse and merge with other women's energy. By doing this, by joining forces (as it were), my intention is to release transformative, creative, positive potential for change into the world's morphogenic-field. It's a beautiful active form of prayer.

This is one of the reasons why I encourage women who seek my guidance, to let menopause 'have her way' with them. And, as far as is possible for them, to steer clear of artificial hormones which block or numb the body's free response. The energy that wants to flow through us at this time is like no other. It's *Her* fire. Its purpose is to cleanse and to de-tox us of the detritus we no longer need, and which we can no longer carry – nor, deep down, wish to carry. I think of hot flushes as immolating my defences until the 'real' me can break free to take her true place in the world.

As I've said before, it's *fierce* grace, and the face menopause wears isn't always pretty. I'm certain that if we want to be truly 'hot' (sassy and sexy) as mid-life women, we need to feel our own heat and to let it burn us from the inside out. If we want to rise phoenix-like from the ashes of our own pasts – we must let ourselves come on fire. The woman who has walked through the flames of her own transforming *ire*, and who stares deep into our eyes when she looks into the bathroom mirror – wow – she is a force to be reckoned with.

I often hear women speak with shamed chagrin of their menopausal anger. I've even heard enlightened or awakening women express the wish to get through the stormy waters of menopausal anger as quickly as possible. So often, holiness or enlightenment is still presented as mostly recognisable through a calm, unruffled, peaceful exterior. I'm a big fan of peacefulness and equanimity, don't get me wrong. However, there's something in that always calm, unruffled, 'enlightened' exterior which, frankly, I don't trust. Maybe I've known too many clergymen who appeared shiny, clean and holy but in truth were cheating on their wives, or were bullies, or homophobic closet gays, or paedophiles, or thieves. These days, I get edgy around a holiness that doesn't get down and dirty with the global mess we're in – a mess that's both an expression and a symptom of our inner turmoil.

In contrast with the ever-popular call in some spiritual circles to let go of our anger, I want to encourage us to stay with it and to work it – especially as mid-life women. I'm constantly on the look-out for places and ways in which we can eye-ball anger and honour it. It's why I began to offer 'wrathing retreats'. This doesn't mean hurling our anger outward at someone or something in unthinking or unconscious ways. It means learning how to harness our fury. It means learning how to ride our wrath like a snarling, smoking, Welsh dragon. If we learn how to ride our rage, creatively and safely, she'll take us somewhere new. She'll guide feelings of betrayal and abandonment - who does not? I knew from the hundreds of funerals I'd conducted that expressing grief ritualistically can be immensely cathartic. This was a very different sort of ritual expression, however, from the one with which I was familiar in crematoria or church.

This was to be the first of many visits I've made to EarthHeart. Jewels has created a really beautiful space there, in which the sacred feminine is central and honoured. A space where the sacred masculine is invited to come and stand alongside 'Her'. Two complementary energies, different and equal. I won't go into the details of the grief ritual because you really need to be there and to experience it. At the time of writing, Jewels offers it annually towards the end of the solar year. Suffice to say, it was the first time I'd experienced women sacred drumming. Wow. Two women drummed throughout the night – one carrying the rhythm sometimes, while the other rested - the sound unbroken and unceasing. The drumming held us. And we sang. We sang an ancient African women's sacred song. The drums and the song carried us as we, individually and collectively, ebbed and flowed in and out of the deep river of grief that flows through womankind.

After the grief ritual had been completed, we were invited to stay in the temple space to keep vigil and, as and when we needed, to sleep. We all bundled our duvets and pillows onto the temple floor. I've kept vigil before, in my role as a priest in church, or alongside the dying, as well as in my role as a mother sitting up with her sick child. But this was different – this time I was not on my own. This time, I was held by a community of women. Some were asleep, some awake and listening – but all of us doing our own grief work.

It was a profoundly safe space. A space in which I dared finally to let my grief rip. And, it really ripped, right through me. I began my vigil by kneeling to pray before the altar to our ancestors which Jewels had created. I'd placed upon it an old photo of my Romany forebears outside their bender tent, and a photo of my birth family. What came through though was a different sort of prayer from the one I was used to making in church. This was embodied prayer. Prayer such as Marlies had shown me, and which I now practise with the women who come to work with me in Sadhana Retreat. I fell forward onto all fours and I howled up my grief. I howled and howled. Fully spent, I crawled over to my duvet to sleep. Then, a few minutes later, I woke as another great wave of grief ripped through me. Up I lurched onto my feet, and back onto all fours before one of the altars. I've given birth four times. The grief ritual was most akin to that experience in the way that I was helpless to resist the intense waves which wracked my body unrelentingly. And, as with birthing a child, when it was done, it was done. In the morning when I finally awoke (the temple had been completely cleared and rearranged around my sleeping form), I felt emptied out, light, and joyful.

Since then, as I say, I've visited EarthHeart many times, participating both in women-only groups and in mixed-groups. It's always transformative. Each time I'm powerfully witnessed as I step ever more fully into my sovereignty as an Autumn Queen. Increasingly I name her 'Wild Woman Walking'. This woman isn't tidy. She isn't tame. She's not polite or easily pleased. She's outspoken and determined. You may not like her – I often don't. She can be uncompromising and forthright in a way that unnerves me and wrong-foots others. I'm getting to know her. Slowly. And, if I'm honest, a little warily. My conditioning from childhood, and from the years spent in the church, mean that 'goodness' is often equated with 'niceness'. And Melanie Wild Woman Walking isn't 'nice'. As I say, I'm just getting to know her. One aspect of her, however, that's instantly and unavoidably obvious, is that she is angry – very, very angry. And so, with knees knocking, to menopausal anger let us now turn.

Chapter Ten

 WRATHING THE TIGRESS AWAKE

Each of us is different, of course, but one of the pieces that I'm called to bring forth (for myself and for you) as we enter our Majesteria years, is the piece about women's anger. My own anger is HUGE. It's a volcanic fire burning deep down in my belly-womb. It's the marrow in my bones. It's the sacred red-katlo thread tied around my ankle that links my blood to my ancestral lines. My ancestors are important to me – and the older I get, the more I feel the need to pay homage to them and, somehow, to give voice to them – especially to the voices of my foremothers.

I have strong blood lines. This blood connects me to my French Huguenot forebears fleeing persecution. It connects me to my maternal English foremother hanged in Kent as a witch. It connects me to my paternal great-grandmother, Corelena – a Romany Gypsy Chovihani wise-woman whose tea-leaf-reading cup was bequeathed to me by my mother. It connects me to all the women in my lineage who were silenced and shamed. Or who were forced to live lives that were less than sovereign. As I've already said, I come from a line of strong women – strong, vibrant, articulate, beautiful, sassy women – and I'm proud of that fact.

Being a strong woman in a world that does not, for the most part, value a woman's sovereignty, strength and sassiness, however, brings with it a price. I'd witnessed the bruising price my mother had paid for being strong-willed, sexy, outspoken, untameable and indomitable. It's a price many women, understandably, choose not to pay. Instead we choose to collude, to pay the price that keeps us protected and privileged within male-dominated structures. Most women, including me, have on occasion chosen the easier option of colluding with what we know to be wrong, because the price of standing up to challenge that wrong is simply too high a price to pay. Our anger helps us to find our much-needed courage.

Like so many of us, I'd been indoctrinated with the notion that for a woman to be angry is unacceptable. Like many women, for almost all my life, I'd kept my anger mostly hidden. It would sometimes erupt unattractively after a few glasses of wine. Or, on occasion, would come unbidden and be hurled at my husband or children. But I did my utmost to keep it under wraps. And, for the most part, I succeeded. As a woman, as a Christian, as a mother and as a priest, I considered my anger to be something negative. It was something of which I was ashamed. It was something I wished I could expunge out of me once-and-for-all, and completely eradicate.

However, as I dived deeper and deeper into the untrammelled, untamed truth of myself during my menopausal years, I discovered something startling. I discovered that I liked my anger – more than that, I relished it and delighted in it. When I allowed my anger to begin to surface, without seeking to edit, control or tidy it up, what erupted in me was an absolutely incandescent energy. It was an energy that carried within it the power of transformational healing as nothing else had. It was mind blowing. I began to practice what I later came to call 'wrathing'. I let myself express my fury through free sound and movement. I danced naked in the wind and the rain outdoors. I rattled my bone-and-feather shaker to the sky and struck the earth with the shamana staff which Peter had carved and decorated for me. It certainly helped having a retreat space which was set a good distance from its nearest neighbour!

At about this time I came across the work of Peruqois. I began to use her CD *Emotional Cleansing* both for myself and with clients. The more I danced and sounded my anger, the bigger and more beautiful it became. I began to cease to be afraid of my fury. I began to sense that here was an amazing source of untapped energy within women. I've enjoyed silent prayer sessions since my teens. But, now, I couldn't keep silent. I began to growl long and loud. I stopped sitting on my prayer stool. I needed to crouch low with my belly and breasts pressed to the earth. Then, as a result, I began to hear a sovereign, sacred, GROWL in reply. I'd sensed that my anger tapped into a life-transforming healing energy inside me. Now what revealed itself to me was the fury of Mother Earth - desecrated and demeaned. Accessing *Her* anger, was a whole different level of potency.

It's a commonplace that many women experience anger in a new way during the menopausal years. The hot flush isn't just something that happens in the middle of the night. For many of us, it rises burning in our soul, in the face of the world's cruelty. Our fuse is shorter. Our gaze is clearer. Our longing for justice is sharper and more to the point. Until I was almost through the seven years of my menopausal journey, however, I'd never had an actual hot flush – or hot flash as some call it. Then I went to Alexandra Pope's three-day workshop on menopause.

There were twenty-three women attending and that, in itself, was pretty potent. On the second evening, we were invited to mull over a question during the night. Alexandra asked us to consider what was our 'calling'? What was the high purpose that wanted to flow through us in this, the third and penultimate phase of our human life? I awoke at 3 a.m. with my entire body feeling as if it was aflame. Energy thrummed through me coming from my core. I felt that I was at the molten centre of planet Earth's heart. I reached for my journal and began to write.

At that exact same time, thirteen other women awoke. They too were experiencing a hot flush and an immense burst of creative energy. I've been familiar since my teens with my menstrual cycle synchronising with other females. I'd grown up in a household of mostly females, after all. But, until Alexandra's workshop, I'd never heard of menopausal women synchronising together in this super-charged manner. Since then, I've had occasional hot flushes at night. Each time it happens, I treat it as an incredibly potent sacred opportunity. I see it as an opportunity - while my molten core-energy is rising - to fuse and merge with other women's energy. By doing this, by joining forces (as it were), my intention is to release transformative, creative, positive potential for change into the world's morphogenic-field. It's a beautiful active form of prayer.

This is one of the reasons why I encourage women who seek my guidance, to let menopause 'have her way' with them. And, as far as is possible for them, to steer clear of artificial hormones which block or numb the body's free response. The energy that wants to flow through us at this time is like no other. It's *Her* fire. Its purpose is to cleanse and to de-tox us of the detritus we no longer need, and which we can no longer carry – nor, deep down, wish to carry. I think of hot flushes as immolating my defences until the 'real' me can break free to take her true place in the world.

As I've said before, it's *fierce* grace, and the face menopause wears isn't always pretty. I'm certain that if we want to be truly 'hot' (sassy and sexy) as mid-life women, we need to feel our own heat and to let it burn us from the inside out. If we want to rise phoenix-like from the ashes of our own pasts – we must let ourselves come on fire. The woman who has walked through the flames of her own transforming *ire*, and who stares deep into our eyes when she looks into the bathroom mirror – wow – she is a force to be reckoned with.

I often hear women speak with shamed chagrin of their menopausal anger. I've even heard enlightened or awakening women express the wish to get through the stormy waters of menopausal anger as quickly as possible. So often, holiness or enlightenment is still presented as mostly recognisable through a calm, unruffled, peaceful exterior. I'm a big fan of peacefulness and equanimity, don't get me wrong. However, there's something in that always calm, unruffled, 'enlightened' exterior which, frankly, I don't trust. Maybe I've known too many clergymen who appeared shiny, clean and holy but in truth were cheating on their wives, or were bullies, or homophobic closet gays, or paedophiles, or thieves. These days, I get edgy around a holiness that doesn't get down and dirty with the global mess we're in – a mess that's both an expression and a symptom of our inner turmoil.

In contrast with the ever-popular call in some spiritual circles to let go of our anger, I want to encourage us to stay with it and to work it – especially as mid-life women. I'm constantly on the look-out for places and ways in which we can eye-ball anger and honour it. It's why I began to offer 'wrathing retreats'. This doesn't mean hurling our anger outward at someone or something in unthinking or unconscious ways. It means learning how to harness our fury. It means learning how to ride our wrath like a snarling, smoking, Welsh dragon. If we learn how to ride our rage, creatively and safely, she'll take us somewhere new. She'll guide us into new realms we've yet to explore and, which – one day – we may choose to inhabit.

So, to this end, I began to offer Rage Retreats, where women could come to practise 'wrathing'. In this space they began to explore how to meet their anger safely, unedited, unashamed and untamed. It was extraordinary. Women cried, danced, painted, sang, smashed and screamed their anger. They let it come, the full force of it rushing through their body while I held the space safe around them. Sometimes this meant they needed me to dance, sing, spit and scream alongside them. And, sometimes, they needed me just to sit quietly and to bear witness.

What we discovered was that shackled to our anger was fear. In releasing anger, we began to feel our fear – to really feel it. It was a fear I recognised. It was the fear that lurks beneath every woman's successes and accolades in an unfree world. It was tempting to turn away, to run and hide – again. It was tempting to play safe – again. Instead, I encouraged us to turn to each other and to lean into our shared sisterly strength. In this way, we became brave enough to keep calling the anger forth.

When I listened to the 'voice' of another woman's anger (and, indeed, my own), I heard and saw something beautiful. I heard us named fearlessly and ferociously in our female glory. I saw us plant our feet on the ground and take a stand on behalf of planet Earth. We stood first and foremost as Protectoress. In this guise, we have many names: the Great Mother Goddess who protects the earth's fertility and the growing of crops; Lady of the Land who hides two-footed and four-footed creatures beneath her skirts; She of Aquaria who purifies the rain; Queen of the Forest who preserves the trees, and all green and growing things; Oceana who swims in the rivers and deep seas, helping them to flourish in spite of pollution and over-fishing; Majesterial Eagle who soars through the skies guarding the sovereignty of air. As I name myself and womankind in this way, I feel a deep longing for the Sacred Feminine to rise up *through us* to replenish the desecrated wastelands of our world.

I want to be absolutely clear here. I'm not advocating that women get in touch with our suppressed and silenced anger in order to fling it outwards in violence at the world - or at our husbands or lovers or work colleagues or girlfriends or the dog or our cat. Far from it. We do, moreover, need to proceed with caution. I wouldn't recommend diving into the deep-water soul-work of wrathing without first checking there's a life-belt, or a life-guard of some description, to hand. No-one wants to drown in a tsunami of anger. And it can be a risk.

The relentless internal pressure of keeping silent, of playing the 'good girl' over most of our lifetimes, can cause suppressed anger to warp into something unpleasant and uncreative. When suppressed anger first surfaces (as my story bears witness) it can be disruptive and ugly. It can lead to self-harming behaviour or suicidal thoughts. So we need strong, wise companions to help hold us steady as the waves begin to roll over us. In other circumstances, suppressed anger can make its presence felt in so-called 'bitchiness' or 'cattiness', or in making our nearest and dearest feel 'hen pecked'. I don't especially like those terms – but I recognise what they're pointing towards. It's easy to see what unredeemed, disconnected male anger looks like. We only have to switch on the TV news or open a newspaper. The world doesn't need a full-blown female version of the same angry violence.

It's why I dislike some of the new movies where females are portrayed as 'super-heroes'. They zap their enemies with the same strength and power as their male counterparts. As far as I'm concerned, they're really just men with tiny waists and big tits pretending to be women. They aren't real and I don't want to be one of their tribe. What I'm talking about here is something quite different. 'Wrathing' (in my practise) is a spiritual high-art. It's about a super-charged anger that is reclaimed, reconfigured and re-connected to our deepest longings. *This* anger is the source of our Wild Woman energy ('wild' as in self-willed). This anger crouches inside us, vibrantly alive, eyes aflame, snarling, claws bared, ready to leap to the protection of the vulnerable, the dispossessed, the voiceless and the lost. She's a mother tigress. Our world needs *her*. She's been absent way, way, way too long.

Some of the women I work alongside, coming face-to-face with their inner tigress for the first time, are afraid of her. She is big, really BIG. And she's fierce. They fear she might overwhelm them, and take over their lives leaving divorce, havoc and mayhem along her trail. I can't promise them that she won't. What I am able to suggest, however, is that if they pick up the scent of their hidden anger and track it back to its lair; they are likely to find themselves there. Oftentimes, it's a frightened little girl they find. And what that girl needs isn't a handsome knight clad in shining armour, riding a white charger, to appear on the horizon – attractive as that might sometimes feel. What she needs is for the grown woman, in whose soul she hides, to step-up and protect her.

This isn't just about us as individuals, of course. It's about our world. It's no coincidence that so many of the grass-roots movements that are springing up around the globe to protect planet Earth - her forests, her rivers, her sacred sites, her oceans, her air - are being led by women. And, yes, *angry* women. Naomi Klein offers an inspiring and informative snapshot into the breadth and depth of these movements in her book about capitalism and climate change, *This Changes Everything*. Naomi documents how many of the ideas embraced within newly emerging alliances to protect the planet, arise from within the ancient wisdom traditions of indigenous cultures and First Nations peoples. The women leaders whom Naomi describes have harnessed the force of their anger and directed it towards a creative end – saving our planet. It's a worthy endeavour.

In whichever direction we look, our planet is in difficulty. We are facing challenges on a global scale the like of which we've never had to face before. Something new (or perhaps very old) is needed. Something radically different from the way we live now. Something that starts from within me, and then moves outwards. I believe, and have done for the past thirty-five years of my professional life, that we cannot heal the planet without first healing ourselves. In fact, my view, these days, is that unless we find a way to heal ourselves pretty sharpish, we'll have left it too late.

Our planet is circumscribed by very real physical laws and limitations. We may have chosen to ignore them largely, since the exciting explosion of human activity initiated by the discovery of fossil fuels which birthed the Industrial Revolution. Yet they remain real nonetheless. William Catton's book, *Overshoot*, though written thirty years ago, offers an excellent analysis of the ever-growing human need to consume the planet's finite and depleting resources. Moreover, it's a kind book. There's no finger wagging. It's an honest, almost clinical, assessment of how we got to where we are. Catton outlines what happened when our (mostly) well-meaning forebears (like us) inherited and developed a system that seemed, on the surface of things, to work pretty well for the greater number of people. It didn't work too well for the minority groups, of course – or for millions of species now extinct, or the environment. But from the perspective of the dominant,

WASP (white Anglo-Saxon protestant) ruling majority at the time, it seemed to be improving the lot of many, many people.

This was the metanarrative the 'western' world inherited. Let me explain what I mean by metanarrative. It's an overarching dominant storyline, told by the 'conquerors', and rendered a permanent truth by virtue of print. We believed what we read (or at least we did until the era of the internet). We believed what we were told by our parents and our teachers. Most of us grew up not knowing there were other, older, untold, hidden or silenced stories. We swallowed the metanarrative, hook, line and sinker, and are now watching nonplussed and seemingly helpless, as that storyline, which said life would just get better-and-better, threatens to drag our species down into an early grave.

So, what to do about it? Well, we can listen to the stories that those who do not belong to the dominant majority are telling. Some of those stories are very old and they predate the metanarrative I've just outlined. It'd be naïve to suggest we can return to an idealised pre-industrial era. We can't. But we can learn from our mistakes. We can get angry about them. We can make different choices now as a result. We can play our part in helping our planet to heal. Planet Earth is as much a self-regulating, self-healing organism as are our human bodies – if not more so. We evolved from planet Earth, after all. Now, that's cause for hope.

Chapter Eleven

AVALON REMEMBERED

In the late summer just before we left Wales, I attended a week-long gathering of twenty-one women at Glastonbury. It was a gathering of high priestesses to re-align and release blocked planetary healing-energy. We came from many different spiritual lineages but when we stood in circle, we were one. We danced, sang, anointed one another and offered ourselves as a portal through which healing love could flow freely. The gathering was called *Avalon Remembered*. It was organised by Kalila Sophia Rose of www.priestesspresence.com and Diana DuBrow www. EmeraldTemple.com. It involved a pilgrimage to visit and reclaim sacred sites within and around Glastonbury. We also visited Kennet Long Barrow and the Avebury stone circles under the guidance of Peter Knight, whose book *Stolen Images: Pagan Symbols and Christianity* is well worth reading.

At each sacred site, we sat or stood in circle and held ceremony. Our task was to 're-set the light codes' in those places. I understood this to mean that we were clearing the spiritual and energetic blockages in the planetary morphogenic field. These blockages are caused by the harm done by humans – to each other and to the environment. Harm is difficult to define of course. I understand it to mean, and recognise it most easily, as violence. I've benefited from acupuncture for over thirty years, so the methodology made sense to me – only this was the planetary 'body' we were unblocking, rather than an individual's physical body. It was an extraordinary week.

The highlight for me occurred after a dream I had a couple of nights into the pilgrimage. I dreamed that I was a high priestess at the temple of Dendara (in what is now Egypt). The temple was dedicated to the Goddess Hathor. Diana DuBrow had greeted me as a high priestess of Dendara when we first met. It was a place I knew nothing about. Later research, however, confirmed that my dream portrayed an accurate sense of what it was like at the height of its influence, two millennia before the birth of Yeshua ben Yosef.

It's clear from archaeological evidence that the priestesses of Hathor were highly skilled and powerful women. They were learned in a broad range of subjects: astronomy, astrology, alchemy (which is the beginning of chemistry and its offspring, modern medicine), herbology and the healing arts, and mathematics. They spoke many languages. They welcomed and learned from many other peoples and cultures. They were in sole charge of the temple of Hathor. There were no priests to defer to or to be demeaned by. There were, however, highly honoured male guards (often eunuchs) whose duty was to protect the priestesses from physical harm.

The temple of Hathor stood within a matriarchal and matrilineal sub-culture within ancient Egypt. Because, like so many of us, I'm formed and shaped within an overarching, almost invisible, male-dominated metanarrative, it's very difficult to grasp what that really means. It's hard to appreciate or to apprehend what that meant for women – ordinary women and girls in their everyday lives.

Let's take a moment to pause. I want to re-imagine (and perhaps psychically remember) what it might have felt like to live in those times.

This is a society in which women are respected and honoured as a matter of course. It's a society in which females are included as primary cultural decision makers, and wisdom keepers. Ruling men turn to the priestesses of Hathor for guidance on matters of politics and war, agriculture and commerce. The archaeological record reveals that within the Hathor temple at Dendara, great councils took place – councils of war, as well as councils during times of peace. Scholars from distant lands came to consult the extensive library there, as well as to consult the knowledgeable and highly respected priestesses.

Still visible within the temple today, the meticulously painted murals reveal the breadth of activity which took place there: the birthing rooms with skilled midwives; the places to bring the dead for preparation for burial; the moon rooms for the sacred act of menstruation; rooms dedicated to the sexual arts where boys would be initiated into manhood; rooms where girls were initiated into womanhood by women; and rooms where the life-force of adult sexual energy was freely celebrated, honoured and enjoyed.

Perhaps those Christians and Muslims who sought to desecrate Hathor's temple were afraid of the power of women? Who can say? What's clear is that they sought to render it an unholy place. They literally *de-faced* the temple – battering and striking the skilfully carved faces of the hundreds of Goddess statues, until no recognisable features now remain. It was, in my view, an aggressive and appalling desecration – a sacrilegious act. Despite the violence hurled at it, those who visit the temple today and stand beneath its soaring columns, say that it still retains a *majesty* - a serenity and a sanctity that two thousand years of brutalisation has yet to destroy.

Hathor's temple at Dendara was a place where the everyday and the esoteric were held in equally high esteem. Where the four stages of woman (maiden, mother, queen and crone) each had their place and were honoured. This was a place and an era where to be ashamed of your menses would be unheard of, for it marked your transition from girl to woman. It was cause for community celebration and ceremony. This was a place and an era where to be denigrated for ceasing to menstruate would be unthinkable, for it marked your transition from mother/matrona to elder. The menopausal gateway was to be celebrated and marked as holy through sacred ceremony.

This was a place where your virginity was not a commodity that added a market-value for your future husband. Virginity was a sign of your own sovereignty. It was within your power to retain or to gift to another. Here, a woman who chose to remain childless was honoured. Here a woman who chose to give birth was honoured. Here the sacred womanly arts of contraception and fertility were discussed and debated by women for women. In Britain, to be called "a cow" is an insult. There, the Goddess Hathor wears the ears of a cow as a symbol of her life-gifting quality. Lactation is not something to be sneered at, to blush about or to be hidden away. It's something recognised as both everyday and yet miraculous. No wonder many people grieve the passing of this era and feel anger towards those who destroyed it.

In my dream I stood in the temple of Dendara before it had been desecrated, its rooms emptied, its priestesses raped, murdered and scattered. I've been a lucid dreamer for as long as I can remember, so I'm normally very awake and aware in my dreams. I usually remember them clearly and I often record them in my dream-journal on waking – as I did on this occasion. This recollection is based upon my notes.

The scale of the temple was awe-inspiring and the energy it contained pulsed through me like an electrical charge. The Goddess was seated upon a throne and towered over me at least a hundred feet high. She was majestic and powerful, beautiful beyond words, both kindly and terrifying. Before Her, I bowed low. I raised my head and looked upon her face. My heart swelled with love. Finally, I was face-to-face with *Her* – the One who had been calling me since I was eight-years-old. She smiled at me and I felt my heart fill.

"You have a question?" she asked.

I nodded.

"Is it time for me finally to lay down my priestly orders and to take up only the mantle of priestess?" I asked.

She laughed and it was a sound that rippled and roared through the temple.

"Tell your story," she said.

I didn't understand.

"Look around you," she said.

Turning I saw a great throng gathering around me. In it were men and women from every human tribe and of every colour. I knew them to be my forebears and my descendants – not just from this lifetime but from many lifetimes. And not just within my physical bloodline but those with whom I share spiritual lineage. Then I understood (and it doesn't squeeze easily into words, so please forgive this clumsy attempt): I knew myself as one soul – one soul passing through many lifetimes and existing in many forms. I knew myself to contain priest, priestess, shamana, shaman, medicine man, witch, druid, spirit-healer, Swimming Forest Seer. One soul called to serve love. As this knowledge landed in me, it was as if a huge burden lifted off my chest. I knew I cannot die. Melanie will die, of course, but this awareness cannot. I was one with life – the life that was both 'me' in this moment, and which was also before-and-after 'me'. I was at peace.

The next morning when I awoke I knew what I needed to do: two things. Firstly, I needed to 'tell the story' of being an Anglican priest to the circle of Avalon priestesses. Secondly, I needed to celebrate the Eucharist (variously called: Holy Communion, the Mass, or the Last Supper) with them. Proposing the first seemed scary enough. The second task was bloody terrifying.

Over breakfast, I mentioned to Kalila and Diana that I'd had a night-time vision.

"Excellent" said Diana.

"Oh goody," said Kalila.

I outlined my dream to them and told them what I wanted to do as a result.

"Well, if it's fine with the other priestesses in the circle, you telling a bit of your story could weave in nicely," said Kalila. She paused. "And I was wondering how tomorrow afternoon wanted to play out. Well, now I know. You're going to lead us in the ritual of Holy Communion tomorrow in the Bethlehem Chapel Almshouses in Glastonbury. Great, that's sorted."

Diana roared with laughter at my stunned face.

The next day, in the morning, we held ceremony at the Red and White Springs in Glastonbury and then, after lunch, gathered in the herbal-healing garden of the Bethlehem Chapel Almshouses. I had asked two of the women to help me with the Eucharist. We set everything up ready inside the chapel and took our places within the standing circle of priestesses.

There, I told my story about being amongst the first women-priests in the Church of England. I spoke of my profound sense of 'doing what I was created to do', as I stood behind the altar for the first time and said the Eucharistic Prayer. The Eucharistic Prayer is the great prayer of thanksgiving into which is woven the story of the Last Supper, when Yeshua breaks bread and pours wine 'in remembrance' of the Great Mystery. I told of how I had stood my ground as mother to my four young children – refusing to be sucked into a work-life pattern that shut them out. I spoke of how I'd smeared my moon-blood on the altar one Sunday morning, incensed by a male priest's refusal to let me near the altar of 'his' church in case I was menstruating. I spoke of being spat at during a service of Holy Communion when heavily pregnant with our fourth child.

I confessed my continuing love of the stories told about Yeshua ben Yosef (Jesus Christ). I reclaimed my commitment to the Christos-Sophia mysteries. I declared my belief that beneath the soul-sapping weight of Christendom lays hidden a 'pearl of great price'. And I named this pearl as wisdom. At its heart, I said, is a vision of inclusivity and belonging and radical self-giving love that I never want to betray or deny. It was liberating to dance this story at the centre of a circle of high priestesses – and to have that story heard, held, and honoured. And when it was done, it was done.

I then invited all the women present to bring into the space anything they were carrying in relation to Christianity, the church, or male-dominated religion that was burdensome to them. I invited them to bring anything from their own experience or from the experience of others which they'd been told about which was hurtful, damaging, or diminishing. I invited them to bring these burdens of herstory so that we could "lay it all down into the arms of the Mother". I opened my arms wide as I spoke:

"I stand here before you as a one-time representative of a male-dominated faith. I stand here among you, my sisters, with an open, fearless heart. I stand here in circle as both priest and priestess. I stand strong and true in order to receive from you the burdens you have carried as a result of the wrongs done in the name of Christianity and male-dominated religion. Only the human heart can heal those wrongs. I offer you my heart, my own sacred heart for the transformation of those wrongs, and I offer it in service of our world. I stand here drawing upon the strength of this sacred circle, that together we may release the abuse and wrong-doings of Christianity and male-dominated religion into the arms of the Great Mother: She who knows all, sees all, and loves all. In so doing, my prayer is that we will thereby help to clear this dense blocked energy from the etheric field. We make this act of love on behalf of all who have suffered at the hands of male-dominated religion."

As I spoke the words I was trembling. It wasn't fear – I'd dropped deeper than that - it was a somatic response to the huge amount of energy thrumming around me in the chapel. And they brought it – woman after woman after woman – speaking her truth and the truth of her sisters and brothers who have suffered at the hands of Christianity and the churches and the Abramic religions. Together we let it pass through our bodies and laid it to rest in the arms of mother Earth. It just kept coming and coming. And when it was done, it was done.

Then Kalila stepped forward and stood directly in front of me, arms outstretched, hips wide and feet solidly planted. She spoke the words that were a balm to my soul – as refreshing and life-giving as rain in the desert.

"I bring before you my wrath", she said, "my fierce rage at what you had to endure as a woman-priest in the church."

She echoed back to me parts of my herstory. She roared her rage, and the circle roared and shook and howled our shared acknowledgement at what I had endured. I could feel it lifting from me – the burden of shame I'd been carrying – carrying without even knowing that's what I was carrying year after year. The shame of being a woman in the church: a sexually active, menstruating, pregnant, lactating mother, and a wild-gypsy-witchy-woodland-naked-swimming woman. The shame that I was still a Clerk in Holy Orders – still legally bound to an institution for which I no longer felt any allegiance.

Kalila stood in front of me with upraised arms shaking, legs wide, feet stamping, connected to our mother Earth. She loudly proclaimed my glory as a woman – my courage, and my deep love, my grit and my huge heart, my resilience and my compassion. She bowed to me in honour of who I had been and what I had done on behalf of womankind by dancing my dance within the church until fierce grace broke me and set me free. The circle echoed her words and also bowed low to me. I stood upright and strong. I accepted the tributes of my sisters with tears pouring down my face. I felt the two halves of my life: priest and priestess join hands. Re-linked: *re-ligio* (Latin) is where we derive the word religion. Religion is meant to be the Great Re-linking of that which is fragmented. The becoming one again of the many.

I then sat down on the floor and told the story of the Last Supper. I wove a new Eucharistic Prayer – that great prayer of thanksgiving which I'd recited thousands of times in church and which I love deeply. I related it as if I was Mary Magdalene herself, sitting next to her beloved at the Passover meal. I told the story of how I'd heard that Yeshua had been arrested. I spoke of the agony of watching as he was crucified. I spoke of that early Sunday morning when I was the first witness of the resurrection. I related how Yeshua authorised me and *sent* me to tell the others. The word *apostolos* in Greek means 'the one sent'. In English we derive from it the word 'apostle'. I spoke and the circle of priestesses reverently listened.

As I remember that re-telling of the core Christian story in the Bethlehem chapel in Glastonbury, I can't help but wonder. What if Mary of Magdala's authority and leadership had been honoured rather than denigrated and ignored? What if the chalice – the grail – that Yeshua had handed to her on the night before his death, had remained in her hands rather than been taken from her? What if Mary and the other women whose status Yeshua recognised and respected, had remained in charge and centre-stage in the years that followed his death? What if the Dead Sea Scrolls at Nag Hammadi, containing a different set of Gospels from those in the Bible, hadn't waited until 1947 to be found (see below)?

So many what ifs … If those things had happened, I wonder what a very different world we might now live in. History would perhaps have included herstory. This knowledge breaks my heart *and* it fires me up to take action. So, 'in remembrance of *Her* story', I broke bread and poured wine. I invited my sisters, the high priestesses from many different spiritual lineages, to partake and to *remember*. To remember who we truly are. We belong here – all of us - Earth's children, made equally from dirt and stardust.

"We remember, we remember," the circle chanted. "We remember we are one heart. We remember our vow to choose Love."

When we 'remember', we literally re-member, i.e. bring back together the broken, lost limbs, the 'members' of ourselves and of our world. The Christos-Magdalena-Sophia story echoes back into the Isis-and-Osiris story. Isis searches for, and finds, the lost limbs of her lover-brother. She re-members him – and thus she

111

restores him to wholeness. In so doing, she re-creates, she brings forth life once again from death. It's a motif echoed again in the Kore-Persephone story. And it's what the Christian 'Easter' story is really about. The word Easter stems from the sacred name of the Anglo-Saxon Goddess of Spring: Oestre. English derives the words oestrus and oestrogen from the name Oestre. She is the Goddess whose sacred animal is the hare - hence 'Easter' bunnies. Spring following winter following autumn following summer following spring – a never-ending story.

Older than the Christ-Magdalene story; older than the Isis-Osiris story; older than Oestre-and-Cerunnos story; this is the story of Earth herself: the seasonal dying and being re-born that we name as the seasonal cycle. Life from death, and death within life. This is our human story. We are not above it, or separate from it, we *are* it. Sharing that Holy Communion with my Avalon sisters was the first time I had done so fully at peace with myself – priest and priestess, 'masculine' energy balanced with 'feminine' energy, child of patriarchy and daughter of the Goddess. One, whole, holy woman. Another threshold crossed. Another turn of the spiral. Another ride at the fun-fair.

Chapter Twelve

THE SCENT OF HOLINESS

One of the many blessings which arose within the *Avalon Remembered* pilgrimage was the reaffirmation of my use of sacred oils. Diana DuBrow teaches women to remember and to reclaim our birthright as those who anoint others at the sacred moments of transition contained within a human life. Amongst these are: birth, death, marriage, menstruation, the sexual union and healing. For millennia women have been the wisdom-keepers of the arts of healing and anointing.

It's said that pure essential oils have the highest vibrational frequency of any material substance on our planet. They are the 'essence' of plant and mineral. I think of them as little light-beings which can transverse cell membranes in a manner that science is only now beginning to understand. I've heard essential oils described as planet Earth's immune system – and, the immune system, of course, is fundamental and crucial for healing. Perhaps this revival of their use is a sign of planetary healing. I hope so.

In the temple of Dendara, five thousand years ago, the 'magic' of essential oils was well known. Among many ancient cultures, the oils were valued as the most precious and expensive substances in existence. It's no surprise therefore that, according to the stories we've inherited, frankincense is among the three gifts which the magi brought to the baby Yeshua. In my wooden Godly Play nativity set, carved by my Finnish friend Johanna, one of the magi is clearly female. This wasn't Johanna being fanciful. Nowhere does it say that the magi were three kings or even males. Perhaps the magi, those mysterious wise ones, were three majesterial women? Who knows?

In thousands upon thousands of Christian churches, millions of people call Yeshua ben Yosef by the name Jesus Christ. The word 'Christ' comes from the Greek word *christos*, which means 'anointed one'. Yeshua is the one who is anointed. That's what confirms and bestows his authority as a divine healer, a wise-man, a sage, and a seer. And who bestows this upon him? A woman. A priestess. A 'Mari'. Mary. Mary of Magdala.

If you doubt the importance of anointing, or are unfamiliar with its place in sacred ceremony, watch the film of the 1953 Coronation Service of Her Majesty Queen Elizabeth II in England's Westminster Abbey. In this rite Elizabeth follows in the footsteps of many, including the pharaohs of Egypt. In order to become queen or king, one must be anointed. The sacred oil which I used as a vicar, and with which I was myself anointed at my ordination, is called the Oil of Chrism. *Chrism* is the oil of anointing. Few Christians know it, but Yeshua stepped into his destiny as the Christ through the anointing of a woman – his beloved 'Mary', high priestess of the Goddess.

In oral folk tradition Mary of Magdala has always been described as having dark skin, dark hair and dark eyes. This oral tradition has now been confirmed through the findings within the Dead Sea Scrolls. She was probably Egyptian. Perhaps she and Yeshua had known each other as children in Egypt. She was certainly a priestess at one of the many temples dedicated to the ten-thousand forms of the Goddess with which that land is blessed. I like to think of her in the temple of Dendara as a young woman, learning the sacred arts of healing and sexuality, perhaps catching glimpses of the little Hebrew boy who sometimes came visiting with his mother, speaking their strange Aramaic language to each other. Who can say? I'm sure, however, that the high arts she learned as a priestess, in whatever temple she served the Goddess, she then shared with and taught to her beloved.

There is a beautiful story in the Christian Bible of a woman who braved the hostility of the Pharisees in order to get close to Yeshua. The Pharisees were strict 'orthodox' Jews who legalistically adhered to the Torah. They were probably well-meaning men but their interpretation of their religion led them to believe that this woman was 'unclean' and therefore unwelcome in their space. They try to prevent her from approaching Yeshua who is reclining at meal. She persists. She then honours Yeshua by washing his feet with her tears and her hair, before dousing them liberally with sacred oils.

Tradition says she does this for love of him because she intuits all that is to follow: betrayal, crucifixion, resurrection. Her prodigious act points to a woman who knew the power of the ritual she was performing – a priestess, a seer. Yeshua's response to this sacred act is succinct and clear. He tells the men who are gathered around him, watching the woman with disapproval, distaste and a total lack of understanding: "wherever this story is told, she will be remembered". *She will be remembered.*

I had the words: 'In remembrance of Her' embroidered on my priestly stole (scarf) as a vicar. I wore it to honour 'Her': this particular woman certainly, but also all the unnamed women in the stories surrounding Yeshua ben Yosef and, behind them, the

Goddess Herself – the feminine divine principle at the heart of creation.

The unnamed woman in this particular biblical story is often associated with the legends that cluster around the super-charged figure of Mary of Magdala. It's worth noting that the women who went to Yeshua's tomb after his crucifixion, did so in order to anoint him with holy oils. These oils, as I've already said, were more precious than gold or silver. The unnamed woman is railed against by the Pharisees for "wasting" the valuable oil by pouring it liberally over Yeshua's filthy, dusty feet. Pah! She knows exactly what she's doing and why.

On that first 'Easter' morning, the women come bearing their sacred oils. They come as priestesses to do what priestesses have done for thousands-upon-thousands of years – to anoint the dead. I am going to name them now as an act of honouring them. They were Mary of Magdala, Mary the mother of Yeshua, Mary of Bethany, Salome and Joanna. The word mis-translated as the name Mary in fact *means* priestess. The term Mari echoes in the many titles given to innumerable expressions of the Great Goddess: Mariamne of the Semites, Mari who was the Syrian version of Ishtar, Maya of the Orient, the Moerae or Fates of Rome, the Persian Mani, and, of course, Maria-Mare who is manifest as the oceans of our world (the energy I like to name as She-of-Aquaria). The presence of three 'Mary's' at the tomb represents the face of the ancient and omnipresent Triple Goddess: birth, life, death.

In the Christian Bible there are several versions of what exactly happened, just after dawn, on that 'Easter' morning, in the garden where Yeshua was buried in a cave. I want to add one more. The group of women approach the cave-tomb where they have laid Yeshua's broken and crucified body on Friday, the eve of the

Sabbath. They had washed him quickly and anointed him in haste because once the sun had set, the Hebrew Sabbath (which lasts from sundown on Friday to sunrise on Sunday) would have begun. It would have been disrespectful of Yeshua's spiritual lineage to have continued with their task after dusk. So they hurried back to the tomb as soon as they could – at first light on the Sunday morning.

What they encountered there that dawn, at that moment when light and darkness touched and embraced, was the Great Mystery. It was an experience of time enfolding eternity, of life entwining with death, of time-and-space breaking free of the limits of relativity and bursting out as … LIMITLESS LIFE. It's a moment which is prefigured by and echoed in the story of The Raising of Lazarus – more of which later. The male authors of the Christian gospels say that the women in the garden on that 'Easter' morning were frightened by the sight of an angel sitting by the entrance to the cave-tomb, and ran away. Rubbish! These were women who were skilled travellers between the realms: midwife, death-doula, mother, priestess, lover, and seer. It would take more than an angel to scare them off. They loved this man.

The Yeshua they experienced in that garden had been *changed*. There's disagreements in the various versions handed down to us, exactly how he was changed – but changed he was. He had broken through the confines of time-and-space – as we all do in death – and he revealed to these trusted, powerful, authoritative women, these high priestesses, what that experience meant for him and for them. He authorised them to "go and tell the world" that death is not the end. Life always follows death. This is planet Earth's sacred mystery: life-within-death-within-life. This is her majesty.

When literature and sacred story is written almost exclusively by men something is missing. Without women's voices, we can't understand what it is to be human – whether we're males or females. The Judeo-Christian 'Holy Bible' is an excellent example of a lop-sided narrative that excludes (and indeed demeans) women's voices. One of my passions is to dig for herstory. I've often thought that if I hadn't ended up a priest/ess, I'd like to have been an archaeologist. Herstory is often hidden within literature and sacred story, and it's worth digging for. I like to dig down deep and find the hidden treasure. I like to press my fingers deep down into the rich, dark, 'dirty' humus of our human stories and have a good old rummage around. I'm convinced that the 'pearl of great price' (wisdom) lies hidden there. Like so many middle-aged people, I've developed a profound pleasure in gardening. When I explore literature and sacred story for women's hidden or silenced voices, I think of myself as a gardener tending a patch of the truth – digging, sowing, weeding, pruning, tending, watering. My aim is to ensure that Herstory is included in the garden and given space to grow strong.

It's worth reiterating at this point that Yeshua ben Yosef was taken as a baby by his parents into *Egypt*. Advised by the Magi, they flee from Bethlehem to avoid 'the slaughter of the innocents'. This was that heinous act whereby King Herod, fearful that a 'new king' had been born who would threaten his power base, ordered all male babies under the age of one to be slain. Can you imagine the terror? From this carnage Mari and Yosef fled with Yeshua into Egypt.

The first we hear of Yeshua again, after the birth narratives recorded in the Christian Bible, is when his parents leave their home of Nazareth to visit the temple in Jerusalem, taking Yeshua with them for the first time. By then, he is twelve years old. His formative years, therefore, possibly until the age of eight or ten, had, in all likelihood, been spent in Egypt. Remember that Egypt is still, at the beginning of the Common Era, a matriarchal, matrilineal culture in which women were honoured and where the Goddess was served and revered in mighty soaring temples like the one at Dendara. The decimation of the Goddess temples under the onslaught of Islam was still five hundred years in the future.

I like to imagine the boy-Yeshua, taken by his mother to the temple at Dendara. He holds her hand, looking around him with his big dark eyes filled with wonder at what he sees. He stands in the incense-laden halls where priestesses and thousands of pilgrims chant and bow in homage to the Goddess, the Mother of Creation. Perhaps his mother regularly consulted with the priestesses there and sought their company and wisdom. Who knows? We know that his mother was a mystic and visionary – her song, Mary's song, known by millions of Christians as the 'Magnificat', attests to that. It makes sense that she consulted and visited with other wise, knowledgeable women, especially as she was living in exile, far from her homeland and family.

We also know that his early life in Egypt left an imprint on Yeshua. Why otherwise would he choose the Mari of Magdala (the priestess of Magdala) as his life-partner? If you doubt that this is what she was, then read the Gospel of Thomas or the Gospel of James, the brother of Yeshua, or the Gospel of Mary Magdalene herself. Precious papyri scrolls – the so-called Dead Sea Scrolls – discovered in pottery urns in the caves at Nag Hammadi near Qumran in 1947 and 1956 – reveal a very different herstory from the one inherited through the official version contained in the Bible.

Let's *pause* here a moment, if we may. I need to catch my breath. This stuff matters to me a great deal, and marked such a significant shift in perception for me, that I want to give it due weight. Okay, I'm ready now. The woman whom Yeshua (Jesus Christ) chose to have closest at his side during his public life, and the first person to whom he chose to reveal the mystery of his resurrection after death, was a woman trained in the sacred art of anointing. She was a priestess. She was, in all likelihood, a high priestess. She was a woman dedicated to, and set apart for, worship of the Mother Goddess – *God the Mother.* As someone raised within the vehemently anti-goddess Judaeo-Christian tradition, it's a pretty momentous realisation. As one of the first women priests in England, it lands in my chest like a time-bomb. As a vicar who always felt more priestess than priest, it detonates with a dynamic explosive force that sends a depth charge through my entire system. For me - *it changes everything.*

As I stood, year by year, in the Cathedral to receive the newly blessed Oil of Chrism to take back to the parish, if I'd known that I stood within the ancient and venerable spiritual lineage of the priestesses of Dendara, how differently I would've felt. It almost doesn't bear thinking about. I look back over the decades of my public ministry in the church and take note of the scores of occasions that I used holy oils to mark a human moment as sacred. If I'd known that by so doing, I joined the illustrious company of thousands of holy women, how changed my self-understanding and self-acceptance would have been. If I'd known that the practise of anointing with holy oil was originally in the purview of women, then maybe I'd have been able to claim my role in the church without fear of exclusion and rejection.

Maybe then, I'd have been able to challenge the Archdeacon (now deceased) who had a habit of pinching and patting my bottom whenever I stood in the processional line in front of him in church. Both of us were robed in clerical holy garb. I was dressed in my cassock and surplice, and the Archdeacon was dressed in his splendidly decorated chasuble. I was thirty-one years old and freshly ordained. As one of the first women leaders in the church, I felt the eyes of many upon me. I wanted to make a success of it - for my own personal satisfaction and on behalf of other women. I kept my head held high as I processed into church in front of the Archdeacon and behind the Cross. Inside my heart though, I felt horribly humiliated. I wish I'd known that my right to be an authorised leader in that sacred space had nothing to do with the 'gifting' of a male bishop. Rather, it had everything to do with the fact that I belong to a long line of holy priestesses.

Then, as the organ music swelled and the congregation rose to its feet out of respect for the clergy – in that pause before the procession into church began - I might have felt able to turn around and knee the Archdeacon in the nuts to protect myself and to ensure he knew to keep his hands off me. Then, perhaps I'd have reported him to the church authorities for repeated sexual harassment in the workplace. If I'd been an authoritative priestess-figure in my own right, maybe the church authorities would have listened and acted appropriately in my defence. I like to think so. This story is *my* Deep-water Dreaming after all.

I deeply grieve that the ancient temples to the Goddess were destroyed. I rage that Her priestesses were raped. I am saddened that those illustrious libraries were burned and the knowledge, gathered carefully over centuries, was trodden into the dust. During this heart-breaking destruction, the cry from the temple guardians was always the same.

"Save the oils!" they cried.

The oils summed up what the temples were about – what the Goddess they proclaimed was about: *healing*, deep, transformational, under-the-skin healing. The surviving priestesses who fled the burning temples took the sacred oils and disappeared with them from herstory into the silent Diaspora. Who knows all the places whence they fled? What we do know is that they will have fled to places which would offer them sanctuary – safe places, places sacred to the Goddess. There are traces of them wherever you look across Europe: in Greece, France and Spain for sure. And, if they travelled even further west, perhaps they found welcome with the Druids at Anglesey and the legendary priestesses of mythical Avalon at Glastonbury. I like to think so.

Wherever the surviving priestesses ended up, we can be sure they had their holy oils in safe-keeping. They also carried with them their oral wisdom-tradition. This wisdom-tradition was preserved and protected by women. Precious, secret and hidden from its persecutors, it was a wisdom passed from grandmother to granddaughter. It was whispered over the bubbling cauldron containing the evening meal. It was shared in the herb gardens of rich and lowly alike. It was respected by the apothecary and the medicine-man. Then came the witch-hunts and much of the sacred lore of women-healers was lost. But not all of it – and today we are *remembering*.

At the *Avalon Remembered* pilgrimage in Glastonbury, Diana led us in a day-long initiation ceremony through anointing with the sacred oils. Our intention was to reclaim and remember the almost lost and forgotten high-art of anointing such as had been practised in Dendara. Afterwards we didn't shower or wash for forty-eight hours so that the oils could fully permeate our bodies.

It would be impossible to describe the impact which that experience had upon my physical system – it was like being re-set back to 'the factory settings'. My whole body thrummed and vibrated, filled with rainbow-light-energy and the dark, fecund power of creativity. I lay naked and whole and ALIVE. I knew it was a foretaste of the mystery which that old-fashioned, churchy word 'resurrection' points towards. It was an intimation of what 'happened' at dawn in that garden outside the walls of Jerusalem two thousand years ago. Suffice to say that within and through that initiation, I landed inside my skin as never before. I like to think of the London 'pop' as the out-breath, and this 'chrism/christening' as the in-breath.

Diana DuBrow and I are sister souls. Meeting her will remain one of the deepest joys of my life. We are amongst the Keepers or Guardians of the sacred oil Galbanum. The gift of Galbanum is both that of 'truth-teller' and of 'light-bringer'. The familiar name for 'light-bringer' is *Lucifer* – a figure most often associated in popular mythology as a 'dark'-negative energy. This popular notion accurately (if perhaps unwittingly) recognises the unbreakable link between light and shadow, positive and negative poles of energy. Light and dark – positive and negative - belong together. Actually they are one.

Interestingly in the Middle Ages, Mary of Magdala was often given the title Maria Stella Lucifer: 'Light-bearing Star of the Ocean' or, alternatively translated: 'Dark Star of the Seas'. I don't imagine the 'Church Fathers' intended the name to be complimentary. More likely it was intended to be condemnatory. However, as is so often the case, countless ordinary Christian folk 'remembered' the Goddess, and continued to offer Her respect and reverence in their daily lives: the adoration of the Virgin Mary and the Black Madonna, which persists throughout Europe to this day, is one such obvious example.

A couple of days before I set off for the *Avalon Remembered* gathering of priestesses in Glastonbury, I had a cobalt-blue star tattooed on my forehead. It was a very deliberate and expressive act of self-anointing. Peter designed it for me. I knew I must be almost through the menopausal gateway which marks the entrance into the Majesteria years. It was time to mark my body ready for the next phase of my life.

The idea of a tattoo on my face caused quite a bit of consternation amongst my nearest and dearest. Sensibly though, I didn't tell them until after the deed was done. The tattoo artist was very nervous. Afterwards, he said that in thirty years of doing tattoos, it was the scariest one he'd ever created. I guess I appear a bit too conventional to have a facial tattoo – after all, I'm still technically a Reverend. He warned me that people would treat me differently if I had a tattoo on my face – and he implied that the difference wouldn't be positive. He insisted on doing my daughter's shoulder tattoo first in the hope (I suspect) that I might change my mind. He asked three or four times if I was absolutely sure. My daughter responded: "If you knew my Mum, you'd know that when she says she's sure, she's sure." When the tattoo was completed and I'd explained to him what it meant to me, he was quite moved and, pressing his hands together in the prayer pose over his heart, he bowed deeply.

Different people bring different responses and interpretations to the blue star I have tattooed on my forehead. For me, for now, it's first and foremost my declaration to myself (and to the world) of my intention to live from my deepest, truest centre. I soon named the tattoo "Star of Avalon". It's a guiding star reminding me of where I've come from, and where I'm heading. It is the mark of a queen, a high priestess of Dendara, of Avalon, a druid of Anglesey, a 'Star Child'. It's a mischievous salute to my free, untamed spirit – and, since it's designed by Peter, it's a statement to the world about us. I absolutely love it. It's a message from me to the male-dominated world of the dying old-order. It says, "Wild Woman Walking - watch out!"

Chapter Thirteen

FALLING HARD

On a breezy October morning not long after I'd left Mind Cymru and opened Sadhana Retreat, I tacked up one of the horses and prepared to hack out from the livery stables on Peter's smallholding. The plan was to ride up into the Cambrian Mountains which lay invitingly beyond his place. My young riding friend, Catrin, was on a pretty Connemara mare. I rode Peter's mare, a mature forward-moving Welsh Cob. I was a little nervous as this was the first time I'd ridden her out without Peter's steadying presence at my side. Usually when hacking out on my own, I rode my very familiar and much-loved gelding called Jackson. He could be a bit of a plodder which, at the time, suited me just fine.

Catrin and I set off up the lane chatting together, enjoying the stunning view below of the coastline stretching from Aberaeron in the south to Ynys Enlli (Bardsey Island) in the north. The two horses were in good spirits, picking up on each other's high energy, both eager to stretch out and test their strides. As Catrin commented, they were perfectly matched, and we agreed to put them through their paces. Once off the road and into the forestry, we kicked them on and set off at a fast trot. We rode for nearly an hour before coming to a sandy track which rose ahead of us in a steady curve – a perfect canter path.

"You ready?" Catrin cried.

"Sure thing," I shouted in reply, laughing.

We took off up the track, the horses cantering neck and neck, stride for stride, in perfect unison. It was a gorgeous feeling. It was the first time I'd ridden a horse so fast and so well. It was exhilarating. I could feel fear in the background but, for once, it wasn't holding the reins. The horses began to increase their pace and we thundered up that hill.

As the track started to narrow, my mare, delighted that finally she was being given her head and wanting to pass the young Connemara, took off. As she did so, my stirrup connected with Catrin's foot and became momentarily hooked. It came free almost immediately but I'd lost my footing and without the stirrup, my balance shifted, my rhythm was lost and I bounced off-beat in the saddle. If you're a rider, you'll know that horrible feeling. You and your horse, who moments before were riding in complete harmony and partnership, one movement, one being, now find yourselves separated and out of balance with each other.

I was too inexperienced at the time to shift my weight and regain my balance without the support of a stirrup, and so I bounced off-beat in the saddle while my horse cantered on. Normally, I would've been standing up out of my stirrups, jockey-like, when cantering. But on that particular day, Catrin and I had been discussing how to canter 'properly' with your seat in the saddle and that's what I'd been doing.

I knew that at the top of the incline, the track re-joined the road before disappearing again into the forest. I tried to get my foot back into the stirrup, but failed. Knowing that I was losing my balance, I tried to pull the mare up. Generally, when I rode her alongside Peter, she was responsive to the lightest touch, but the circumstances and the energy now were very different. I felt her resisting me. Again, inexperience was my enemy. Rather than softening my grip and releasing my body into the saddle in order to slow her down, instead, I pulled harder and tensed up. I felt the familiar uprush of fear flood my system. The mare felt it too. As we reached the road she panicked. By tightening on the reins, I'd pulled her head up and the result was she didn't know which way to turn. She clattered out onto the road, spun around, and went down a ditch. I somersaulted over her neck and crashed my head and shoulders down onto the tarmac. I lay completely still, winded and in pain.

My companion, sitting relaxed astride her horse, witnessing this undignified descent, laughed loudly with the innocent amusement of an extremely proficient nineteen year-old rider. The forty-something year-old woman lying on the tarmac, however, was feeling something quite different.

"You alright, Melanie?" Catrin asked between guffaws. "God, for a moment I thought you were dead! Peter will kill me if anything happens to you."

"Don't worry, I'm fine," I lied, trying to smile gamely.

I pulled myself up to sitting, shakily got to my feet and went to retrieve my horse. Her reins had snapped so Catrin cobbled something together sufficiently safe to get us back to the stables, and helped me to mount.

My face was cut and scratched from hitting the tarmac but nothing had been permanently damaged by the fall. It took months, however, for the bruising across my back to disappear totally, and over a year for my neck and shoulder to recover fully. During that year I committed myself to uncover, understand, tune into and tame my fear around riding. I'd been carrying this fear around since childhood. It had the potential to get me into dangerous situations and, more than that, it was getting in the way of the thing I most enjoyed doing: riding out with the man I loved.

Up until that point, riding was, and always had been, a battle to overcome fear. I covered it well. I repressed it well. I overcame it well. Yet still it was there – tucked away, deep down, ready to erupt and ruin my ride. I'd learned to ride when I was a young child on my sister's pony, but had never become a particularly confident or proficient rider. My sister was a brilliant horsewoman and helped to train the seventeen hands-high Windsor Polo Club ponies. She would sit me, age ten, upon her little pony, Rueben, and tell me to relax and enjoy myself as she put me over tiny jumps.

"Remember, Mellie, he can feel your fear," she'd say. "He knows your every thought" - which really didn't help.

She was right though. Rueben could feel my fear very clearly. Time and time again, he would take off across the field with me on his back. I'd grip onto his mane for dear life, knowing that the only way this would end would be me falling off; which I frequently did. I loved grooming him and feeding him, but I was nervous of riding him. My deep desire to please and impress my older sister, however, kept putting me back in the saddle again and again. It took me decades to realise that I envied her. I wanted to be able to ride like her – to look like her on horseback: an elegant and upright, well-turned-out and fearless horsewoman, who was classically trained in English-riding. I wanted that so badly. It took almost thirty years for me to stop wanting to ride like her. For me to start wanting to ride like me (which is very different). And then to begin to discover and to enjoy what that feels like.

After my parents' divorce when my horse-loving older sister left the family home, I stopped riding. Then, when I was in my thirties and my children began to learn, I took it up again. During the weekends at our holiday cottage in Wales, I'd go with them for a riding lesson at a farm half-way between Aberystwyth and Machynlleth. It totally reawakened my love of being around horses. And when my daughters began to show a real interest too, I found us a pony on loan which we stabled as near as possible to the Vicarage.

As I've already mentioned, after I moved full-time to Wales, I began to help look after a hefty Shire/Dray horse for a family in the village. During that dark first year after I left the church, that huge horse, aptly named Merlin, was my therapy. Grooming him and feeding him each day, occasionally riding out on him, grounded me like nothing else. I'd chat to him and tell him all my woes, weeping into his glossy flank and breathing in his warm, reassuring hay-sweetened breath. His silent, accepting, kindly, strong presence helped the healing process. A year on, by then beginning to feel stronger and less afraid, I bought my beautiful Welsh Cob, Jackson. And began to ride in earnest. Moreover, as you may remember, it was through looking for a companion pony for Jackson that I met Peter.

When I began to date Peter, we had eight horses between us. Like me, he didn't learn to ride seriously until in his thirties. Unlike me, however, he is a natural and fearless horse rider. We've hacked out for five or six hours at a time and after I moved my horse onto his smallholding, we rode out together several times a week. When riding out with Peter, I felt safe – safe in the way I described in a previous chapter – where I can simply be present in a non-violent situation with nothing being asked of me. He never asked me to do anything I didn't want to do, or push me beyond my limits. On the rare occasion when I felt suddenly afraid; without comment, Peter would pull up and wait for me to dismount. I'd take a moment to let the adrenalin flush through my system. Then, once my heart rate returned to normal and I was breathing easily again, I'd re-mount and we'd carry on with our ride.

I feel it's time to introduce you properly to my husband Peter – this beautiful man with whom I'm deeply in love and with whom I delight to share my life. I met him soon after I'd begun the descent that marks the beginning of entering the Majesteria, and he's been the most significant companion along that long journey. Peter is a rare breed. We often joke about it – but I'm totally serious. I've spent time with all kinds of people from many different cultures and countries, and I've never met anyone quite like him. He has an inner depth and spaciousness that is like the deep, dark mountain lake-water I love to swim in.

Let me give you a brief sketch of Peter's back-story – about as different from mine as is possible. Peter grew up with his brother and sister on a dairy farm on the edge of a village near the river Teifi in a Welsh-speaking family. His father worked for the Forestry Commission for forty-eight years and his mother was in charge of the cows. Days were long and involved manual work on the farm before and after school. In spite of the fact that he belongs to a huge extended family, he and his siblings were shy with other people and when visitors came to call, the three of them would run out the back door to hide.

Peter was twenty-four years old before he ever used a telephone. He still hates them. He is, for the most part, uneducated and untouched by cultural expectations or parameters. He spent his school career climbing out the windows to go fishing or hay-gathering on nearby farms, or sitting on the school roof watching the teachers trying to find him. As a result, he is free from much of the baggage of cultural convention and pressure, which warps so many of us out of our true shape.

He will patiently build, make or mend anything I ask him. With his strong muscular hands and careful artist's eye, what results is always something beautiful. He is most at home in the wild where, climbing, fishing, hunting or tracking, he moves with the focused energy and grace of a dancer. As I've said, I sometimes call him my Fisher King or Wild Man of the Mountains. A huntsman since boyhood, with a sharp eye and a steady aim, he's physically fit and agile. He exudes a masculine, raw, sexy energy. The archetype he's closest to, in my mind, is Puck - for there's a sparkling, mischievous, untamed quality about Peter.

A deeply private person, he loathes crowds of people (even celebratory family gatherings can swamp him) and avoids towns and cities if at all possible. Beneath his quiet exterior, there's a steely strength that allows for a clear, non-judgemental, unfaltering, but not unkind, 'No'. He's a man who knows his own mind, and this, perhaps surprisingly, is actually very restful to be around. He belongs to himself and he belongs to place. Attachment to people, even close family, is almost absent. A pristine, pure soul, he nightly dreams textbook Jungian archetypes, and mytho-poetic stories drawn from the collective unconscious, in spite of never having heard of Carl Jung. As is typical of someone whose expressiveness is embodied rather than verbal, oral rather than literary, he is a consummate and entertaining story-teller with a phenomenal memory for detail. He is intuitive and deeply intelligent, rather than bookish or intellectual.

In spite of the many differences in our backgrounds, we fit together laughably easily. He seems to embrace the complex totality of who I am (which, in its natural unrestrained state, is constantly in flux and as swiftly changing as a weather-front). Towards me he demonstrates an easy, uncomplicated, simple acceptance. Having had to fight for the right to be myself in a variety of external contexts, Peter's easy unquestioning acceptance of me is still a cause of wonder. A man of very few words, he's the least opinionated person I've ever known.

We can spend entire days utterly contented in each other's company without ever needing to speak. We don't listen to the radio, read the papers or watch the TV (unless it's the rugby). To our offspring that's sometimes amusing, sometimes baffling, and oftentimes boring. But, for a wordy, mentally busy, woman like me, our quietness is a haven of rest. We frequently call ourselves "Mr Yin and Mrs Yang" (deliberately swapping the 'feminine' and 'masculine' titles). We are very different and yet comfortably complementary. We belong together – from our first date I knew this - I knew I'd grow old with Peter. He says we're two halves of one soul, and I think he's probably right.

One of the reasons Peter is so easy to be around, is that he doesn't need to assert himself or promote himself because he is quintessentially happy and at peace in his own skin. And, which is so rare nowadays, he is also deeply at home within the natural world, where he shines luminous. All of the qualities I've described are an antidote to so much that I carry: the need to be competitive, self-assertive, self-promoting. Deep insecurity and the disabling experience of being overwhelmed by fear are traits that I have, and he doesn't. So that, slowly, slowly, without even trying, just by being alongside him, those qualities which were deeply rooted in me, gently let go their suffocating grip upon my soul.

Peter has his own shadow side, of course; and his own wounding. He has his own experiences of being humiliated and betrayed. He also knows what it's like to feel powerless and afraid. This surfaces sometimes if he's swimming in deep water - but more of that later in the story. Truth to tell, he's the easiest man in the world to live with: a kind, gentle, strong, protective, clear-seeing, sensitive soul. As I write those words, we've been together seven years, including nine months living full-time in a two-berth motorhome over a long hard Scottish winter. And it just gets easier, and more and more fun.

When I first met Peter, he was the horse expert and I was the novice. As I healed more and more, in part through loving and being loved by him, I discovered in me an authority and skill around horses. This meant that, as in every other aspect of our shared life, we came to stand in that arena as equals. I still sometimes feel the fear - in a way that he doesn't and never will. But it's become so familiar, and dear, to me – this fear of mine – that I now can embrace it. I now know that it has the capacity to enhance rather than deplete who I am. It no longer prevents me from enjoying life to the full – including riding a horse very fast out in the wild with my beloved at my side.

The story of how this transformation came about is very much at the heart of my menopausal journey, and, therefore, well worth telling. I met Peter because of our horses. I wouldn't be the woman I am today if it weren't for our horses. Soon after I had the nasty fall I've just described, I began the practise of what I came to call 'horse-sistering'. Before I dive into the detail of that particular process of transformation, I want to re-wind a little and tell you about my beloved horse Jackson. Without understanding my relationship to that horse the 'horse-sistering' won't fully make sense.

Chapter Fourteen

KICKING OUT AND BROKEN BONES

As I've said, during that first dark year after I'd left the church, got divorced and moved full-time to Wales, I began to help look after a big Shire/Dray horse called Merlin. The woman who owned him, and who knew a little of my story, though she kindly never pushed me on it or pried, saw how much I loved being with that horse. As I became more confident as a rider, hooking up with other women in and around the village who also rode, she suggested I might consider getting my own horse and stabling him, at no charge, with hers. It was a delightful idea and, together with my youngest daughter, we began the search.

We were directed to view Jackson by a friend who was a horse breeder and trainer whom I'll call Maggie. We went to the farm where he was and fell for him instantly. We thought he was a bit over-priced for an unschooled horse, but seemed to have a willing nature and was clearly ready to be brought on. He was a registered Welsh Cob with a Dartmoor grandsire and so had a very pretty face. More importantly, he had a kind eye and was easy to handle. Maggie generously offered to stable Jackson for a fortnight while we trialled him. At the end of the fortnight, we bought him.

This was a big step up for me; but with the support of my new horsey women-friends, I was soon hacking out regularly and thoroughly enjoying him. Each day, morning and evening, I walked the couple of hundred metres from our cottage to his paddock, to feed and groom him and Merlin. If you're not a horse lover, or if you've never been around horses, it's difficult to describe how deeply satisfying it is to develop a friendship with a horse. For someone like me, raised around horses and with Romany blood, the connection I feel with them is profound. Jackson smelt like home. There's no other way I can think to put it. When I was with him, I felt settled in my skin and although at times I experienced fear when out riding, I trusted him absolutely. I must have said it a thousand times: that horse had not a single unkind bone in his body.

One evening, as the winter was approaching and the horses were therefore getting hungrier, helped by my daughter, we prepared their feed. The routine was that Merlin was fed first and then, once he was settled into his feed, we'd place Jackson's bowl on the ground a safe distance away. As the larger, dominant horse, Merlin could be territorial around the food bowls. That evening I carelessly placed Jackson's bowl too close to Merlin and as Jackson approached, Merlin kicked out hitting Jackson hard on his right foreleg. Jackson retreated and we rushed over to examine him. The skin was broken below the knee and the injured area was already beginning to swell.

I stayed with Jackson and my daughter ran to get Merlin's owner who as a long-term horse owner, plus as a nurse and midwife, I knew would be able to help make an informed judgement about what to do next. After examining him and walking him around to see whether he was walking lame – he was not – she made a cold compress and support bandaged the leg. We agreed to meet first thing in the morning to see how he was getting on after a night's rest. Merlin, who was clearly sorry at having hurt his friend, stood close by, gently nuzzling Jackson.

The next morning the leg didn't look any worse and Jackson wasn't showing any lameness but the impact site was still swollen so we decided to call the vet. On examination, the vet diagnosed a sprained tendon. I was so relieved that nothing was broken. Merlin had sizeable hooves. We were given some antibiotic cream to prevent infection, and told to keep applying a cold compress to reduce the swelling and, if we wanted, to continue with the homeopathic remedies. Weeks passed with several further visits by the vet. Jackson was not getting better, and I was worried. He stayed immobile where he was, looking sorry for himself, with Merlin standing sentinel at his side. The horses knew something was wrong; I knew something was wrong; but the vets had been convincing in their diagnosis and I didn't know where to go from there.

My friend Maggie came to have a look at him, and she agreed he looked very poorly. By then, it was six weeks since the injury. He was standing at the top of the paddock, head lowered and when I stroked him, I could feel his distress. It made me weep. I decided to call the vets again. A different vet arrived and on examining Jackson she quickly became very concerned. She said that although the injury site had superficially healed over, she feared there might be an internal infection in the leg. She recommended that he be taken immediately to the equine hospital in Liverpool for an MRI. She phoned and made the arrangements for him to be admitted at the weekend.

Merlin's owners lent us their horse trailer and drove my daughter and me to Liverpool. Jackson was examined by various vets and an MRI was taken. During the examinations he kept his head pressed into me. If I moved away, he became distressed and so I held him, just as I would hold one of my children when sick, soothing and comforting him for the time it took to complete the initial examination. When it was finished, I led him to a stall and settled him down before going to find my daughter who was waiting anxiously.

When the vet walked in, I knew instantly, it was bad news. He said they needed to operate immediately. Jackson had a splint bone fracture, which in itself, although serious, is a condition from which most horses can recover and which rarely proves fatal. However, an infection from the wound had spread from the splint bone into the canon bone. We were devastated. The canon bone is the thick weight-bearing bone in the horse's leg.

The vet explained that he would operate and try to scrape away the infected tissue from the canon bone. He wouldn't know how far into the bone the infection had spread and what damage it had caused until Jackson was in theatre. He said that they would operate with Jackson in a body harness suspended from the ground so that after the operation he could be gently lowered onto the leg. If he was lying prone, then the force of trying to stand upright could snap the, now thinner and weakened, canon bone.

He then said, what we most dreaded hearing. If during the operation, he found too much of the bone had become infected, so that scraping away the infected bone tissue depleted the bone to such a degree that Jackson would be unable to stand upon it, he would need my permission to euthanize him. He said he had every hope that the operation would be a success but he suggested that we go and make our goodbyes to Jackson. It still makes my heart ache with grief to remember. When the vet left us, my daughter and I clung to each other and wept. We then made our way to Jackson's stall with heavy hearts.

A couple of torturous hours later, the surgeon reappeared in the waiting room. He was carrying the dried out old bones of a horse's leg. My heart lifted and I smiled at my daughter. She smiled too. We both knew that there was no way this kindly vet would appear in that manner if he had just euthanized our beloved horse. He sat down and told us that the operation had been successful and he demonstrated with the bone what precisely it had entailed.

Jackson needed to remain a week more in the hospital so that if the canon bone proved too weakened to weight bear and snapped, they would have the option of a second operation to pin the bones together. He said he doubted very much that would be the case and the prognosis was good for a full recovery. Jackson was awake so we went to visit him. We kissed him and snuggled him and wept over him. Again, he pressed his head into me and I held him, and then he snorted in my daughter's face, making us both laugh. He was so pleased to see us and we, of course, were over-the-moon to see him.

When Jackson was discharged from the equine hospital he convalesced for a month in the care of Maggie. For the first two weeks, he was on complete stable rest. Over the next month he had superlative care: allopathic and homeopathic treatments, a magnetic boot wrap around his injured leg, gentle exercise and practically twenty-four hour attention. Merlin's owner was understandably anxious that Jackson might get injured again, so suggested I find a new paddock for him. When the first month of convalescence was over, we moved him to a field on his own just outside the village.

For the next three months, I walked him out each day, gradually going further and further. This enforced period on the ground with my horse was exactly what I needed. I didn't have to face my anxiety around riding. I could simply relax and enjoy being with him week after week. I remember this period with Jackson with great fondness. We walked for miles together. Jackson, me and my dog Black-beauty. After six months, he was well enough to be re-introduced into a herd and so I moved him closer to the village into a paddock with two mares.

When I began to ride him again, it was like starting over for both of us. We took it very slowly, riding at walk, with two or three rest days in between. Eventually, his leg was strong enough to move forward into trot on fairly soft ground. And soon after that, I was able to lift him into a slow, gentle canter. On Boxing Day, eight months after the accident, I rode out with a group from the village. Jackson and Merlin were delighted to be reunited and we had a fabulous ride in the fresh snow. At one point the two geldings raced each other up a gentle slope amidst much laughter and hollering. Jackson was fully recovered and I could not have been happier. Six months later, when I met Peter and introduced him to Jackson, he commented on my deep love for my horse. He'd once loved a horse like that.

"You never forget," he said, "it changes you."

Being on horseback is the greatest teacher of embodied awareness which I've yet come across. It has the capacity to force me back into my own skin with a single-pointed focus that brooks no distractions. When I'm on horseback, I'm not thinking about anything else apart from the act of riding. I'm a hundred times more aware of my body than when I'm simply standing or walking or even swimming. It's closest to my experience of yoga. I can feel my muscles, where I'm holding tension, where I'm stretching;

where I'm in balance and where I'm out of balance. My senses are alert. I can see more, hear more, and smell more. Not only is there a heightened awareness of my own sensate body, there's also a heightened awareness of the sensate body of another being. This, partly, is the gift hidden in my fear of riding.

The relationship with a horse is a very particular kind of relationship with an animal. Humans have ridden, lived alongside, and worked with horses for thousands and thousands of years. Most people have a strong visceral embodied response to being close to a horse. It's in our ancestral memory to connect with this creature. Our amygdala fire within the limbic system, and most of us have an instant, strong, emotional response in the presence of a horse. I've watched person after person spontaneously begin to weep within minutes of standing next to a horse, often without even touching it, and without a word being spoken. The person will then look at me surprised and slightly apologetic. But, for me, what I'm witnessing is a natural response. We are remembering; remembering something tucked way back in our genetic hard-wiring. We *know* this animal; and this animal *knows* us.

A horse is a highly sensitive, intuitive, subtle communicator. It needs to be. It's a prey animal - a herd animal. A horse is designed to graze the grasslands of the plains with a constantly vigilant awareness of the predator that might creep up towards it through the long grass, leap upon its back and sink teeth into its jugular vein. Within the herd, horses communicate with each other all the time. If you make a connection with a horse, you become part of that field of resonant awareness. To be so closely connected with an animal as big, powerful and intelligent as a horse is both humbling and a constant privilege.

Every practised rider has the experience of thinking something, and the horse instantly responding. My sister was right; a horse can feel your every thought. It's partly that, like them, we're somatic creatures: our muscles, our pulse, our ligaments, tendons, nerves, glands and hormones all react instantly to a thought or feeling. My conscious mind is often left lagging far behind when I'm horse-riding. I'm in 'flow'. My conscious mind takes a back seat and my animal-body takes over. This is why, when fear suddenly has me in her grip, I dismount. My horse doesn't know something has triggered my PTSD. He just knows I'm afraid, and he's instantly up on his hocks, ready to flee the sabre-toothed tiger lurking behind that farm gate post.

This acute sensitivity of the horse is why we can't fake it around them. Our bodies don't lie. I've learned when out riding to try and not even to think fearfully by anticipating a problem before one actually appears. Jackson knows exactly where we are when we return to the place where previously a dozen mountain bikes suddenly hurtled around a corner right in front of him, causing him to spin around in a panic. If I think fearful thoughts, it'll reinforce his – which is what my older sister was trying to teach me. If I think it, my body will respond to the thought, and the horse will pick up on it instantly.

My horse trusts my judgement. If he didn't, he wouldn't let me ride him. He puts himself in my care and expects me to make good decisions for the both of us. I've never subscribed to the notion that as the rider, I'm the 'alpha horse' – Jackson knows I'm not a horse – but I do see it as a true partnership, where both sides bring different strengths, skills and affinities into the relationship - like a good marriage. This isn't about masking your true feelings, or desperately trying to bury them way down where even the unconscious mind and the parasympathetic nervous system can't reach - which is what deep trauma teaches us to do. It's about being open and honest with your feelings and with your horse.

Nowadays, there are many, many different sorts of equine therapy on offer. Many of these are offered by people better qualified and with far greater horse-experience than I have. So, I want to be careful here not to inflate the 'horse-sistering' practise I engaged with into something bigger than it actually was. It was huge for me personally because it was profoundly transformational. If you're interested in learning more about equine therapy, I would recommend you begin by reading *Tao of Equus* by Linda Kohanov. So, let's now climb aboard and have a ride on the carousel and I'll tell you about my practise of horse-sistering.

Chapter Fifteen

BEHIND THE MASKS OF PERFORMANCE

After the nasty fall off Peter's horse, with which I began chapter thirteen I invited two women from the Deepening circle, whom I'll call Ginny and Violet, to come and spend some time with me and my horses. They both already had a deep affinity with horses, and welcomed the chance to work with them in a new way. We weren't sure, to begin with, exactly what we were seeking to do, but the three of us each wanted to spend time with the horses differently from riding out on them. For me, it was about tracking back to the source of my fear of riding.

Peter had built an outside horse arena at his place, and it was within that space that I took my herstory with the horse back to its beginnings. One of my 'horse-sisters', as we called each other, came to work with me on Jackson. We led him into the arena in just a halter (no saddle or bridle) and, to begin with, I just stood close to him. The aim was to slow it right down so that I could notice exactly what was happening in me.

Jackson was a little unsettled. We hadn't done this before. Like me, he can be a bit of a people-pleaser and he wanted to get it right. I began to move around the arena and, as was his habit, he followed me. I just kept trying to feel into what was happening for me in that moment – and that moment only. It was like I was pushing against something inside me – a membrane, a veil, a kind of numbness – that was preventing me from reaching what I really felt. Whatever it was, it had the effect of separating me from my truest expression.

The veil I was trying to push through and which caused a kind of inner numbness, was my propensity towards 'performance'. As I've already mentioned, from the age of six onwards, I performed in many ballet shows. There's nothing quite like being on stage in a darkened theatre, curtseying to an audience erupting into applause, for giving you a buzz of validation. In that moment, your worth seems incontrovertible; and, therefore, as an experience, it becomes desirable, and, potentially, addictive.

It took me a long time of honest self-observation to realise that when I was being watched, if I sensed any expectation or anticipation or approval on the part of the observer, I'd begin to perform on some level. This is part and parcel of that early conditioning: to please, to impress, to perform and, preferably, out-perform, my sisters. As a vicar, of course, this is what I did every Sunday – I put on a 'costume' and 'performed'. It's probably worth saying that obviously this isn't the only thing I did. There were many layers and levels to all that was going on for me in church on a Sunday morning. But, certainly, performance was part of it.

The act of performing put up a barrier between what I was feeling inside and how I was presenting myself outwardly. It's a bloody hard habit to break. Like many people when on stage in front of a live audience, on occasion I could be inwardly terrified, but outwardly I always appeared confident and assured. There are advantages to this undoubtedly, and, 'putting on a brave face' has its place. When it becomes habitual, however, an emotional incongruence occurs. After a while, if left unattended, we can lose touch with what's really going on inside ourselves.

By the time I left the church, after twenty years of standing in front of a congregation week by week, of sitting at the front chairing hundreds of committee meetings, I'd lost myself somewhere. I'd become horribly entangled within the folds of my flowing clerical robes. I wouldn't have known how to 'drop the pretence' even if I'd wanted to. I lived most of my life in full view of others, many of whom felt they had the right to judge, comment on, and discuss me and my family. Inner and outer lives were both tied into knots of self-protection and fear. Goodness only knows what it'd be like to be famous – for me, I reckon it'd be a living hell.

I've lost count of the times that someone with whom I'm working has replied to the question, "how are you feeling right now in your body", with the words: "I don't know. I'm just sort of numb". In my experience, this emotional discongruity and disconnection is particularly acute in women. Unlearning the art of 'performance' is commensurate with entering the Majesteria. Those who walk the world as Autumn Queen, as high priestess, as Wild Woman Walking, or whatever name you choose to give her - these women are not performing. They are what they appear to be – women at the height of their powers, who are in charge of and responsible for their own life choices, their relationships, their own bodies and their own fulfilment.

It took several sessions in the arena with Jackson before I could slough off the costumes of performance. Firstly, I had to feel into them. I needed to recognise that this was what I was wearing for protection, like a version of Harry Potter's Invisibility Cloak around my shoulders. In order to feel the weight of that cloak, I had to recognise the ways in which I'd hidden behind a mask of self. I'd been presenting a smiling, amiable, ever-understanding Melanie to the world. It was like peeling away onion skins – it seemed never ending.

The turning point was the session when I sat on Jackson bareback, in loose clothing, barefoot and without my riding hat. I often rode him bareback and he was quite steady and safe with me. I was proud of how responsive he was with nothing but a loose halter and I began to show-off a little. My horse-sister, Violet, gently brought us to a halt.

"Melanie, I want you to stop performing," she said. "You don't have to do or be anything. Just sit on Jackson exactly as you are."

I looked at her, the child in me disbelieving her words. She saw the disbelief and mistrust in my eyes and her next words responded to it.

"You don't have to ride well, or sit up properly, or do anything at all. You cannot get it wrong. Simply sit, just as you are."

"Really?" I asked.

She nodded.

"You cannot get it wrong", she repeated.

I closed my eyes and the tears came, wave upon wave. I let go of the constant effort of 'trying' - trying to be someone likeable and acceptable and successful - trying to get it *right*. Finally, I melted into the undemanding safety of sitting on the horse I loved, without the fear of getting it wrong. Something inside of me that had been held clenched tight, softened, opened and let go. As with so many transformative moments, this was one I'd need to revisit again and again for a good while before the new experience of safety could take root.

In several other sessions we worked imaginatively with my memories of horse-riding with my sisters as a child. It was at this point I began to understand how much I'd modelled myself on my older sisters and how there were parts of Melanie – things *I* liked, or wanted, or enjoyed, or hated, that had never seen the light of day. I was familiar with shamanic soul retrieval practises and knew that this was what I was doing – calling parts of my soul back home. I began to discover my own way of riding a horse – a softer, more fluid pelvic posture. I cultivated a conscious and aware connection through my spinal column to the horse beneath me. And, most of all, I gave myself a profound permission to feel whatever I was feeling.

In addition to the horse-sistering sessions, I began to go for bodywork: massage, McTimony Chiropractor and acupuncture. My shoulder, upper back, and neck were still contused after the fall from the horse, and deep-tissue massage helped to release the holding. My body therapist and I began to allow whatever arose while she worked my muscles to be given full rein. I howled and shook and screamed and vomited. I let the repressed, denied, silenced and hidden faces of Melanie finally have a voice.

At the end of each session we'd chuckle together about the amount of noise I'd made and she'd reassure me that it was okay. The clients in other therapists' neighbouring treatment rooms had been told to expect to hear some noise. My 'homework' was a twenty minute 'psoas muscle rest' twice a day. I lay supine on the floor with my legs resting on a sofa at a ninety degree angle. If you've never tried it, I can't recommend it highly enough. It's become part of my regular self-care routine.

The psoas is the largest and most important muscle. It connects the two halves of our body. Every major nerve runs through the psoas. It holds muscle memory, especially around trauma. I hold a tremendous amount of grief in my diaphragm, which is, of course, the area of the heart chakra, associated with self-preservation and safety. Relaxing my psoas took weeks of daily practise. If you're interested in working with your psoas, I recommend Jo Ann Staugaard-Jones' book *The Vital Psoas Muscle*.

Six weeks after the fall from the horse, I awoke in the night with a terrible migraine. I decided not to take any medication (which is a choice I make increasingly) so that the migraine could do whatever she needed to do, and show me whatever I needed to see. I was spending the night at Peter's and the pain became so bad that he wanted to take me to the hospital. He was afraid I was suffering a brain haemorrhage or something, caused by the fall from the horse. I, however, recognised what was happening – an emotional unleashing. It was a threshold - an invitation to dive deep into my fear. I asked him to support me while I let go into my body, trusting her to do the work which my conscious wordy mind couldn't manage on her own. He agreed and went to get me a bowl in which to vomit. He then sat silently behind me, legs astride so that I could lean back into his strength, while I let the pain flow freely through my system. It was intense. But, with Peter at my back, I dared to let it come. It took several hours and once it was done, it was done.

We rested the next day and then arranged to ride out together the following weekend. As we rode along the driveway towards his front gates, I realised that I was sitting on the horse differently. My stirrups felt too short, so I lengthened them. I could feel my pelvis moving much more freely with the horse and I got Peter to come over and watch me. He agreed that my legs, which were resting against Jackson's flanks, were lying differently. They had relaxed and lengthened. A tightness which I'd been unconsciously holding at the base of my spine was gone. My seat had deepened.

If you're a rider, you'll know what that means: my body had settled and balanced into the saddle. My skull floated lightly on the neck. My shoulders were relaxed, elbows aligned, hands soft, each vertebra of the spine resting on the one below. Most importantly, my pelvis was loose, free to move in unity with the horse's movement. My legs were hanging loosely, ankles flexing, toes spread, eyes shining and my smile was HUGE. I'd finally arrived on horseback.

From then on, my riding began to change. I noticed the difference and the horses noticed the difference. My riding became increasingly confident, fluid, supple and enjoyable. I supported my new-found confidence by up-skilling myself through returning to weekly riding lessons at an excellent local riding centre. I gave myself permission to be the rider that I wanted to be. A year on and I'd grown into a pretty proficient horsewoman and I loved it.

After five years, Peter and I got married and went for our honeymoon to the Azores on a riding holiday. We rode each day for six or seven hours on the most beautiful Lusitanos – just Peter and me, plus our guide. I rode five different horses – all spirited, well-schooled and expecting the best from their rider. I have so many wonderful memories from our honeymoon – but perhaps my favourite is Peter and I at full gallop, racing along for over a mile, splashing our way along the edge of an azure volcanic lake, taking corners at speed, jumping ditches, our horses with their tails high. They, like us, relished every moment.

Our Swedish guide took a photo of us and it's still my favourite screensaver. I was exultant. I came off our honeymoon accepting that at last I'd become a good rider. I didn't need an older sister or a friend or a teacher to validate me – I knew it for myself. I'll never be an elegant and upright, well-turned-out, fearless, horsewoman who is classically trained in English-riding, like I thought I wanted to be. What I am now is me, Melanie-on-horseback: passionate about my horses, sometimes afraid, but oftentimes not. I am a woman who absolutely loves riding, very fast, in the wild, with her beloved at her side.

I was going to end the chapter here – with me happily galloping off into the proverbial sunset. However, this book seeks to bring into the light that which I've been afraid to reveal about myself. I made a promise to myself to be radically honest. I made that promise because honesty has proven again and again to be the gateway to my soul's freedom.

That image, of me finally free to ride freely, is the positive aspect of the story. We could call it the 'light' aspect. Where there's 'light' though, it needs to be balanced by 'darkness' - otherwise the light can become blinding, or scorching and destructive. Night always has to follow day. It's a natural law that applies to us too.

There was a final difficult episode in the horse-sistering experience which occurred later in the story. I'll hold fire on telling you about it at this point, because the chronology of the unfolding story is important. Chronos (clock) time weaving with kronos (sacred) time makes the telling a bit of a challenge, so I need to weave back and forth, spiralling slowly in towards the truth of my story, which I seek to share with you.

First there's much more to tell of the great adventure with Peter that took us from Wales to Scotland. And, before that, there's a spiralling back in time to face the shadow behind all other shadows – the shadow of death. As we buckle up again for the next exciting ride on this roller-coaster experience called The Change, I'd like you to hold in mind that there is a 'dark' aspect of horse-sistering waiting in the wings, tacked-up and ready to come out onto the stage of my life and bite me hard in the butt. I didn't see it coming – but then we rarely do. Hold that thought, and hold on tight, the roller-coaster is about to become The Ghost Train.

Chapter Sixteen

 # SHADOW-DANCING WITH DEATH

In earlier chapters I focused on my journey through menopause in relation to learning how to ride my fear. In this chapter I'd like to share with you my experiences around, and reflections upon, the shadow that lurks behind or below all our other fears. It is the fear of death. I've been a death-dancer for thirty years. Recently, there's been a wonderful new/old resurgence of the role of women as death-doula and 'soul midwife'; i.e. someone who helps people to cross the threshold into death peaceably. For more on this, you might like to read the work of Felicity Warner, *The Soul Midwives' Handbook*. Being a death-dancer is somewhat similar, but a little different.

I want to tread gently and carefully here because most of us carry a heavy burden of grief over the loss of someone we love. Whilst honouring that, I also want to give an untamed, full expression to the wonders I believe lie hidden behind death's grim mask. Grief is real. It is painful. It is life-long. And yet, when we allow ourselves to be carried on its tides, it is also natural, healthy and wholesome. It may be an unconventional idea, but grief – even the deepest grief – can enrich and enhance our lives immeasurably.

This chapter isn't about grief though, it's about death. I'm going to explore death by sharing several of my 'near-death' experiences. Well, here goes. Perhaps I should warn you that I'm about to remove the veil of propriety and social acceptability, and to give myself full permission to go unapologetically and unashamedly 'woo woo'. Snap on that safety harness; the menopausal roller-coaster ride is about to climb high enough to touch the stars.

You don't need me to tell you that one day you will die. We all know this. We live in a culture, however, that lures us into a whole range of distractions to try and avoid, deny, postpone, and ignore that fact. The dream of immortality and the myth of eternal youth are both alive and kicking on twenty-first-century planet Earth. I'm very well aware that my first numinous, ecstatic, spiritual experience coincided with my first apprehension of my own mortality. I was eight years old. From many people's perspective, religiosity is merely a knee-jerk reaction at best, and a cop-out at worst, to the human fear of death. From this stance, spirituality - from cave painting to Chartres Cathedral – can be considered nothing more than a fear-based response arising from our resistance to the frightening notion that 'I will one day die and thereby cease to exist'.

In my forties, during that year-long 'dark night of the soul' which followed my exit from the church, I would have possibly agreed. This was in spite of the scores of numinous incidents I'd by then experienced but which I chose to dismiss as faulty memory, fantasy, escapism or self-deception. It's certainly true that our eventual demise acts as an incentive to enquire about what happens after death, which for many leads inevitably to considerations of a religious or spiritual nature. When our impending demise is imminent, it gives those explorations a certain degree of urgency, if not downright panic. Death unavoidably begs the question: 'Is this it?'

I cannot prove what I am about to tell you. During that dark year, as I say, I even stopped believing it myself. However, in the last seven years whilst I've been undergoing this radical, transformational menopausal initiation, these supra-normal incidents have multiplied and become almost-daily phenomena. They are so insistently real and so unutterably beautiful, that I refuse any longer to deny or doubt the truth of them.

People have said to me that they wish they could see what I see and hear what I hear. They say that if they'd had the sorts of visions I've had, they'd a hundred per cent believe in life after death. They'd *know* that there's more to life than just this brief, transitory existence, apprehended through the five senses. But I reply that these experiences do not of themselves eradicate doubt and self-questioning. I have to choose to 'believe' in exactly the same way as they do. These days the choice has become so habitual that it's now an intrinsic foundational part of whom I am. I'm no longer consciously aware of it. But it took a lengthy spiralling journey to get to that point – as this story attests.

Before I begin, I'd like to present a caveat to what follows. I once wrote a blog post on my website in which I spoke about the fact that, for the most part, I no longer fear death. A dear friend, on reading the blog, wrote me a slightly acerbic response. What she'd detected in my blog was a smug, self-satisfied, 'I'm alright, Jack' sort of attitude. It'd left her, understandably, irritated. I know myself well enough to admit that the tone could well have been present, even if undetectable by me.

I was too many years in a pulpit, looking down upon a silent, passive, rapt (or so I liked to hope) audience, not to have been shaped by the experience. Firstly, there's the liking of the sound of my own voice. Secondly, there's the thinking I know better than you. And thirdly, there's the difficulty in accepting challenge - because in a pulpit, it never happens. Preaching from a pulpit is a mind-bogglingly privileged -and therefore potentially abusive - position to be in. Its underbelly is that it can condition you to feel that you are 'superior' to others because you are, literally, superior to them Sunday by Sunday while you stand several feet above them in a pulpit.

However, I won't deny it's one of the aspects I most enjoyed about my life as a vicar. To stand and share one's deepest core beliefs week by week with an attentive, open-hearted and receptive audience was immensely rewarding and personally satisfying. So, these days I'd be the first to admit that I can, on occasion, get a bit preachy (a bit? I hear you say), and, when faced by verbal challenges, I can be tempted to retreat into a safe space that is both sanctimonious and slightly pompous. Fortunately, having Peter around in this regard has been wholly beneficial.

The things about me which some people love - others dislike. Part of my personality is that I'm an enthusiast and I can exude highly-charged energy and positivity. It comes in intense bursts, like an animal hunting. And then I need retreat, rest, quiet and solitude. As I mentioned earlier, I recognise myself in descriptions of the trait HSP (Highly Sensitive Person) with the pitfalls and blessings that brings. My highly-charged energy can attract people - some of whom put me on a pedestal.

It can also provoke envy and even spite – especially when it's discovered that, despite having mystical visions, I also have lumpen feet of clay. I can be impatient, intolerant and judgemental of people. I can be forgiving, highly sensitive and easily hurt. I'm sometimes slow to recover from a perceived injury or insult; and at other times, I bounce back immediately. I'm an instinctive optimist so I tend to look for the best in people. More often than not, I seek to understand rather than to condemn. I can also be curt and dismissive of those who see things differently from me.

I have a beautiful purple cloak which I wear sometimes in ceremony. There's a photo of it on the Retreats page of my website: www.melaniesantorini.org. It was made for me as a wedding gift by my women's circle. Sewn onto the back of the cloak, read from the ground up, is one of my many names: *Melanie Exuberant*. It's very much part of who I am. I get fired up and impassioned about the things I really care about (hence this book), and I make no apology for that. I would invite you, in the pages that follow, to hear the passion beneath any pomposity, and the exuberance beneath the exclusivity of a smug 'I'm alright, Jack' attitude, if indeed you detect those unpleasant traits. In spite of the mass of contradictions that swirl around inside, at the heart of me is the very simple belief that love is at the centre of *everything*. This is the unbreakable diamond at the centre of my being, to which I return again and again and again.

So, after that lengthy preamble, let us spiral back in time to an early 'near-death' experience. By 'near-death' I mean literally that, when death does a brush-by. This can be our own death or the death of someone else. What the experience does though, is it forces us to eye-ball death in the face. When I was in training for the priesthood at theological college, I was required to go on a four-month placement with a secular organisation.

I arranged to work for the Co-operative Funeral Service. I was in my late twenties with two beautiful young children at home. It may appear to have been an unusual choice, and certainly my college supervisor thought so. I was clear that my Christian faith, if it was to count for a jot, needed to be able to deal with the harsh reality of death. I knew that as a vicar I'd be taking funerals, so it'd be good to see how others conducted them - but it was deeper than that. I wanted to spend time around death to see what it really was/is. I was curious about it. The theological reflection I wrote afterwards is called: *Staring death in the face.*

It was the most extraordinary four months, and I am so grateful to the staff of the Co-operative Funeral Service who accommodated my inquisitive presence with such grace and good humour. Over those four months I attended about seventy funerals – often two or three in a day. I went to collect the deceased from the hospital morgue. I prepared the deceased for burial or cremation. I watched the process of cremation. I witnessed the process of embalming. I met with the bereaved and helped with the funeral arrangements. I have nothing but respect for those professionals who work as undertakers.

Since then, in the intervening years, I've conducted nearly four hundred funerals. Even after leaving the church, I continued to offer this service as a funeral celebrant – though not as a vicar, nor indeed as a humanist. I am neither. Quite what I am these days, I'm not sure. I haven't yet found a meaningful label for it and perhaps I never will. I deeply value taking funerals though. A funeral needs to be done well - with care, compassion and a focused attention. And, if done badly, leaves a wound that is hard to heal.

Back to the Co-op funeral service with me aged 29, and to the first of the spiritual experiences which sometimes unfold when I'm in the presence of the dead. These experiences are central to the core beliefs I've come to live by, which is why I'm spiralling back to share this particular one with you. I'd gone with an undertaker to collect the body of a young man who had died from an injury incurred when falling off his skateboard. He was eighteen years old. It was a tragic accident and you can imagine the devastation and grief that his parents were enduring. While preparing the young man's body for burial, the undertaker was called out to the phone and I was left alone with the deceased. My heart ached with the sadness of the situation. I placed my hands upon the young man's chest and, with my eyes open, I began to pray - by prayer I don't mean something verbal but rather a heightened attentiveness and focussed awareness, placed gently upon him.

The room we were in was suddenly filled with light. I was overcome with a sense of love and peace that was so all-encompassing and powerful that it seemed to burst outwards through the pores of my skin. I could hear an unimaginably beautiful singing and I knew with absolute certainty that beneath this ghastly, tragic 'appearance', all is well. I knew that this lovely young lad before me, although dead, was somehow okay – more than okay, much, much more. Although I was gazing down at his dead body, I could sense his presence close by and that he was, in some mysterious way, still 'alive'.

This experience has been repeated over and over again when I am in the presence of the dead or the dying. I sometimes see them. I sometimes encounter them in my dreams before going to meet their families. I sometimes hear messages from them. I'm sometimes requested to help them 'pass over', if they've got stuck between realms. As the years have gone by, the more I've used this faculty, the more sensitive I've become to their presence, and the easier it has become for them to communicate with me. On occasion I become aware of their presence because I see a blue or white floating orb in the room with me. Other times, it's less a physical seeing than an intuited awareness of them.

I once heard Carolyn Myss describe the intuitive faculty which allows her to diagnose illness over distance without ever needing to meet the person. It resonated with how I most commonly 'see' the dead. The easiest way is to say that they leave an imprint on my imagination. I liken it to the effect you get when you gaze at a candle, blow it out, and then close your eyes – an imprint of the light is still visible behind your eyelids but if you open your eyes, it is gone.

About three years ago in 2015, I began to hold ceremony to release the 'sea of souls' which clog the etheric space around the planet. I've been shown that victims of war or violence are often bewildered by death and don't know where to go after death or how to get there. A death-dancer or shamana like me guides them safely to where they need to go. Nowadays many ordinary people die without having seriously thought about their own death, and certainly without having prepared for it. They too can benefit from some simple support and guidance. Otherwise, there can be a tendency to get 'stuck' here. Since the First World War there's been a huge build up of 'lost' souls – a sort of psychic pollution clogging up planet Earth's aura, which exactly mirrors the physical pollution in the atmosphere.

Moreover, the fear of death which underlies the frenetic, frantic life of so much of 'western' culture, means that the bereaved, often unwittingly, 'hang onto' the dead and won't let them go. Though this is understandable, it's actually unhelpful. The dead need to move on. Our greatest service to our loved one is to release them. A simple way of doing this is to picture your loved one and tell them that it's okay for them to let go of their earthly life and to move on. Perhaps imagine them travelling away from you on a beam of light, further and further away. It may take several days – three is usual – but you'll know when they're gone. You may find it harder to picture them, or the beam of light will have disappeared, or you may feel lighter inside. You could finish or close by sending them your love and wishing them every blessing as they travel on. It doesn't matter if you feel silly doing it. I sometimes do, but I do it anyway.

I've also been shown that there are souls who wish to return to help with the great change that is underway on planet Earth. I've held ceremony to open a portal so that these kindly ones can return. They wish to align their energies with ours in order to support the planet as she struggles to hold steady against the onslaught of destructive actions which humanity has let loose upon her. I've also held ceremony to release from the planet that dense energy (force, spirit) which is attracted to the sleeping-unaware and contracted energies of unawakened humanity.

My psychic sense is that things are hotting-up for planet Earth, not just on the physical realm with global warming, but on every level of being. I believe this is why so many more people are tuning into the unseen realms in a myriad of ways which are creative and beneficial. The churches and synagogues and mosques may be emptying, but the number of people spiritually awakening on the planet is rising and rising.

Menopause is one opportunity to plug into this new, rising tide of healing energy, to align ourselves with it, and to place our lives at the service of planet Earth. There are beautiful beings and energies all around us in the (mostly) unseen realms, waiting and willing to help us at this crucial juncture in our planetary life. I tell the story of my encounters with angels in my forthcoming book *Blood Sacrifice*. Suffice to say here, whether or not you've ever seen an angel with your physical eye, use your mind's eye and your imagination, and call them to your aid - to our aid.

So, if you're someone who has latent psychic ability, please consider using it in the service of our planet and for the benefit of all. My advice is to keep your intention clear and your practise, whatever it is, simple. Avoid the esoteric and over-complicated; and trust your intuition and your own judgement. If something doesn't feel right, then it probably isn't. If someone who purports to be a 'psychic expert' asks you to do something that makes you feel uncomfortable, or that you wouldn't want to tell your best friend about, don't do it.

Sad to say, that with the upsurge in fresh, freer expressions of spirituality, and with the cascade of etheric energy flowing through this realm, there are inevitably some charlatans out there, ready to make a fast buck by spouting nonsense. In the last few years I've worked with several people (mostly women) who've handed over large sums of money to someone who purported to be in contact with their dead loved one - and perhaps they were. The long and the short of it, however, is that the grieving person came away from the encounter emotionally, psychologically and spiritually, as well as financially, depleted. It's not a pleasant experience getting lost and confused in a House of Mirrors.

Chapter Seventeen

THE GODDESS CAVE

I've had several brushes with my own physical death. The most recent occurred just after I met Peter. My youngsters were at their father's, and I'd booked to go for a week's holiday with a friend to the beautiful Maltese island of Gozo. When the arrangement with the friend didn't work out, I decided to go on my own. I found Gozo quiet and restful, and surprisingly tourist free. I stayed in a tiny self-catering villa in a small village with a few houses, several huge churches and a zillion cats. The people I greeted as I walked to the village shop for daily provisions were, for the most part, goat-herders, farmers and fishermen.

Each day I followed the sandy tracks for three miles down the cliffs to reach the sea where I would swim. My love of deep, wild water follows me wherever I go. I can hear the call of Tiamat, the Babylonian goddess known as 'the Deep', most clearly when wild-swimming. "Come deeper, come deeper", she sings. I'd pack up a picnic for myself, take a book, and spend the entire day by the nearest cove in contented solitude.

A few days into my holiday, I was out swimming in the deep azure water beyond the cove, when an elderly man swam out passed me with a knife between his teeth. I was a little taken aback and watched with interest. He was diving for squid. Back on the beach we got chatting and he invited me to join his family for supper. His name was Mario and he said that as well as the fresh squid, he and his wife would serve me home-grown olives, sun-dried tomatoes, freshly caught sardines and the local goats' cheese wrapped in vine leaves. How could I refuse?

A couple of days after that pleasant evening, I saw him again on the beach. He waved to me and I waved back. Coming over, he asked what I was reading. I explained that it was a book about the ancient Goddess who was once honoured on the island. He became quite animated and told me that there were 'goddess caves' dotted about everywhere – ones, he said, that the tourists know nothing about. He asked if I'd like him to show me the most beautiful, which was nearby. He warned me though that it was quite a swim. I was intrigued. We swam out of the cove and along the coast for about half a mile. The cave was only accessible from the sea. He pointed out some rocks on the cliff-face which he said hid the entrance to the cave.

Just as we were approaching the shore, something extraordinary happened. The water around us began to seethe and boil as if in a cauldron. Mario grabbed my hand and began to swim to the rocks. Scrabbling out of the water, he let go of me in order to pull himself up to safety, before turning back to try and grab me. A wave sucked me under and I tumbled head-over-heels through the boiling sea. I had no idea which way was up and which was down. The noise was roaring in my ears as I was flung to the surface of the water, gasping for breath.

I struggled towards the shore where Mario stood with his arms outstretched, calling to me. Again, just as I reached the rocks, a wave sucked me back down into the depths and I somersaulted through the water. The suction was terrifying and as it plunged me to the depths, I was close to drowning. The third time I surfaced, the wave flung me towards the rocks and Mario was able to grab my swimsuit and haul me out. He yanked me, coughing and spluttering, away from the crashing sea and wacked me hard between the shoulder blades to make me cough up the sea-water I'd swallowed.

Once I'd caught my breath and stopped trembling sufficiently, we began the climb up the cliffs. I needed to move to stop from going into shock, and I guess Mario knew this. We headed up the cliff-face towards the sandy track I'd so often walked. Gozo is a volcanic island and the rocks are larval, sharp against bare flesh. My feet were soon cut and sore, but we had to keep clambering upwards. I dislike heights since I suffer occasionally with vertigo, and, after about twenty minutes of scrambling up the rocks, I was as high as I dared go. I sat down on a tiny rocky ledge and told him I couldn't go any further. He tried to urge me on but I was adamant. I knew I simply couldn't climb any higher up the cliff-face. I was too frightened. Reassuring me that he'd be back with help, my companion disappeared up the cliff, scaling the rocks in his bare feet with the speed and agility of a goat.

I sat and looked down the way we'd come. It was steep - just looking at it made my stomach churn. The sea had calmed and returned to its azure blue beauty. I could hardly believe that such a short time before it had been a seething, angry cauldron seemingly intent on sucking me down into a watery grave. Still trembling, I shuddered from the memory. I focused on thinking about my four youngsters – using them like a life-raft to keep me from sinking into full-blown panic.

After about half-an-hour, I heard voices above me. Looking up I saw Mario, plus two other men. The three of them descended and hunkered down on either side of me on the thin ledge. They introduced themselves as Italian divers who were visiting Gozo on holiday. They asked me to tell them a little about myself. It was a way of calming me, helping me to relax and to trust them – having done it several times myself with a frightened individual, I was aware of their strategy.

"There are only two ways out of here," one of the men said to me, "you have either to climb or jump. We're here to help you, and we won't leave you until you are safe. Okay?"

I nodded and he smiled reassuringly.

"Good. Now, which do you feel you can do, climb or jump?"

I looked up at the rocky cliff above me and then down into the sea.

"I think I can jump," I said.

"Okay, excellent. I am a diver, and so is my friend here, so that is an excellent choice."

We all laughed. I slowed my breathing and tried to overcome the feeling that I was about to throw up.

"I will explain what we are going to do," he continued. "We are going to sit here together, while you continue to get stronger. Your friend borrowed a phone and a boat is on its way towards us. When it reaches us, we are going to jump into the water. My friend here will jump first so that you will know it is safe, and then you and I will jump together."

I must have looked terrified because he took my hand.

"See, I will hold your hand like this, and I will not let you go. Okay?"

I nodded. I nodded but I wasn't convinced. The sea was way, way below and in the sea were jagged rocks. We sat waiting, the three men talking quietly together. As promised, my new-best-friend never let go of my hand.

A boat appeared around the headland and made its way towards us. It was a full tourist boat that had been contacted by the coastguard and, as the nearest vessel in the vicinity, re-directed to come to our aid. The two men either side of me stood up and helped me to my feet. My legs were like jelly. It looked a long, long way down.

"Okay, Melanie - my friend will jump in first, and then I will count to five and we will jump together. I want you to jump out as far as you can. I will hold your hand and I promise I will not let it go."

I looked down at the sea and thought of my four precious children waiting for me back at home. I could do this. For them, I could do this. The man on my right-hand side gave a thumbs-up and leapt out from the cliff, away from the rocks below, and landed with a splash in the water. He resurfaced and waved up at us. The two men on either side of me on the cliff waved back. I didn't. I was trembling from head to toe.

"Okay. I'm going to start to count now. When I get to five, you're going to leap out as far as you can. You're going to be fine. Here we go: one-two-three-".

I grabbed his arm and vehemently shook my head.

"I can't," I said breathlessly. "I'm too frightened." I could feel myself about to cry.

"Yes, you can do this. You will be safe. I will not let you go. I promise."

I took a breath, offered a silent prayer, and nodded. He squeezed my hand and gave a thumbs-up sign to his friend waiting in the sea below.

"One-two-three-four-five!"

He leaped out from the rocky ledge and I leaped with him. I felt him tug my arm as I plunged downwards. Then I crashed into the water, feeling a rock brush the back of my head like a whispering caress. As I surfaced, both men were immediately at my side keeping me buoyant and afloat. We swam together towards the tourist boat to the sound of cheers and applause from its passengers.

I was hauled aboard and wrapped in a huge dry towel. The captain came to check me over.

"Are you hurt?" he asked.

I shook my head.

"I'm a bit shaken, but I'm absolutely fine," I replied.

"But your neck - you must have hit your neck on the rocks."

I touched my neck confused. I could feel no pain or discomfort. Then it dawned on me and I smiled.

"Oh that," I giggled. "That's my new boyfriend. He was a bit too passionate."

The captain threw his head back and laughingly relayed the information in German to the passengers. Everyone erupted in laughter, stamping their feet and clapping enthusiastically.

You see, just before I'd left for Gozo, Peter had stayed a couple of days with me in my little cottage. Half-jokingly, he'd left a circle of 'love-bites' around my neck.

"Just to mark you as *my* love before you disappear on holiday," he'd said.

Our offspring had been somewhat disparaging about this OTT pseudo-teenage behaviour. We'd just laughed, too in-love to care what they thought of us.

Back on Gozo, the next day I rested in my villa. In the afternoon, Mario turned up with his wife. She carried a bunch of wildflowers for me. He was very apologetic.

"I have swum in those waters since I was a boy," he said. "Never before has anything like that happened. It was an underwater earth tremor."

"An earthquake?"

"Yes, we sometimes get them on land, but I've never known one to happen like that in the sea. No-one in the village felt it. Strange, very strange."

I couldn't have agreed more. His wife spoke to him in Maltese and he translated.

"Sophia says to tell you that we are very sorry and will you please join us for the fireworks on Thursday in honour of Sante Maria? It is the biggest firework display in Gozo and I am in charge of organising it. We will be honoured if you would join our family to watch it."

I said that I'd be delighted to attend. It was indeed an impressive display of fireworks accompanied by classical music, which lasted over an hour – all in honour of the Sacred Feminine principle in the guise of Saint Mary. Just perfect.

A couple of days after the fireworks, I saw Mario diving for squid. He waved at me and came over to show me his catch.

"I have something for you," he said. "A gift."

He reached deep into the pocket of his dripping swimming shorts, and opened his hand to reveal what looked like two white stones. I peered more closely and looked up at him enquiringly. He picked up one of them and placed it in my palm.

"It's a fossil," he explained. "A shark's tooth. I found it yesterday. There's loads of fossils round here. I've got hundreds of them. This is for you."

"Thank you," I murmured as I looked at the two inch long tooth nestling in my hand.

He put the second item in my hand.

"This is -, you know, for hunting?" He made a gesture as if throwing a javelin.

"A spear-head?" I said, delighted.

He nodded.

"I've had this one for a long time. I found it many years ago in the cave I wanted to show you. People have been going there for thousands of years. It's for you. A souvenir. I know you like history."

"Herstory," I corrected automatically, though he didn't understand.

I looked at the small flint spear-head and wondered about the man or woman who had fashioned it. Years ago I'd read the novels by Jean Auel, *Clan of the Cave Bear,* and loved the fascinating insight they gave into prehistoric life. It was an imagined version of herstory, of course - though I'm convinced that our imagination leads us into deep ancestral genetic memory.

Mario left to go and gather his things together as it was drawing towards the end of the afternoon. After a few minutes reading, I got to my feet and went over to him.

"You know, I'd still really like to see the Goddess cave," I said. "Would you show it to me? Maybe tomorrow?"

"You're not frightened after what happened?"

To my surprise, I wasn't.

"I think I'm ready," I said.

"Well, if you're sure."

He threw his head back and laughed showing his white teeth bright against his tanned and sun-lined face.

"There will be no more sea-earthquakes. One in a lifetime is enough. I will take a buoy with us and if you get tired, you can hold onto it and rest. You will remember our little island Gozo all your life, I think – eh?"

I nodded emphatically – yes, I would definitely remember tumbling in the Goddess's bubbling cauldron while she cooked me alive in her sea-earthquake. I'd survived the initiation and it was one I was unlikely ever to forget.

The next morning, before it got too hot, we set off and swam without incident to where the cave entrance was hidden. Mario helped me ashore and we clambered across the rocks towards the dark slit that marked the threshold. I turned to face the sea and offered my prayer to the Goddess of life-and-death. Then, while Mario waited respectfully outside, I descended into the deep dark womb of the cave of the Great Mother. Strange to tell, I remember absolutely nothing about the interior of the cave. It's as if that memory has been blotted out. I remember entering and exiting. I remember swimming back. The rest is silence.

Caves are places sacred to the Goddess. They're the places where our ancestors sheltered from storms or other predators, and where they buried their dead. They're very special sacred sites to me. I've many potent memories of visiting them with my children to see prehistoric paintings or stalagmites or underground lakes. They're dark places, burial grounds yet womb-like, both inviting and scary. They root me and remind me of the words which I used to recite every Ash Wednesday when I was a vicar. I'd make the sign of the Cross in ash on a person's forehead. Then I'd say very softly and quietly to the man or woman or child kneeling in front of me: "Remember, O mortal, dust thou art and to dust thou wilt return." We are Earthlings. Humans - Humus-beings. Children of the Earth. Made as much from dirt as from star-dust.

Chapter Eighteen

DUST THOU ART

There's no getting through the menopausal gateway into our Majesteria years without facing our mortality. It's not easy, but it's got to be done. We're in the third of the four phases of our life. Our hair is greying, our menses are ceasing or have ceased; our bones are thinner and are bodies need more rest. But before I fill you with too much doom and gloom, let me say that, as far as I can make out, our inner self is becoming brighter and more exuberant. On a soul-level I feel 'younger', more alive and vibrant and adventurous than ever before.

To step across the threshold into our Majesteria years takes time, as I've repeatedly said. For me it took seven years. So be patient. Be patient and yet be persistent. Don't give up. Eye-balling death may not appeal as a hobby or weekend activity – but nothing frees us up more completely than grasping this thistle and learning how to dance with it stuck into our cleavage. My experiences are, in all probability, not your experiences. But, whatever your experiences are, I'd encourage you to grapple with them and cleave them to your bosom for they are uniquely your own.

I reckon that the only universally shared, and essential, element in getting through this menopausal gateway in such a way that we win the crown of an Autumn Queen, is our honesty. Honesty takes courage. And, like everything else I've been sharing with you - it takes practise. Part of my honest commitment to you is to admit that for a long time (a very long time), the fact that I experience visions made me feel 'special'. I thought maybe I was a mystic. And maybe I am – but that doesn't make me special, it just makes me a little bit unusual. And then, when I lost my faith and experienced a 'dark night of the soul', I thought I was a liar and a bad person who'd led good-hearted people astray. I feared I was mad. None of these labels is particularly helpful. To reach the truth of who we are, we need to get below the self-labelling. We need to dig deep in our own grot and grit and shadow.

All those little deaths: my first marriage, my life in the church, my PTSD diagnosis, my cherished convictions and notions about myself; all of it, is grist to the mill of self-knowledge – and, ultimately, wisdom. Nothing is wasted. It all helps us to spiral around and around towards a deeper and deeper self-understanding. Every hurt, every failure, every betrayal, every accolade and every success, all moves us inexorably closer to the day when we wake up and know our place within the world and within the realms of being. We wake up and find we're home.

A way to help this process along, while simultaneously preparing for our own death - that big ugly one looming at the end of this physical existence - is to practise 'dying' daily. By this I mean the practise of letting go. Learning to let go is an art form. And, as every spiritual tradition tells us, it's the primary requisite for finally landing inside our own skin within this lifetime.

Up until my menopause, I thought I was pretty accomplished at letting go. I'd even raised my kids to 'let go' of old toys in order to donate them to the church Christmas Fayre each year. "Making room for the new", I told them. They still struggle to forgive me for encouraging them to give away their Thunderbirds and Tracy Island models. But I had absolutely no clue about how deep this menopausal letting go needed to cut. It has to, if it is to free us up, to loosen the ties that bind us to the past, and to liberate us to follow the strange, winding path that will, in the end, bring us home to ourselves.

Letting go is the lesson, beyond all others, of the menopausal initiation. Let me try to describe for you what I mean by using an analogy from yoga. For someone like me – at least the person I was prior to entering the Majesteria – raised to be high-achieving, driven, and competitive – yoga subverts and challenges my early-years conditioning. I'm an achiever by up-bringing, so for many years I tried hard to 'achieve' even in yoga. I remember one yoga teacher saying to me, "Melanie, stop trying not to try." I laughed at the time and I still chuckle with the recognition of what he was pointing out in me. What yoga is *really* about is another of those annoyingly ungraspable concepts - par for the course for any spiritual practitioner – which make you feel like your head is about to bust apart. Let me try to explain.

There's a moment in yoga when, if you want to enter fully into the asana (the body-posture) you have to let it go. You have to release the muscles that are holding the posture. It sounds paradoxical and, of course, as with so much in the spiritual life, it is 100% a paradox - in order to hold the posture correctly, you have to let it go. You know this is happening because what you experience during the asana is ease. There is the feeling of stretch still, but there's no tension, no holding - the breath rides the body and the body rides the breath. It's very beautiful and very like prayer.

Letting go, as I say, is the key lesson of the menopausal journey. It's not an easy lesson to learn – and, in reality, it's not a lesson at all, it's a practise, a craft. The learning of this craft is life-long, of course - and it's repeatedly going to test us to our limits. As with an asana, you have to reach your limit first, and then you release the holding that accompanies it. A word here about 'reaching your limits' because what I'm talking about is often confused with a sort of internal bullying that pushes us beyond what our body is wisely telling us is enough. This kind of internal pushing most often leads either to an increased holding or to collapse and is, in my view, a form of self-harm. I should know. Trained in classical ballet as a child, my default has been to push through physical (or inner) discomfort and to try to ignore or override it – even if my body (or soul) was screaming at me. I was raised in the erroneous 'no pain no gain' era. What I'm talking about here is something much softer and more subtle.

In the yoga I practise, the limit is the moment I feel discomfort. As the stretch tips over into discomfort, I pause. (That pause again.) I don't push through it. I don't ignore it. Neither do I retreat from it. I hold the asana exactly there, and then … I let go. I release the holding by breathing into the stretch – riding my breath like a beautiful Welsh blood-red dragon, so that increased oxygen flows through my rich red blood into the cells that need it. The muscles, tendons or ligaments then naturally and easefully lengthen and the stretch deepens. There is a feeling of weightlessness and vibrancy and calm and flow all rolled deliciously into one. As I say, it's very like prayer.

If you're a spiritual practitioner of any description, you'll recognise what I'm talking about here. It's the potent moment of surrender – the moment when the little 'me' expands and wakes up. In that moment, I know myself to be something freer, wilder, more exuberant, expansive and wondrous than I'd dared to believe. This surrender is the opposite of grasping. From childhood onwards, in so many ways, we're taught the belief that in order to live-life-to-the-full we need to acquire (and to keep re-acquiring) a whole load of stuff. The shopping list is endless: clothes, accessories, achievements, status, more sophisticated electronic gadgets or taste in food, bigger and better houses or cars or jobs. "Consume, consume, consume" is the materialistic world's mantra.

Menopause, by contrast, teaches us the opposite. In order to be ready to embrace the next portion of our life, we need to "let go, let go, let go". By the time the seven year initiation was over for me, I'd crafted letting go into an art form. Or perhaps it'd be more accurate to say that it had crafted me. There was so much that I needed to unlearn and to relearn. So much I needed to face, to forgive and to embrace about myself. It was a long old haul.

If I were to describe to you in full my own practise of letting go, it'd take another entire book. So here, I'll offer one juicy snippet. I hope it'll inspire you to do your own soul-work in those places where you're still grasping tightly. And I hope it'll encourage you to honour and recognise the tremendous amount of letting go you've done so far. The area in my own practise I'm going to focus upon is jealousy and envy.

Let's start by making a distinction between these two states because they're related but not the same. When I was dancing honestly and consciously with my own demons of jealousy, I searched far and wide for guidance and support, but found little. Most people seemed to conflate jealousy and envy, but I knew them to be distinct. I'm rarely envious of other people but I do get jealous – fiercely jealous – and it's a very different emotion from envy. Moreover, during my years as a public figure I was often on the receiving end of envy but only twice (to my knowledge) of someone's jealousy.

On both occasions, there was an intensity and focus to the emotion which rained down upon me that was unmistakably jealousy. Envy can accompany jealousy - but jealousy, it seems to me, is a much more stand-alone emotion. Envy is often described as wanting what someone else has - whereas jealousy is often targeted and personal. I feel jealousy deep down in my womb-belly. It's a burning hot energy that can rise instantaneously and be quite overpowering. On an extreme occasion, it can even make me feel nauseous. I become 'sick with jealousy'. Envy, by contrast, is slower burning, more diffuse. It often involves thought, including comparisons of material wealth or advantage or beauty. Envy most commonly relates to things - jealousy most commonly relates to people. It's jealousy that drives a man to murder his wife's lover, not envy.

I've mentioned several times that as a girl I was envious of my older sisters. In actual fact, I realise that I was also jealous of them. At the time, and for many years afterwards, I was unaware of this dynamic. I love my sisters deeply and because I love them, it's hard to get below the love to what lies beneath – to reach into the reactive, difficult places where they trigger me. I find so often that the deeper I go into my own psyche, the murkier it can get, so the slower, more attentively and carefully I need to swim.

My envy and jealousy of them was the hidden face of my love for them. It was an energy which had the power to motivate me to stretch myself beyond my perceived limits - to get up on that scary pony or to attend ballet classes that challenged me beyond my competency. In that sense, the energy of envy was positive – it helped me to stretch and expand towards *more* of who I am. Yet it was also an energy that had the power to make me belittle myself and to undervalue myself - to play the underdog and the victim in a way that diminished me and caused me to contract. It conditioned me both to love the company of females and also to be wary and competitive in that company. It sensitised me – for good and ill – to the nuances of female rivalry and sisterhood.

When I grew up, I ceased to be envious of my sisters. I no longer needed to be envious of them because I'd 'outdone' them in terms of my outward accolades and achievements. But - I continued to be jealous of them. On occasion, I still am. The jealousy I feel in relation to them is part of the protective mechanism that comes into play to keep Melanie 'safe'. It's not that they're out to hurt me – they love me as much as I love them – but by virtue of the fact that they're my older sisters (with our ancient shared story), I get hurt. Having worked as hard as I have to let go of this particular sticky emotion, it's no longer as obvious or as damaging as it once was, but I suspect it's with me for life. Well, we'll see what my post-menopausal Majesteria years hold for me. I'll make sure and let you know in the sequel to this volume. I plan to call it *Wild Woman Walking*.

Before I leave the subject of sticky emotions, I want to say something about alcohol consumption. My dance with alcohol has been another of those little deaths. The over-use of alcohol seems to be part and parcel of 'having a good time' for the majority of people these days. It was certainly the case in my first family. I grew up in a household where family celebrations were defined by free-flowing booze. At different times different members within my birth family have danced dangerously close to alcohol dependency – including me. My maternal grandmother was a diagnosed alcoholic and almost died from cirrhosis of the liver. I've vivid memories of how she looked when she was very, very poorly. She, like so many of the women in my genetic family, had an indomitable will and a profound love of life, so she was able to recover and go on to live many more years after her illness. However, she continued to struggle with the lure of the sherry bottle until she died.

During the final year of my menopause I chose to live entirely AF (alcohol free). I found my body couldn't handle very much alcohol anymore – it contained far too much sugar. It took me a long time though, of working honestly and kindly with my own over-use of alcohol, before I was ready to let go of it. The strong line of women who are my foremothers all share an intense dislike of being told what to do. "Don't tell me what to do", is a familiar refrain in my family – try to control us, and we'll rebel, even to our own detriment. So, my attempts to 'force' myself to give up alcohol were destined to fail. Going AF wasn't sustainable over the long-haul because the feisty, independently-minded Melanie rebelled from being 'told' to stop drinking.

I knew that I needed to have done the soul-work. I needed to understand and release the story that lay beneath my need for the second or third or fourth glass of wine, before it would truly release its grip. And it had to be done kindly. Any hint of self-loathing, guilt, punishment or condemnation, and the inner-me would run off and hide – and, in all probability, she'd reach for a glass of wine.

In relation to the sticky emotion of jealousy which I was outlining above, alcohol was a blue touch paper. After I met Peter - who rarely drinks, and then usually it's "a pint of bitter-shandy" - I knew I wanted to be free of jealousy and I knew I wanted to be free of the over-use of alcohol. Over-use of alcohol and spiritual clarity are, for me anyway, mutually exclusive. I'd reached a point in my life where it was clear that a new era was opening up, and I wanted to step across the threshold alcohol free.

My way of getting to the root of my story with alcohol – to find out what was really going on deep down inside of me where no-one (including myself) stood in judgement – was to make it the focus of a series of 36-hour-intensive-solo retreats which I made in Sadhana Retreat. I drew a huge spiral on a piece of flipchart paper and then wrote along that spiral every memory I could think of relating to my own and my family's use of alcohol. I worked it and worked it and worked it. It helped.

The lynchpin, however, that enabled me finally to let go of the need to have a glass of wine, was when Peter told me that sometimes when I drank too much, I became "sharp", and that he didn't like that Melanie. I was mortified. I'd been telling myself for years that when I had a few drinks I became attractively forthright, expressive, and strong-minded; cleverly opinionated, well-informed, and amusing. I felt it made me more sociable and put me in the centre of the fun. His word "sharp", however, struck true. He had sensed a shadow lurking behind the loud, frivolous facade, and he was rightly wary of it. It was a hard pill to swallow. As soon as he said that word "sharp", I felt the truth of what he'd intuited - that behind my fun and frivolity lurked an unkind shadow.

The shadow which Peter intuited as being present behind the third or fourth glass of wine was cast by my fear - that I wasn't good enough, that I wasn't enough, that I was too much. Basically, it was the fear that I wouldn't be loved just as I am. That Peter wouldn't (couldn't) really love the mess, the pickle, the muddle that is Melanie. His gift to me actually, is that he does. In accepting the truth behind Peter's challenging words, I knew that it was time – time to unravel the knot of my fear – the fear which lay beneath the desire for that innocuous-seeming glass of wine.

So, I took the plunge. I decided to choose to become alcohol free (AF) for a year. I was curious about what was asking to come unravelled in me, especially in relation to Peter. How deeply could I trust our love? Could I trust it enough to allow it to heal my well-hidden wounds of self-doubt and self-harm? That was definitely something I wanted to explore. That was definitely something worth finding out. I remained AF for two years. I know, without a shadow of a doubt, that we would not be where we are today, if I hadn't. These days, I encourage those menopausal women who ask me for guidance, to seek to live alcohol free lives. It really does seem to help with many of the unpleasant physical symptoms with which some women suffer. It's probably as much to do with reducing sugar intake as anything else. It's certainly something well worth considering.

After I'd passed through the menopausal gateway into my Majesteria, I chose to cease being AF. I've never forgotten that word "sharp" though – and I keep a look out for her, that sharp, shadowy Melanie. She wears the mask behind which a frightened, angry young girl hides. If I sense her stepping into the room, I reach out to hold Peter's strong hand and I make the self-loving choice to pour a glass of something delicious and alcohol free. Freedom, after all, is the goal beckoning beyond the menopausal gateway. Freedom is the life-blood that pulses through the heart of every majesterial woman or man I've ever met.

Chapter Nineteen

THE RAISING OF LAZARUS

I'm going to close this exploration of death with another near-death experience – but of a different sort. It occurred the year before Peter and I left Wales. During one of my solo retreats in Sadhana, I had an out-of-body experience. It sums up the truth which, more than anything else, I want to convey. It was an experience of what I've come to call 'The Divine Chuckle'. Let me set the scene for you. I was sitting on my little wooden prayer-stool, which I've had since I was eighteen years-old, in the living-room of the static caravan. I'd lit a candle on my altar and was looking at an icon called The Raising of Lazarus.

The icon is made from the trunk of a Dutch Elm. It's one of those lovely trees that fell victim to Dutch Elm disease in the 1980s. Even if I said no more than that about the icon, it would be rich with meaning. The icon stands solid and heavy at eighteen inches tall and eighteen inches wide. It's painted in blue and gold, white and rose-pink. You can see a photo of it on my website: www.melaniesantorini.org. I purchased it when I was in my late twenties at theological college. Although I've let go of almost

everything else from that period of my life (books, clerical robes, title, networks and friends), the icon has travelled with me.

It was carved and painted by Sister Theresa Margaret, a Christian nun with the Order of the Holy Name based near Derby. In later life she spent several years as a hermit on the Lleyn Peninsular in north Wales. Close by her hermitage is Ynys Enlli (Bardsey Island) where I'd spent several summers with my young children. We'd holiday there while I fulfilled the role of Chaplain. On Bardsey, there's no electricity, no hot water and no flushing loos. Pure gorgeous simplicity – but I digress. I'll save the stories of Bardsey to tell you about in *Blood Sacrifice*.

As a relatively poor theological college student, it took me two years to buy the icon of The Raising of Lazarus, paying just a few pounds a month. There's a dynamic energy to the icon which I love. The colours move and swirl. Yeshua is young and beardless. This is how he's portrayed in the earliest visual representations we have of him, which are preserved in a Roman mosaic floor in Briton, and on a wall in the catacombs beneath Rome. In the icon Yeshua reaches forward, stretching his arm out towards his friend Lazarus who is emerging from his tomb. Around Yeshua's head, a golden halo echoes the shape of a dove. The dove is a traditional Christian symbol of the Holy Spirit. The golden energy around Yeshua's head arcs outward along his outstretched arm to embrace and surround the head of Lazarus. The icon captures a magnificent moment in a magnificent story.

Lazarus, a man who had been one of Yeshua ben Yosef's dearest friends has died. He's been dead and buried for three days. It's the only time in the stories we have about Yeshua that we're told he weeps at the loss of a friend whom he deeply loves. It's a beautifully humane moment and one that gives full permission to our grief - for even the enlightened grieve.

Then the story ups a gear. Yeshua commands the onlookers to roll away the stone in front of the cave in which Lazarus is entombed. Lazarus's sisters resist for they fear there'll be a stench. Yeshua insists, and the stone is rolled away. Then... he reaches out towards the dead friend he loves and has lost. He stretches himself to the utmost in order to make a bridge of his love from this realm into the next. And, in a mighty voice, he commands Lazarus, "Come forth!" Energy erupts from deep within him. It's visible on the icon as a gold line along his torso echoing the gold of the halo and the arc of light.

The strain shows in the young Yeshua's face. Lazarus emerges from the tomb bound in his grave-clothes, looking like a mummified chrysalis waiting to be transfigured into a glorious air-born butterfly. In the foreground are three witnessing women. One with her arms flung wide, caught up in this dynamic dance of Love. This Love which, the story tells us, has the power to transform and transfigure everything - even death. Death, that densest of all mysteries, reveals itself here as a shimmering, diaphanous dance.

Then, in the story, Yeshua says the words that are the reason that this icon, and this particular story, has stayed with me for over thirty years. Yeshua says to the women:

"Unbind him and let him go free."

And within those words I hear, "unbind *her* and let her go free". Now, as I write, it feels significant that it's the women who perform the act of unbinding and of liberation. I never tire of looking at the icon. This 'unbinding' needs to happen for all of us – on so many levels - women and men, human and non-human. And, indeed, it needs to happen for our entire planet.

Back to that particular day in 2015, sitting meditating in Sadhana Retreat, gazing at the icon of 'The Raising of Lazarus'... Suddenly I was outside my body, hovering near the ceiling of

the caravan, looking down at myself. Everything went silent. Not quiet but SILENT. It was as if the volume dial for the whole of creation had been switched to 'off'. Total and utter and complete silence. A *pause*. Expectant. Pregnant. Then I heard a chuckle! A chuckle that was so warm and all-encompassing and GOOD that my whole being was filled with delight and reassurance and joy. To this day my eyes fill with tears and I smile every time I remember the sound of it. There was a joyous lightness in the sound, a playfulness, a kindly mischievous energy that showed me – yet again - that, in spite of appearances – in spite of all the bloody mess that surrounds us – at the deepest, deepest, deepest level, all is well. Then I was back in my body, back on my prayer stool and back in a noisy world. What a privilege - to hear the Divine Chuckle – the sheer, unimaginable *delight* at the heart of existence. It reminds me of the old creation story where God looks at *Her* creation and sees that it is GOOD. What a relief.

This is my human freedom: to choose to believe and to live from within this truth. It could be that I'm delusional. I cannot prove that I am not. However, I know with absolute certainty that the deeper I've rooted myself in my core beliefs, all of which stem from these sorts of experiences and the more I've lived from the implications of those core beliefs, the happier and healthier I've become.

By the time the seven years of my menopausal journey was almost complete, my mantra was "I'm done with doubt". The cobalt-blue star facial tattoo, which Peter and I had designed together, is a physical expression of my commitment to make this my daily choice for the rest of my life: to live henceforth from within my deepest truth. It's pretty difficult to forget that daily intention when it's painted permanently on the centre of your forehead.

I hope that you've enjoyed the contrasting stories of my 'brushes with death': at the Co-op Funeral Service, on the island

of Gozo and in Sadhana Retreat. I hope the stories have made clear the contradiction that lies at the heart of my own feelings about death. On the one hand – at one level - I no longer fear death because I no longer believe myself to be a separate 'I' who will cease when my body dies. On the other hand – at another level – I continue to feel fear in the face of my own physical death. Embracing contradiction seems to be the menopausal and majesterial way, so I'd probably better get used to it.

As I've been relating, letting go isn't easy. So, the greatest letting go of them all – which is death – is inevitably going to take some courage and an almost unfathomable depth of trust. When this body dies and I let go of earthly existence – in this form anyway – I'll have to let go of everything I most love. The list makes my heart ache: my children, my grandchildren, Peter, sunlight on water, autumn leaves falling in a silent forest, the blaze of red on the woodpecker's underbelly as he feeds on the bird-table, the smell of freshly brewed coffee, the taste of garlic – you get the picture.

When I die, I hope I'll be able to let go of all these beloveds peacefully, and with a heart over-flowing with gratitude for all that has been given to me to love – including this physical-soul-expression called Melanie. I've watched enough people die, however – including light-filled holy souls – to know that the act of dying isn't just a spiritual art, it's a physical event. And it's one which often involves pain, discomfort and quite a bit of mess. Like menstruation, like childbirth, like menopause, dying is rarely tidy. I often say to people who are anxious about witnessing the dying of their loved one, that the animal-body will visibly do what s/he needs to do, just as the soul-body will invisibly do what s/he needs to do.

Sometimes, dying is as easy and natural as breathing out. It isn't always though. So, when sitting with the dying, it's best to adopt the humble attitude of "what will be, will be". What I hope for, in anticipation of my own physical death, is that I'll die with a modicum of equanimity, a generous dollop of good humour and a liberal sprinkling of grace. Whether or not it looks tidy or feels comfortable – well, I'll just have to wait and see. I trust though – deeper than words can convey – that, despite appearances, *all will be well.* Heard or unheard, the Divine Chuckle will be present.

To conclude, I believe that every experience we have – whether as part of our childhood conditioning or as something that comes along later in life – bears a dual aspect. You could say that all of life is two-faced. Every experience has the potential to become blessing, however negative it might appear on the surface, because through it, we can learn more about ourselves. As I write that I can hear a dear friend whispering in my ear that she disagrees. She tells me that I can only make that claim because I've been blessed with an easy and happy life in comparison with her experience of childhood trauma and sexual abuse. She has a valid point. I cannot know what is the deepest truth for you – I can only know what *I* know and dare to share it with you in the hope it will help you along the journey to finding your own dear self within your own skin.

In letting go of the fixed notions of self – I am *this*; I am not *that* – and embracing the plurality, fluidity and contradictory nature of self, I began to deepen into self-acceptance. I've had to learn to let go of layer upon layer of who I thought I was. I needed to stop battling with myself - beating myself into shape trying to be something or someone that felt more socially acceptable. I needed to make peace with myself – the bits I like and admire, and the bits I don't. That's easy to write but in actuality very difficult to do. We're all fed a drip, drip, drip of notions of superiority and inferiority each and every day.

As I've said, it's like shedding skins, peeling away the layers of who I think I am, until I am left with an empty husk of who I thought Melanie was. Around me, the discarded notions of self lie scattered at my feet like fallen autumn leaves. When I am empty of who I think I am; no longer subscribing to the myth of my uniqueness or specialness, I stand naked – raw, vulnerable, scraped clean. This is me in my natural state – my *wild* self (i.e. the self-willed-self) - viewed for perhaps the first time. She's not very attractive, possibly; not very glamorous, probably; and as far away from the 'celebrity image' of self as it's possible to be. But it's me, and, finally, I'm mine. I am she who is becoming who she is. Now, I see myself mirrored in the face of every other human being – and, if I'm lucky enough to spend sufficient time in nature, I begin to discern my kinship with everything around me – rock, root and river. I'm on my way. I'm coming home.

Chapter Twenty

PARTYING AND PACKING UP

The summer after we were married, Peter and I threw a weekend-long party for family and friends on our thirteen-acre smallholding. People rocked up with tents or in motorhomes, and the house and static caravan were full to overflowing. We hired Portaloos and set up wash-stations outdoors – just like a proper mini festival. We cooked outside, went for horse-rides, chatted and laughed, ate and drank far too much and occasionally burst into song. It was tremendous fun. Peter had constructed a stage at the front of the barn for the Saturday evening.

It was fancy dress and the theme was 'the Sixties' with a prize for the best outfit – won, to his delighted surprise, by one of our middle-aged neighbours. We'd booked the Aberystwyth-based, all-female band, *The Hornettes*. Before their gig began, everyone toasted us with a glass of champagne. They cheered as Peter and I whirled and twirled through our 'first' dance together. We'd chosen the Joe Cocker version of *Love lifts us up where we belong*. We all boogied enthusiastically in the outdoor marquee well into the small hours, young and old together – it was magical.

On the Sunday we held a triathlon - a little tongue-in-cheek for the less serious participants, but with enough edge and zing for the competitive and physically fit to get their teeth into. It involved swimming a stretch of a small mountain lake, cycling three times around another smaller lake and running some distance or other – I can't now remember as I never got that far.

It wasn't all champagne and laughter, however. Peter's younger sister had completed her own dance with death less than a week before our planned wedding party. She had been struggling with cancer for five years. I was privileged to conduct her funeral service. Doreen was the same age as me and Peter loved her dearly. We thought about cancelling our wedding party which was going to take place just three days after her funeral. So many people had already made arrangements to travel great distances to be with us, however, that cancelling it at that late hour really wasn't feasible.

Then, Doreen's partner, Phil, said he was coming to the party in memory of her. When we'd sent out the invitations, six months before, Doreen had said how much she wanted to be there. Phil was convinced the party needed to go ahead. He gave a little speech and we toasted her memory, and then he flung himself wholeheartedly into our celebration – it was moving and generous-hearted and absolutely right.

Though we didn't say it at the time, Peter and I both knew that, as well as being our wedding celebration, the party was also our farewell. Several of my women-friends intuited this to be the case, but nothing was said at the time because of Doreen's death which had left Peter's parents distraught and grieving. His Mum and Dad were used to having him around – he still lived less than twenty miles from the family home in which he grew up and, until he met me, he'd left Wales fewer than a dozen times in his life. Although we'd been talking about our dream of moving to the wilds of Scotland, most people thought it was just that – a dream. Peter and I, however, were never more serious.

The very first time Peter visited Scotland he fell in love with it. We went on a fishing trip and travelled in an ancient T25 VW campervan. We explored salmon rivers and mountain glens with the excitement of a couple of teenagers on their first trip together away from home. I watched as Peter's wings began to unfurl. In that wild, untameable landscape, he could breathe, stretch, and inhabit himself in a way he felt he'd never been fully free to do before. We began to talk about the possibility of taking early retirement from waged employment, leaving Wales and moving to Scotland. We had two youngsters in their final years at school for whom we were still responsible, but the others had already flown their nests.

Peter began to research Scottish properties for sale and over the next three years, on our annual fishing trip, we went to visit potential dream places. We had a pretty clear wish-list: riparian rights to enjoy more fishing, increased acreage in which to set up a rough shoot (pheasant, wild duck, woodcock, pigeon) and in which to enjoy our horses, more time for my writing and on-line businesses, wilderness, privacy, a small house with just enough space to welcome visiting youngsters, mountain view and (a key factor) no mortgage. We thought what we wanted was simply *more* of what we already enjoyed. As a fly-fisherman, Peter's passion was salmon rivers, so the properties we viewed had to have access to a river.

I've often said that watching Peter fly-fish is like watching a classical ballet dancer – focused concentration and strength in a fluid, measured, graceful form. To be taught how to fish for salmon by such a skilled practitioner was a privilege and a pleasure. I haven't landed a salmon yet (and in Scotland, it's worth pointing out, there's a strict and necessary catch-and-release policy). Having a powerful salmon on the line is an incredible feeling. Losing them off the line – again and again and again – is also an incredible feeling, and not a pleasant one.

Peter can read a river (where the brown trout and the salmon will lie hidden) with as much ease and contentment as I read a book. He loses himself in a river, becoming one with it in a manner which I recognise from deep prayer. In keeping with his fear of deep water, however, we never looked at anything with loch frontage. He was dismissive of loch fishing anyway because, in his view, hitting a fish on a lake or loch was simply a matter of luck rather than knowledge and skill.

We'd probably still be looking for the dream property with river frontage and extensive acreage had not two significant, but seemingly disconnected, events occurred. The first was we watched a DVD series in which the British actors Timothy West and Prunella Scales sailed around Britain and northern Europe on canal boats and motor cruisers. Happily married for forty-plus years and now in their eighties, for some reason, this delightful couple's adventures struck a deep chord with us. We watched several other series about canal boats and boat touring and we were hooked.

To my astonishment, Peter announced that we needed a boat. For a man who is very, very afraid of deep water, his new and unshakeable desire to have a boat was a completely unexpected turn of events. I used to water-ski as a kid, I'm a strong swimmer and we've been out a few times on a dory (small rowing boat used for fishing) - neither of us, however, has any proper boating or sailing experience. This sudden, burning desire for a boat was so uncharacteristic of Peter – who's the least materially minded person I know – that I was convinced. The fact that we knew nothing about boats wasn't going to put us off, and we began visiting marinas in Wales, and then further afield, on a day-trip out.

One weekend, we came across an exquisitely outfitted 33' Dutch steel motor-cruiser for sale. She was beautiful. Her name was Pegasus – which could not have been more perfect (I often experience dreams of riding a horse with wings). To our disappointment, she was already under offer – which was just as well really because she was far, far too big for a first boat. That was it however, the Scottish dream had shifted. A new element now had to be included in our already long (and seemingly unrealistic and unattainable) wish-list. We now wanted a place with all that I listed above, plus close enough to deep water for us to have a boat. It seemed to me an impossible (and possibly greedy) dream. Peter, being Peter – he just kept on quietly doing the on-line research and taking me for day-trips out to view boats.

The second event which had fundamentally shifted things was Doreen's death. A couple of days after she died, Peter had said to me: "This is it; the time to do this is *now* before we're too sick or too old to enjoy it". Suddenly, everything shifted into another gear. We were now married, our two youngest were both about to finish school, and both sets of elderly parents were still in good health and actively enjoying life. If we didn't do it now, we'd end up like so many people our age. People who, having fulfilled the obligations involved with rearing school-age children, now found themselves tied into the obligations involved with caring for aging and infirm parents.

We chose differently. We chose to put our dreams into action and to fly the nest ourselves. Let me be clear here, it was a radical (and, I suspect, rare) choice to make. Some whom we loved deemed us selfish. Some envied us. Some were hurt by us. Some have never fully forgiven us. To the credit of our various aging parents and our eight youngsters – they were amongst those who cheered us on and encouraged us to dare to live out our dreams to the full. However, it wasn't easy to leave all that behind – especially our two youngest sons who'd shared home with us. They were both clear that they didn't want to move away from Aberystwyth – and, since they were both now legally adults - albeit very young adults - we wanted to honour their choices. But leaving them behind in Wales was hard on them – and hard on us. So, this was no easy, glib choice. It was the right choice though – we were always one hundred percent clear about that. It was a costly choice, but its prize was our happiness. We hoped that in making such a radical bid for freedom in pursuit of our own deepest happiness, we'd hold a model up for our youngsters - all eight of them - that would give them permission and inspire them to follow their own deepest dreams.

We both put our properties on the market. Mine sold within ten days and Peter's within a couple of months. It seemed like a sign from the universe that we were doing the right thing. We raced up to Scotland to view a loch-side property on Loch Awe. It was a small two-bedroomed cottage with about four acres of land and the option to lease four more. It was called Church Cottage, which felt both amusing and serendipitous. The sale of the smallholding was almost in the bag, so we cleared out the farmhouse, put all our furniture and worldly goods into storage, and moved into the static caravan that I'd been using for my Sadhana Retreat work. Both our lads had moved out, and it felt we were nearly there. Scotland beckoned and we decided to take a leap of faith and jump. We made an offer on the loch-side cottage on Loch Awe. We were excited and pleased that everything seemed to be going so smoothly to plan. Peter headed off to work, and I sat by the phone to wait to hear from our solicitor in Edinburgh.

Early that afternoon, she phoned to tell us that a higher offer had been received and to ask did we want to increase our offer – it would need to be a substantial increase. We had until 5 p.m. to put in our bid. I couldn't reach Peter by phone – he was out on a job and out of signal range. I paced up and down in the caravan, wondering whether or not to increase our bid and, if so, by how much. I spoke again with the solicitor and was able to ascertain what sort of figure we were looking at. It would take us slightly over the top of our budget, and leave very little left in the kitty to do the renovations we'd planned. I paused, had a cup of tea and sat watching the red kites soaring over the farmland that lay between us and the sea. Putting down my cup, I picked up the phone and instructed our solicitor to make our top offer. She put in the bid on our behalf and said we'd hear tomorrow whether or not it'd been accepted.

We spent the evening pouring over Ordnance Survey maps of the area. The offer we'd put in was a good deal more than the asking price and so we felt that we were in with a good chance. The next morning Peter delayed leaving for work and we sat anxiously by the phone. Just before lunch our solicitor in Edinburgh phoned to tell us that we'd been outbid. We were stunned.

It's funny isn't it, how you can think something's in the bag, when it clearly isn't? You'd have thought that my experience of repeatedly hooking and then failing to land a salmon, would've taught me something. Suddenly our plans seemed to be going horribly awry. The sale of the smallholding was still proceeding, albeit slowly, but we'd seen nothing else on the market in Scotland within budget that looked even remotely suitable. Homelessness loomed. We were floundering and wondering what to do next. Should we give up on the dream, and settle for something less, we asked ourselves and our loved ones. The answer from all quarters was a resounding "no". So we decided to set off for Scotland anyway, even if we didn't have a clue where we were headed or what would be our destination.

Peter and I had talked, half-jokingly, about buying a motorhome, letting go of everything in Wales, and setting off to search for our dream place, and now we found ourselves having to do just that. I was quite energised at the prospect of living on the road – it connected me with my Romany gypsy ancestry. Living in a 'vardo' (a horse-drawn gypsy wagon) had been an idea I'd played with around my children for years.

Peter began to research motorhomes for sale on the internet. If we were going to be living in it full-time, it needed to be spacious, warm and comfortable. I wanted a luxury one with a separate toilet and a proper shower, central heating and – most important of all – a fixed bed. He found us a Fiat Bessacar in Lincoln and we set off to take a look.

The dealership agreed to take our T25 VW campervan in part-exchange, which was just as well because the Bessacar was expensive. It was perfect though, and I fell instantly in love with my new motorised home – thoughtfully laid out with plenty of storage space, cupboards in smart oak veneer, a full size oven and fridge, gas central heating, and a proper shower with a sliding door in the bathroom. It had everything we could possibly need. It looked clean, comfortable, light and airy. At the rear of the motorhome was a fixed double bed adjacent to a large side-window.

I could imagine sitting there to write or to read, enjoying stunning views in the early morning light with Peter asleep beside me - which is, of course, exactly what happened. It's just as well the motorhome was so comfortable and snug. What we didn't know on the day we bought her was that we'd be living in the Bessacar, not for a few weeks, as anticipated, but for nine long months. Four months of which would be in the snow over the longest, hardest winter Scotland had known in a very long time. Expensive maybe, but the Bessacar proved herself to be worth every single penny.

With the motorhome parked up and ready-to-go in front of the farmhouse, we finished packing our goods into a storage container and prepared to leave. The date for the completion of sale on the smallholding had been set for a fortnight's time. We were still struggling to sort out what was going to happen to our beloved horses. We'd planned to take them with us to Scotland. A farmer friend had reluctantly agreed to have them for a few weeks – two months max, while we settled in. Then, when the property on Loch Awe fell through, we needed to re-think. A friend near Machynlleth stepped in and offered to have them at her place for as long as we needed. When we went over to check it out, however, her fields proved unsuitable. Other well-meaning friends generously offered to help, but didn't fully realise what would be involved.

Horses take some serious looking after, and need a very particular kind of environment in which to thrive. Non-horsey people can see a horse in a field contentedly grazing and think that's all there is to it. What isn't seen is the never-ending maintenance of fences (horses love to rub up against the posts), the removal of ragwort and other poisonous plants, the need for a constant supply of fresh water, the high quality of mixed pasture required for grazing and the removal or chain-harrowing of the horse-dung. A horse needs to be checked and groomed daily and exercised regularly. In winter, horses need to be fed twice-a-day with hay and possibly rugged, at least at night. They're hard work, and if they get injured or become unwell, even harder work. I love it, absolutely love it. But when I outlined the commitment needed to look after our horses, friends sensibly withdrew their offers. I looked into full-time livery but the cost was prohibitive - plus the livery yards weren't prepared to take responsibility for our horses while we were so far away in Scotland.

In the midst of dashing hither and thither to try to find a solution, the owner of the riding centre where I took my weekly class, suggested I pause and turn to face what I already knew, but didn't want to have to admit.

"You need to sell them, or put them up for loan," she said gently. "I know it's hard."

With a heavy heart, I put the horses up for sale. When I talk about letting go, and call it the high-art of entering the Majesteria, it might perhaps sound a bit lofty or abstract. The reality is that it's as down-to-earth as it gets. It is kissing goodbye to the warm, sweet-smelling, soft nose of an animal you love and who trusts you – an animal who's been your unfailingly loyal best friend through some seriously challenging times. It hurts. I'll say it again - menopausal letting go hurts. I imagine you nodding your head in agreement. The fire of menopausal transformation definitely leaves scars.

As soon as I posted the horses for sale on Facebook, we instantly had masses of enquiries. It was especially difficult to manage the enquiries because I was away on the *Avalon Remembered* pilgrimage (see chapter eleven). When I'd booked the retreat, I'd felt it would be perfectly timed to mark the threshold that was our transition from Wales to Scotland. And it was - as well as a stretch for the both of us. Miles away in Glastonbury, I had to let go and leave Peter to suss out potential buyers for our horses. He's a good judge of character and I was happy to be guided by his intuition.

Although, in the initial flurry, no-one suitable came forward, after a few days someone who was experienced with veteran horses got in touch. She already had a couple of veteran horses and had been seeking to buy another one for almost a year. She was excited by the prospect of buying two horses who were good friends. She sounded like a serious contender and after a lengthy chat, I arranged for her to go up to the smallholding to meet Peter and to have a trial ride. Peter phoned me afterwards to say he thought we'd found a decent buyer and we agreed to sell her both our horses. I didn't meet her until the morning of their departure – time was running out, we were leaving in a fortnight, and, anyway, I trusted Peter's judgement.

On the morning that the horses were to leave us, I went into the field to catch them. Gosh it was a huge wrench. I'd always assumed that they'd be with us until they died. Peter's mare had been with him for sixteen years, including giving him a foal, and I'd had Jackson for seven years. The tears wanted to come but I refused to be overwhelmed. I did my best to hold myself strong, clear and resolute – I told myself, this needs to happen and therefore I need to trust it.

Jackson was stressed during loading into the horse box, and I stepped back to let Peter do it. When I went in to say the final farewell, Jackson bit me – hard. It was only the second time that had ever happened – the previous occasion was after he'd fully recovered from his splint-bone fracture. I carried the bruise from his farewell bite like a badge for weeks.

The two horses quickly settled into their new home on the Welsh-English border. Their new owner absolutely delighted in them and sent me regular photos showing all their new adventures.

I still miss them hugely. When we briefly returned to Wales the following Spring I suggested to Peter that we call in on the horses, as we were crossing the border fairly close to their new home.

"Don't, it'll break your heart to see them," Peter said.

I opened my mouth to disagree and then paused to think about it. He was right. As much for myself as for them and their new owner, I needed to let them go.

Chapter Twenty-One

TRAVELLING THE ROAD
TO FREEDOM

In late September 2017 my youngest son and his girlfriend waved us off as we left our life in Wales behind and headed for Scotland. They'd parked their car in a lay-by just outside Aberystwyth so we'd see them as we set off on our adventure North in our motorhome. It was a lovely gesture. In typical unpredictable fashion though, the first thing we did on leaving Aberystwyth for Scotland was to turn right towards the south coast of England.

After months of research, Peter had finally spotted a boat for sale in Southampton which seemed to fit the bill. He knew exactly what he was looking for and we were thrilled to have found her. She was a Channel Island 22 Motor Cruiser in impeccable condition; two berth with twin Volvo Penta engines, 43 HP each (which makes her strong, steady and reliable); a snug galley; a sea-toilet; and an 8'x 8' rear deck – plenty of space for fishing; and, with a diving platform for me, we anticipated lots of fun family times ahead.

Peter produced a wad of cash for a down-payment (part of his legacy from his sister's estate), and the boat was ours. It was agreed that we'd leave her dry-docked where she was, under the careful and kindly eye of her previous owners, while we found our dream place in Scotland.

We named her *Star of Avalon,* partly in memory of Doreen, and partly in recognition that, like my facial tattoo, she was part of the Deep-water Dreaming in which we were now swimming and to which we had committed ourselves. There was no going back – the dream had shape-shifted: the perfect property now had to include loch or sea frontage. We were asking the universe a lot – I quietly wondered whether we were asking for too much – "you're being greedy" is one of the conditioned negative hyper-critical mind-tapes that sometimes play in my head.

On leaving Southampton, we headed north straight up the centre of England towards Leeds. We'd hoped to pop in and see one of our daughters at University there, but the timing was off as she was away in London. We parked up overnight in a tiny village deep in the countryside not far from Rugby. In the morning before leaving I gave her a quick call. It turned out that she was just fifteen minutes drive away at her boyfriend's in Coventry. He drove her over and we had two hours of solid high-speed chatting while Peter drove us up the M1 motorway to drop her off in Leeds. We even managed to stop en route for Sunday lunch in Wakefield. We had a proper traditional roast beef dinner, which Peter tucked into with gusto. This was one of the many happy synchronicities with which our road-trip was blessed.

Later that day, as the sun set, Peter and I crossed the border into Scotland amidst much whooping and hollering of "FREEEEDOM!" The Scottish Adventure had begun.

◆

We had two house viewings lined up near Loch Awe, the area we'd already settled upon as a real possibility, and we rapidly got caught up in an intense process which at times felt quite pressurized. The Scottish system for buying a house is different than in Wales or England. It seems to me that it's easier on the person selling property and harder on the buyer. If you're seriously interested in a property then you're required to submit a formal offer via a Scottish solicitor. Once all the offers have been received, they're opened in the presence of a solicitor and the vendor can settle on one offer, or invite further bids. As we'd already experienced, it can then turn into a bidding war. On the positive side, once your offer has been accepted by a vendor, then it's pretty well binding on both parties. With the Scottish market experiencing a bit of a boom – there being too few properties on the market for the number of interested buyers – the whole process can skip along at a fair speed.

One of the properties we'd booked to view near Loch Awe seemed perfect: it had a stretch of a salmon river, 48 acres, and plenty of potential for a rough shoot. Its proximity to Loch Awe meant we could arrange a mooring there for our boat. On the negative side, it had no house - but it did have planning consent for one. We spent three hours walking the land. Peter, when in company, can be hard to read, and I was unsure what he was making of it. Once we were on our own, I asked him.

"It'll be the death of me," he said with his usual bluntness.

I grinned from ear to ear.

"Oh, I'm so relieved to hear you say that. It seems to have everything we've been looking for but there's so much mud! I can't imagine living here and I was dreading that you might like it."

He shook his head slowly.

"You know," he said. "Now I'm here, I don't think I want anywhere as big as this. The fencing alone will cost us twenty-five thousand and it'd be six months hard graft for me. It's very wet, anyway. And, they've had cattle grazing on it, which has ruined the land for horses."

He paused.

"You know, I don't think I'm up for a new build neither. Too many people need to get involved. I want to get away from all that stress with people. I want to enjoy my retirement in peace."

I nodded vigorously – I couldn't have put it better myself. I linked my arm through his as we walked slowly to where the Bess was parked up for the night.

The next day was the second viewing. This also had river frontage, about seventeen acres, two dwellings and plenty of outbuildings. Part of it was a registered croft, and the croft house, though needing restoration, was delightful. We sat drinking tea in the Bessacar discussing its pros and cons. It wasn't perfect, but was it good enough, we wondered? It had only just come back on the market and we knew that if we wanted it, we needed to move quickly. The estate agent in Oban was confident it'd be snapped up sharpish.

We talked around and around it, until we were quite dizzy. Neither of us wanted to make the wrong decision – would we regret it if we let it slip through our fingers, or would we regret it if something better came along later? We very nearly ended up panic-buying the place out of sheer exhaustion. Leaving Wales and negotiating all that we'd had to negotiate: including letting go of houses, sons, jobs, dogs and horses, had left us exhausted.

What we needed to do was to stop – to *pause*. On the advice of a good friend, we headed to the island of Mull and stayed there a week simply resting and allowing the months of letting go to land

and settle inside us both. Our thinking was that if, after a week's holiday on Mull, we were still interested in the property, we'd put in an offer but, for now, we both agreed that we were just too tired to see straight.

To say that we were bone-weary would still be to understate the depth of the exhaustion we both carried. We were not aware of it at the time, but, suffice to say, during those first five months that we were travelling in the motorhome, we both slept twelve to fourteen hours a night – every night. I reckon we were, for the first time, giving our bodies exactly what they needed: REST - deep soul-restoring, body re-booting, bone-healing, solid, undemanding rest. Peter is a relentlessly tireless worker and it's more often than not hard physical work. He sleeps long hours at night anyway, but I usually don't – or didn't pre-menopause. This was a whole new experience for me. I hadn't slept this well since before I'd borne my children.

Looking back, I can see now that the nine months travelling in the Bessacar was the *pause* within the pause of my menopause. Nine months - the perfect gestation period. Living on the road, simply and quietly with just the two of us, was the enforced pause which I needed in order to enter my Majesteria years healthily and happily. It was the pause that allowed me to loosen my grip on my role as 'mother' – a role that was fundamental to how I perceived myself as a woman. Looking after youngsters is what I do. It's not all I do, but it's what I do an awful lot of the time. It's what I've been doing for nearly thirty years and what I enjoy doing. I have in my life four of my own and four of Peter's – and now a grandchild as well.

To leave them behind and to migrate to Scotland, as I've already pointed out, was a challenge - not just for them, but for me as well. It was a challenge that went bone deep into who I thought

I was and, most fundamentally, what I thought made me a good mother. Loving my 'children' and my step-'children' is easy. We're blessed with a great bunch of youngsters – all very different and all good company to be around. However, to begin with, it was a relief not to feel responsible for them. Peter and I felt like we were on an extended vacation.

But after a while, I missed my contact with them. Although they're all technically adults, they're young and they're facing those challenges appropriate to their stages of life. I enjoy being there for them. It validates me in some ways, I guess – and it's appreciated. It's a thoroughly ingrained habit. It is, however, a difficult habit to indulge from a motorhome in the Highlands of Scotland where (even with a smart-phone) we were usually without phone signal and internet for weeks at a stretch. By the end of the first month, I'd begun to feel the pull of that stretch and, as with any good stretch, I'd started to touch places that I hadn't reached before.

In those early days on Mull, however, the stretching was yet to come and we were content to relax and enjoy the unexpected beauty of the island. We drove round the entire island travelling in a clockwise direction. It was stunning. In the morning on the first day, we walked a mile across a bog to find a beautiful circle of prehistoric stones tucked away and hidden. No-one there but us two. It was very special. Then after lunch we walked for over three hours along the rocky coast looking for an elusive castle, only to discover it the next day in totally the opposite direction. It says it all really and was prophetic - though we didn't know it at the time.

We enjoyed a couple of solitary nights parked up on a headland beach looking out over the Sound of Mull. I spent many hours, just as I'd envisaged, sitting on our bed reading and writing, being reinvigorated by the stunning view. One morning watching the tide go out, Peter spotted two bottle-nosed dolphins playing with a fish they'd caught. We then watched an otter tumbling and diving across the bay for about twenty minutes and then – oh wow - we saw a Minke whale, thirty feet long, slowly, languorously swim across the cove with her calf, leading it out to sea. Mind-stoppingly beautiful. We felt we were ready. The holy Isle of Iona called. A threshold from the old life into the new.

Braving a seriously rough sea crossing (which put Peter keenly in touch with his deep fear of deep-water) we landed on this tiny patch of ground. The island of Iona is understandably described as a 'thin' place; a place where heaven and earth are separated by only a tissue-breadth of material existence. The light there is like nowhere else I've ever visited. The turquoise seas and white sandy beaches make it a pilgrim's haven. The name 'Iona' (the Irish form is Shona) derives from the Hebrew word for 'dove'; it is synonymous with the word 'peace'. Many years previously, just after I was ordained, I'd stayed on the island of Iona with a group of clergy so this visit with Peter was resonant on many levels.

A heavy downpour, however, greeted us as we disembarked, and so we headed straight for the Abbey. We stopped first at St Oran's church, the oldest building on the island and traditionally where pilgrims paused before they entered the Abbey to kneel in prayer before the shrine of St Columba. Peter and I sat on the prayer stools immediately in front of the altar of the tiny stone chapel. Peter leaned towards me and whispered, "Look behind you."

On the edge of a pew, only a foot away from my right shoulder sat a robin. It cocked its little head and eyed me quizzingly. I began to speak softly to it and it answered me, chirping and trilling. We chatted together a good while before it flew to the altar and sang its heart out to us. Peter and I were in awe. Without taking my eyes off the robin, I reached into my back pack and fished around for my picnic lunch. I held out a morsel of bread which the robin gobbled up. We heard someone behind us enter the chapel and the robin stood on tiptoes – literally – elongating its little body to have a good look – before giving us a final chirp goodbye and flying out the door. In this state of grace, we entered Iona Abbey.

We had only a brief look round the interior of the Abbey. Peter felt disconnected from all the churchy stuff inside and I felt unexpectedly triggered – the space felt heavy, tamed and contracted - it made me want to growl and stamp and shout and swear. We left before I began to behave in an indecorous and unseemly fashion.

After visiting the gift shop – I wanted to replace the chalice I'd bought there 21 years earlier - we sat in the cloisters to eat our picnic lunch, peacefully watching the torrential rain pour over the stonework before heading back outside. By then the sun had burst through the clouds and graced the landscape with a rainbow. I love rainbows. They speak to me so clearly about the mystery of light - and, indeed, of life. We cannot 'see' light until it is fractured by rain-water (is 'God/dess tears' too fanciful?). Light is broken open by water to reveal the spectrum of colour that lies hidden and invisible within it. Scotland abounds with rainbows.

As we crossed the island, we saw numerous rabbits and wild geese ("where's a gun when you need one?" winked Peter) and finally arrived at an empty beach on the other side. The sun shone through the clouds, the white sand glistened and the turquoise waves rolled and crashed, as screeching seagulls soared free and true overhead. It was simply glorious.

There, in that resonant landscape, we invoked Cerunnos. He is Peter's earthy Celtic guiding spirit whom he meets in dreams and held a ceremony at the sea's edge to ask for blessing and guidance for our journey. The crossing back from Iona to Mull was even rougher. I didn't say anything to Peter, I just quietly noticed how less afraid he appeared to be of the tossing, heaving movement of the boat on the return journey.

After leaving Mull, feeling fully restored and absolutely certain that we weren't going to buy the property we'd been dithering over, we arrived back on mainland Scotland and set off along the coast looking for 'For Sale' signs. We knew our dream-place was out there somewhere, but where?

The following episode will give you a flavour of how thorough (not to say desperate) our search became. One day, a couple of weeks after leaving Mull, we were driving along a lovely single-track lane bordering the sea loch, Loch Creran. We spotted a guy half-way up a ladder painting the outside of a somewhat dilapidated farmhouse.

"I wonder if he's doing it up with a view to selling?" I said.

"Why don't you go and ask him?"

"Oh, no, I couldn't possibly to that. It'd be cheeky."

So we drove past. Then we pulled up and had a conflab. Peter drove us back round the six-mile loop to bring us to exactly the same place and pulled up once again. The man had gone. Sighing, we agreed it wasn't meant to be and Peter went to pull away. In his rear-view mirror he saw the guy reappear carrying a fresh pot of paint and begin to climb the ladder. Speedily pulling on my wellie-boots, I leapt out of the camper. Although the guy wasn't the owner of the property, he took our details and promised to pass them on to the owner. We never heard anything back, but we were determined to leave no stone unturned. Our dream property was out there somewhere calling to us. We just had to keep faith.

Our search took us right through a hard snowy winter and out the other side. We freedom-camped all the way, sleeping for free in lay-bys or in quiet lanes. The only time we paid for a pitch was on a campsite on the Isle of Mull. We needed to use the internet to update the laptop overnight. While we travelled on the road, we ate good local food - masses of fish, sea-food and venison. We drank gallons of loch and gin-clear mountain river water.

We followed up every *RightMove* and *OntheMarket* email alert that vaguely fitted the bill and covered most of Scotland - 12,000 miles in total over nine months. We saw incredible sights that convinced us again and again that this stunningly impressive land was where we wanted to be.

Finding the perfect home, however, proved much more of a challenge than we'd originally thought. As well as enquiring at local solicitors/estate agents in most towns we passed through, we knocked on doors, wrote letters, and even chatted up strangers. Several times we stumbled across 'For Sale' signs on properties that had somehow slipped our net, but which had potential, and so we'd follow up those.

If we saw an empty property that looked interesting, we researched the owners and tried to contact them to see if it was for sale. We went at it with gumption and gusto. This led us to knock on the doors of Roman Catholic presbyteries; secrete a letter of enquiry in a Christmas card to a landowner in Sutton Bassett; assail a Dutch baron; approach squatters through a broken window; and knock on front doors to startled homeowners.

We walked miles and miles in snow, rain, hail and fog, leaving no stone unturned and few lochs unexplored. And still, nowhere we visited felt right. The Scottish housing market was tight and getting tighter - with fewer and fewer properties available. Places such as we desired - with a mountain view, privacy and loch frontage for our boat – were getting snapped up within days. Most were simply way beyond our budget. Several times we phoned to book a viewing of a property fresh to the market, only to be told that it was already under offer.

During those long nine months we visited Loch Maree in the north and Loch Eck in the south. We spent ages probing the area around Fort William, and viewed property on lochs Linnhe, Leven, Eil, Arkaig and, of course, Loch Ness. Increasingly we found ourselves drawn to the west coast, especially the sea loch of Sunart and the impressive inland lochs of Morar and Shiel. The clarity of the light on the west coast is incredible. Peter kept saying he needed sunglasses – even on cloudy days. It was like nowhere else we'd ever been.

We returned again and again to the little fishing village of Mallaig and to Loch Morar which had rapidly become Peter's favourite loch. It's the deepest fresh-water lake in Europe and, legend has it, the home of Grendel's mother's mother. Grendel's mother is the She-force who seeks to slay the hero in the Old English alliterative poem *Beowulf.* Morar is a dark loch. It's surrounded by majestic snow-capped mountains on all sides and, except at its western edge, is almost inaccessible apart from on foot or by boat. Several people described it to us as "menacing" or "sinister" and the people there "unfriendly". We loved it. It's a wild place – incontrovertibly inhospitable to us puny humans. Perhaps because of that, it remains unbounden, unspoilt and free. Freedom is exactly what we were tracking.

Chapter Twenty-Two

GRANDMOTHER TIMING

In November 2017, three months after we'd set off in the motorhome and thirteen moons after my last menstrual bleed, I held a ceremony on the shores of Loch Morar to mark my passing into my Majesteria years. I lit a fire outside under the full moon and laid out my altar. Peter anointed me with sacred oil from *Avalon Remembered* and I burned rosemary for remembrance before washing in the icy dark water. It could not have been more perfect. It was a simple ceremony, almost silent. Potent. Sufficient.

I stepped across the threshold and smiled. The ceremony marked a particular moment in time. I knew, however, that this threshold into my Majesteria years wasn't a line to cross, but a deep, dark mystery to inhabit. A few days later, we left Loch Morar for Fort William. From there I caught the sleeper-train to London to hold my first grandchild in my arms for the first time. Timing, as they say, is everything.

PART III

Chapter Twenty-Three

DEEP-WATER DREAMING

We spent Christmas on our own on the Isle of Arran – a full Christmas dinner cooked in the Bessacar oven - though we cheated a bit by buying a whole cooked chicken. This was followed by a long walk on the beach to find a signal and phone the kids. And the perfect Christmas Day ended with the DVD of David Attenborough's series *Blue Planet 2* watched on the laptop. New Year we spent in Abernethy with good friends who were poorly with the flu. Peter did some maintenance on the Bess and I delighted in having a large well appointed kitchen to play in, plus thoroughly enjoying two of our daughters' company for a few days.

From Abernethy we revisited the central part of Scotland around the Cairngorms which had once been a favourite haunt when we first began visiting Scotland. Here were the wonderful salmon rivers which first caused Peter to fall in love with this magical land: the Tay, Tummel, Garry, Lyon, Lochy and the Dochart. We watched the sun set on the river Tay where it flows into Loch Tay, while two fresh spring-run salmon leaped. It's a sight worth living for. Within those fifteen minutes as the sun set, we saw wild salmon, deer and pheasant. Our love for Scotland simply grew and grew.

Snowdrifts (and the sniffles we'd brought with us from Abernethy) forced us to hold up at Kenmore near Loch Tay for a few days. Each day we were able to walk a bit further into the snow-clad forest above Kenmore until we were well enough to have a full throttle snow-ball fight. Once the roads (and our noses) were a bit clearer, we moved a little way north to explore Loch Tummel.

One nearby Loch we had never visited was Loch Rannoch, bang-smack in the centre of Scotland – so, off we went. We were instantly captivated by it, arriving just as the sun set in the distance over its western shore. The Loch is eleven miles long and up to a mile wide, banked on its southern edge by the largest fragment of the original boreal temperate rain forest which once covered most of Scotland and Europe. The native Caledonian Scots pine-trees are very beautiful. We fell in love with them wherever we went. They're nearly always surrounded by silver birch, which has to be one of Britain's most elegant trees.

The road around the loch goes nowhere apart from the six miles across Rannoch Moor to Rannoch train station – a stop on the London to Fort William line for the Caledonian Sleeper (a train which I use and heartily recommend). Loch Rannoch is quiet and peaceful, popular with outdoorsy tourists. There is a small village at the eastern end called Kinloch Rannoch, with a primary school, shop/P.O., country house hotel and a marina offering boat trips to holiday visitors – some of whom come to walk the magnificent mountain of Shiehallion which overlooks the loch. At 3,400 feet Shiehallion is not as high as Ben Nevis, but is so very much more lovely – and, when snow-clad as we first saw her, simply stunning.

We spent a couple of days parked up at Loch Rannoch, still nursing our colds. On the second day we set out along the southern shore dotted with a few properties and a large castle which, on the market at several million pounds, was a trifle over budget. Then, three miles further on, we turned a corner, close to where the forest ends and the farmland begins, and we saw an unexpected 'For Sale' sign.

We parked up and had a look around. It was a bungalow – which we both agreed wasn't what we were looking for. It didn't have much land – it looked about an acre – so, clearly not at all suitable. Moreover, a large new house was being built next door, privacy, we guessed, would be in short supply. Full of cold and feeling pretty poorly, we both quickly dismissed it. The bungalow did, however, have loch frontage, an additional self-contained one-bedroom guest cottage, and the garden opened directly onto the primeval forest.

Hoping that some fresh air and exercise would help move the cold virus through our systems, we walked slowly into the dark forest on the watch for the mighty herds of deer that roam freely there. Soon we felt much better; utterly captivated by the ancient trees, the quiet and the sense of peace there. We agreed it was a truly magical place and decided to have a look at the bungalow after all. I phoned the next day to book a viewing, but was told that an offer had been accepted that very day. Typical, we both commented grimly.

We had to leave pretty sharpish, anyway, as an interesting property had come up for sale on the sea loch, Loch Leven. It was a fifty mile drive northwards towards Fort William with more snow forecast. I booked us a viewing for three days hence, and the following day, around midday, when the roads were clearest, we set off. The drive tested us to the limit. The Glencoe Pass through the mountains was still open and we needed to get through it before nightfall made the driving conditions too dangerous.

The Bessacar has a heavy rear end (poor lass), and with the compacted snow on the roads – in spite of the gritters and snow ploughs being out-and-about day and night – we knew getting up Glencoe Pass would be a real challenge. We were not disappointed. The Glencoe Pass is the only road through the mountains and so, even in snowy conditions, there's a lot of traffic. Normally, we'd pull in to let traffic behind us go past, but in these conditions we had to keep on the road following the route cleared by the snow plough. At one point, with a tailback behind us, the Bessacar began to slide. I popped on the hazard lights to warn oncoming traffic that we were straddling lanes.

Added to this was the (very Scottish) challenge of deer on the road – and I mean hundreds of deer, wandering with stately grace across the road. The deer come down from the mountains to graze close to the sides of the road where the warmth from the traffic melts the snow revealing the grass. They ambled along serenely grazing and crossed the road at will, seemingly oblivious to the slow moving traffic in both lanes. Our problem was that we couldn't stop – not even for a deer. If we stopped, Peter was clear, we wouldn't get started again. I prayed that a deer wouldn't cross in front of us. I didn't want to hurt one of these beautiful creatures, nor did I want to be stranded thirty miles from the nearest house in the dead of winter high up on a mountain pass. This was decidedly not where we wanted to spend the night – even in our snug Bessacar.

Fortunately, Peter is a good driver, and managed to get us safely to the top of the pass and down the other side just before nightfall. It really was a close call though. As we slowly made the steep descent towards Ballachulish, the opposite side of the road had just become blocked by a line of HGVs unable to make the ascent. Glencoe Pass was closed to all motor vehicles soon after and remained closed for the next two weeks.

We spent the night in the Long Stay Car Park in Fort William. A familiar, if unattractive, place we've often had recourse to as a base. It was in Fort William we did our laundry, had leisurely hot showers, updated the laptop and the smart-phone, and did our re-supply. The temperature outside was minus fifteen degrees at night and minus eight in the day. We were snuggled up cosy and comfy in the Bess, glad to have arrived at our destination safely. The next morning we awoke to frozen water pipes. Peter had filled a water container and put it inside with us, so we could still make tea – he knows how I like my pot of tea with breakfast.

Around midday, when the roads had thawed a little, we carefully negotiated the road to Kinlochleven. The property on Loch Leven had real potential. We parked up the day before the viewing and walked the area. It looked suitable for riding. It looked suitable for the boat. It had no neighbours. It had good mountain views. It had two acres, sufficient for stabling. It needed a complete re-build though which looked doable - plus it was well within budget.

Adjoining the property was a parcel of land about ten acres in size. It had been a campsite and had clearly once belonged to the property, which, if we could buy it, would suit us for the horses to graze on and for rearing pheasant. All looked very hopeful. We sent photos to our youngsters scattered across the globe and got enthusiastic 'thumbs up' all round.

Around 3 p.m. it started getting dark, so we found somewhere sheltered from the wind to park up for the night, and settled down to trawl carefully through the property's Home Report. Having done this many times already, we knew what to look for. One alarm bell rang when we read that planning permission had been applied for which affected the property in some way.

I phoned the estate agent to ask who owned the adjoining parcel of land and was told that it was Liberty Aluminium. There used to be an Aluminium works in Kinlochleven which was closed in the 1990s. They'd bought the land the previous July. So, I phoned Liberty Aluminium. Just as well I did. They'd obtained planning permission for a Hydro turbine to be installed in the loch channel opposite the property, with the plant building to be positioned on the parcel of land we were hoping to buy. Moreover, they were in the process of applying for planning permission to set up a boatyard too. I phoned to cancel our viewing appointment.

We'd bought some sea-bass for supper, so Peter chopped sweet peppers, onions and garlic to sauté, while I boiled some rice. Once everything was almost cooked, I pan-seared the sea-bass and we sat down to a delicious meal. Over supper, we chatted through the past few days. Yet again, what we'd hoped would turn into the perfect property, had failed to materialise. With nothing pending, we decided to head once again towards the west coast, to Peter's favourite loch. There we could lick our wounds and reassess the situation. It was hard not to feel disheartened.

We parked up in a favourite spot on Loch Morar and spent the day walking and talking. There were a couple of building plots for sale but neither had loch frontage and we both agreed we didn't want a new build. We were too old for it – we wanted to start enjoying our retirement now and not in two or three years' time. That night we slept on the sea-front at Mallaig, buffeted by the westerlies blowing in hard from across the sea. At one point we feared the motorhome was going to overturn and Peter had to drive us into the centre of the village so we'd be protected a little from the wind. Neither of us slept much. The following day, bleary-eyed, we drove along the coastline near Arisaig and watched seals and otters playing. We both really loved this area, but agreed it was too remote, and would make it too difficult for friends and family to visit.

We then headed a little way south to view a property in Acharacle near the gorgeous Loch Sunart. This didn't have loch frontage but had plenty of land. The drive-by the day before our viewing, however, quickly revealed that the land was too poor to sustain either horses or pheasants and was surrounded by neighbours. From Sunart – at my insistence - we headed to view a building plot with its own beach and mooring on Loch Ailort. It had absolutely incredible views and a delightful couple showed us round the plot. Afterwards, over a pot of tea, Peter gently reminded me that we'd agreed a new build was not what we wanted.

"I can't do it," he said.

"I know," I said softly, reaching for his hand. "It just seems that whatever we're looking for keeps slipping out of reach. I don't know how much longer I can keep doing this. I feel I'm ready now, ready to begin our new life, but where is it, Peter; where's home?"

He shrugged.

"I don't know either. I just know what I don't want. I don't want a new build. I don't want neighbours. I don't want deep tidal water which I'll drown in. I don't want noise and stress and people."

I smiled at him.

"Your 'no' is always so very clear," I said. "It's your 'no' as much as my enthusiastic 'yes' that'll guide us to where we're meant to be."

He reached across and kissed the end of my nose.

"I know. Let's see what tomorrow brings, eh?"

Well, what tomorrow brought was something neither of us had foreseen or expected.

The figure of the Shadow-dancer, who'd been patiently waiting in the wings during all our to-ing and fro-ing across Scotland, quietly stepped out onto the stage of my life and bit me hard in the butt. To this unpleasant experience I must now turn.

Chapter Twenty-Four

DOGGY FRIENDS

I invite you to cast your mind back to chapter fifteen, that moment when I rode off into the sunset of the Cambrian Mountains at full gallop with Peter at my side – riding my fear with exuberant delight. Part of the journey which had brought me thus far was the transformative process which I called horse-sistering. You will remember I warned you that a 'dark' aspect of learning how to ride my fear was, unbeknownst to me, waiting in the wings ready to step out onto the stage of my life to bite me sharply in the butt. We've come to the part of the story where this episode needs to be told.

But before I proceed to tell you about the 'dark' aspect of learning how to ride my fear, you need to know something about me. I like to be liked. I work very hard at being liked. It's important that I remind you of this because I've spoken at length about 'wrathing', and wooing the tigress within, Wild Woman Walking, and being a Death-dancer. You might have come away from those pages with the impression that I'm unshakeably strong and fearless. And that I'm girded about the loins and ready to grab the Son of Patriarchy by the short-and-curlies, tussle the blaggard to

222

the ground and raise the banner of The Goddess Resplendent over his prostrate form.

If I've given you that impression, then I'm glad – because it's true. But only in part, and only sometimes. The other side of the truth about me, as I cross the threshold into my majesterial years, is that I'm still very conventional in many ways - not least in my desire to be liked by as many people as possible. I'm not a massive fan of social media's 'likes', though it's very clear to me why two billion other people on the planet are big fans. We all like to be liked.

The 'dark' aspect of learning how to ride my fear and thereby enter my majesterial years with aplomb, involved – to my surprise - the art of learning how not-to-mind-so-much about not being liked. Another way of putting it is to say that I needed to learn how to welcome and wear the face of the Dark Lady. She is the one who lives deep in the wild forest. She is the stuff of ancient (pre-Disney) fairytales and the source of our nightmares. She is the dark fecund soil. In fact, she is our very own night-soil – our shit.

When she calls to me, I turn my back on conventional niceties and walk barefoot and bare-breasted into the dark forest. When I speak in her voice, expletives (which I don't commonly use) come fast-and-furious. We've met her before in these pages and we meet her again now. She's the one who will show us how to work our hidden shit until it transforms into fragrant compost supporting new growth. She refuses to be ignored, silenced or tamed. She waits patiently in the wings of our life until that moment when the curtain rises, the jester tumbles onto the stage amidst uproarious laughter, we get a custard pie in the eye and we fall flat on our faces.

Earlier in my story I called her fierce grace, but I could just as easily have called her Lucifer or the Holy Spirit. She is the witch waiting in the woods. Young children are instinctively right to be fearful when they sense she's around. In Robert Bly's poetry, she's aptly named the Teeth-Mother for she devours and destroys our detritus. I wrote a master's degree thesis on the poetry of Robert Bly when I lived on Vancouver Island in British Columbia during my mid-twenties. I still enjoy Bly's work immensely. My reading of his poetry is interwoven with memories of the dark, feral, primordial forests of northern BC - where beaver and black bear, coyote and cougar, wolf and wildcat still roam free. The presence of the Teeth-Mother can be felt instinctively in such places - our senses are heightened when other alpha-predators are in the vicinity. I think it's good for us – it humbles us and reminds us of our place on the planet.

It's the face of the Teeth-Mother, eyes staring, snarling with teeth bared, which looks down from many of the totem poles carved by the First Nations peoples who've lived for millennia along the north-west coast of North America. She is the fearsome Owl Witch of the Kwakiutl, and the unfaltering gaze of Sgat'iin of the Nisga'a. It's her fierce protective energy, I believe, which has ensured the survival of the ancient boreal rainforests of British Columbia and of the ancient peoples who live within them. It's her strength and determination which now rises to inspire people from every lineage to stand together and oppose the oil-industry's plans to lay hundreds of miles of gas pipelines through her sacred ground and under her sacred rivers across the globe. In Indo-Asia she's instantly recognisable as Kali. In Western Europe she's known as the ancient Celtic goddess Cailleach.

Let me share with you an example of how she invites us to dig deep into our night-soil and how she lures us into working our own shit – doing the soul-medicine work we've avoided or never noticed before. It's time to reveal the 'dark' aspect of my experience of horse-sistering. It involved my horse-sister whom I've called Violet. I'm aware of the need to respect someone else's privacy, but there really is no way to tell an honest tale of menopausal transformation without including this portion of it. This obviously is the tale told from my perspective and will only reveal the truth of what was going on for me. I cannot know the truth of what was going on for her as, sadly, she didn't share it with me.

The difficulty arose in relation to my dog. I'm going to call her Black-beauty for the purposes of this story. Peter and I were packed up and ready to leave Wales when, as I've already told you, we were outbid on the house we were planning to move into on Loch Awe. Our decision to buy a motorhome, set off for Scotland anyway, and travel around looking for our dream-home, meant that we couldn't take our dogs with us. They were primarily outdoor working dogs. Part of the difficulty surrounding Black-beauty was that really she 'belonged' to my youngest son – you know that special bond that can develop between a boy and a dog? Well, my son loved her to bits and I was hoping we could find a way to hang onto her for him. One of our daughters had offered to have Black-beauty when she returned to the UK from overseas, and so we just needed to find a stop-gap. Out of the blue, Violet and her husband offered to have Black-beauty for us. We were delighted.

We set off for Scotland in the Bessacar and left Black-beauty behind in the care of Violet and her husband. Three months later, just before Christmas, Violet contacted me to say that she felt she'd looked after Black-beauty long enough and could I come to collect her. She mentioned that the noise in their village caused Black-beauty to bark during the night and the impression I got was that she and her husband had reached their limit with the dog. Fair enough, I thought.

Our daughter had extended her stay overseas and didn't know when or if she'd be returning to the UK, and so clearly wasn't in a position any longer to offer Black-beauty a home. We asked around amongst friends and family, and no-one was able to take her in. We couldn't have her with us, she was too big. Peter was clear it wasn't doable – it was one of those rare occasions when he gave a non-negotiable "No". So I asked Violet if she could help me to re-home Black-beauty through The Dogs Trust. We'd been impressed with the canine charity when we'd re-homed Peter's Jack Russell terrier.

In response to my request, Violet's husband emailed me and demanded that we come immediately to fetch Black-beauty from Wales. He reminded me that it was a temporary arrangement and said I needed to honour that and come get the dog. I explained that it wasn't feasible for me to drop everything and make the thousand-mile round trip. I pointed out that the process of assessment with The Dogs Trust took at least two weeks to complete, and we were in the midst of viewing properties. I offered my reassurance that I would do my utmost to find a solution as quickly as possible.

I phoned The Dogs Trust to see if they could help us sort out the situation but they explained that unless Violet agreed to become the legal owner of the dog and presented Black-beauty for re-homing, their hands were tied. I asked Violet if she'd consider doing this. She replied that she'd already thought about this possibility, but that she wasn't ready to commit to a strategy for re-homing Black-beauty until some issues which she said she "sensed" around my relationship with the dog had been cleared up. From my perspective, the conversation now shifted into another gear. Violet's agenda came to the forefront and blocked mine. My agenda was to get the dog's long-term future appropriately sorted.

Violet told me that she'd been listening to Black-beauty's unspoken story. She said that she sensed that the dog was trying to communicate that her move from inside-dog in my cottage, to outside-dog on Peter's smallholding, had caused her unacknowledged suffering. She said that in keeping the dog outside Peter's farmhouse in a kennel, I'd caused Black-beauty mental distress and physical harm. And she cited the evidence that the dog displayed discomfort in her hip causing her to limp. Violet then went further and said that the issue wasn't only about my dog, it was about my care of my youngest son. She sensed (from her one conversation with the lad) that he also felt pushed "outside" by my relationship with Peter. I was deeply shaken and I went away to think about all this very carefully. These were serious accusations. Perhaps you are wondering why I didn't just laugh in her face and tell her to f-off. Well, she had my dog for a start. But it went much deeper than that.

The accusation of my wrong-doing, my self-deceit, my 'bad-mothering', triggered in me a cascade of responses which tracked straight back to my 'shadow'. What woke up in me was a hornet's nest of fear. Buzzing loudly inside of me was that early wounding of witnessing my step-father's violence, my failed marriage, my row with the bishop, my diagnosis of PTSD, my fleeing the church - i.e. all my shit - call it by whatever name you will.

Experiencing this cascade of emotion was like following the breadcrumbs left by Hansel and Gretel in the forest. You may remember that in the fairytale they leave a trail of breadcrumbs in the hope that it will lead them to the devouring wise witch's tempting gingerbread house and back again, all the way home.

That cascade of emotions, that trail, was the footprints of the Teeth-Mother leaving a track for me to follow. At its destination was the Teeth-Mother's devouring maw, symbolised by the witch's oven (the daunting cauldron of transformation). The Holy Spirit was prodding me in the back, forcing me to venture out onto the half-hidden track through the dark, frightening forest of my innermost fears. She was wearing the deeply kind face of fierce grace – only it didn't bloody-well look or feel like it at the time – it rarely does.

Two earlier signposts had already pointed out the direction my relationship with Violet would inevitably take – only I didn't have eyes to see them at the time. Firstly, just before we set off for Scotland, Violet and her husband, whose home had impressive compost toilets, had lent us a book describing how to compost human manure – how to turn shit into fertiliser. As I've said before – you couldn't make this stuff up. Peter didn't like the idea of shovelling his own shit, however, so we never took it further.

Secondly, a year earlier, Violet had lent me an audiotape of a workshop led by my favourite American poet Robert Bly. Violet had no idea, when she lent me the audiotape, that I'd written my master's degree thesis about his poetry. Looking back, I can see the trail of breadcrumbs, portents of the Shadow-dancing that was to come. Hindsight, as they say, is indeed a wonderful thing. During the recorded workshop Bly tells the story of the Lindworm dragon – a story all about the incredibly painful process of shedding skins in order to reveal the hidden true-self within. Once again, a true gift – though one I couldn't yet see. If you want to sniff out the presence of Shadow-dancer, be alert to these 'coincidences' – they're a sure sign that divine grace is present, however fierce a face she might be wearing.

Back to the story: I was horrified by what Violet had said and I immediately felt guilty, in some way to blame, and that there was truth in what she'd said. There *was* truth in it, but much deeper than the mere surface bombardment of accusations. My first response was fear. Deep inside, I felt that I'd been 'found out'. I felt that my 'performance' had been seen through, and that the truth of Melanie as the 'self-centred bitch' had at last been revealed. Again.

The ostensibly negative narrative which I'd heard from Violet, confirmed and triggered that insistent negative inner audiotape that'd been sounding inside me since my early teens: "I'm bad, I'm bad, I'm bad". It was the voice which I'd worked so hard to muffle through distractions, and to mute through compassionate, loving service in the world. I instantly assumed that Violet knew something about me that I didn't know about myself, and that I'd been blind to my faults. After all, I respected Violet. We'd done helpful soul-work together in the past, including some very beautiful horse-sistering. I wanted to give the matter the attention it deserved.

I wondered whether the notion of insider/outsider would reveal an avenue of possibly fruitful, even if distasteful, soul-medicine. I wrote in my journal. I consulted with those who knew me well. I dug deep into the relationships between me, my dog, my son and Peter. Basically, I did the work. I did it carefully, diligently and in an unhurried fashion. I spoke at length about it with my youngest son who, out of all of us, had the deepest love for our nine year-old dog. What was mirrored back to me was what I knew (on one level) to be true: I'd looked after our family dog with appropriate love and care.

I then messaged Violet to say that while her assertion that my dog had suffered because of the changes in her circumstances after I'd met Peter, had felt initially "painful but true", it wasn't the whole story. I recounted all the benefits the dog had enjoyed as a result of my relationship with Peter. Violet's reaction to my words was equally clear. She stated that she believed I was in deep denial. We were at an impasse.

It was mid-January. Peter and I were snowed-up in the motorhome on the edge of the Tay forest, unable (on various levels) to move on. I arranged with Violet that I'd walk to the nearby village to get WiFi so that we could have an unhurried phone conversation about Black-beauty. I very much hoped that the conversation would clear the air between me and Violet, and allow us to move forward in making the practical arrangements concerning the long-term re-homing of the dog. I didn't sleep much the night before our arranged phone call. I lay awake listening – listening for the deep truth, whatever it was (and however shitty it might feel), which might want to surface from the murky depths of this difficult situation. Nothing arose apart from a sense of calm stillness and peace, and a softly held certainty that I stood by my words.

The conversation with Violet lasted an hour-and-a-half. I think it mattered to her, just as it mattered to me - and it's important to acknowledge that. I took notes during the phone call so that I'd be better able to reflect later upon what had been said. The PTSD can still scupper my short-term memory under stress, and I wanted an accurate remembrance. During the conversation I was honest with Violet that a lot of what she was saying didn't ring true for me. I told her I wasn't going to pretend to agree in order to give her what she was pointing towards (i.e. that I had neglected to take proper care of my dog), and she agreed that it should be so. It was a gentle enough conversation though we struggled to maintain connection – on every level, and it got us no further along the path of actually sorting out Black-beauty's need to be re-homed.

When I asked Violet at the beginning of the phone conversation to tell me what was going on for her in all of this, she was insistent that we stick to the agenda (her agenda as it seemed to me) of dealing with my so-called hidden and denied stuff. By the end of the conversation, I felt pretty frustrated and somehow wrong-footed, though I couldn't yet put it into words. One of the things that Violet said was, "It is time to listen to what is not easy to hear". Was there a soul-level blind-spot here which meant I simply couldn't see what she was trying to show me, I wondered? And so I faithfully went away once again and thought about her words very carefully.

I let it lie for a couple of days and then I awoke one morning with an absolute clarity sounding inside me. I realised that I utterly refuted Violet's repeated accusation that there was an unacknowledged 'wound' in my relationship with my dog, and, moreover, possibly with my son. I texted her to that effect, and awaited her reply. It was clear to me by then that Violet and I were dancing together in the Shadow-lands, and that this was the 'dark' face of the healing process which Violet and I had shared together a couple of years earlier in the form of horse-sistering (chapter fifteen). Days went by and I heard nothing back.

When the response came, it was scathing. Violet accused me of many things, amongst them: that I'd left my dog freezing outside in the snow over a severely cold winter; that I chose love of Peter over love of my dog *and my son*; that I had repressed overwhelming guilt; that I lacked trust and courage; that both my son and my dog experienced 'non-acceptance' at Peter's place; that I'd neglected the dog to such an extent that her skin was raw and scabby, and that she was therefore too smelly to be kept indoors; that the dog only 'woke up' to the truth of all this awfulness when she was at Violet's – I could go on, but enough is enough. The text ended with these words: "Most of what I have brought to your attention has not only been denied, but justified as an act of costly love. [Black-beauty], with the least power to choose and the quietest 'voice', was appointed as the sacrifice. I hope you read this in the spirit of truth and love, of tough love, in which it is offered… a telling of, not a telling off. Much love to you."

My instant reaction to it was a physiological response of fear – no, more than that – terror. My heart-rate shot up, I couldn't breathe and I had a full-blown panic-attack – the first in six years. Perhaps, had Violet been present, she might've explained my body's response to her words in terms of deep denial and repression. However, before any of us are tempted or cowed into an acceptance of someone else's interpretation of our soul's deepest truth – especially if it's a condemnatory or unkind interpretation - let's remind ourselves to *pause*, breathe deeply, seek support from those who know and love us well, and remind ourselves that: *I am the sovereign Queen of my own soul – I and no other.*

Peter's response was also instant. He was furious. He couldn't get his head around how Violet could make such wild and unfounded accusations about a part of our shared story that occurred before we'd even met her. To him, the whole thing seemed bizarre, and he rapidly concluded that Violet must be "deranged". This wasn't my interpretation, however, as I knew from my own experience that there's often magic hidden in seeming-'madness'.

I'd finally begun to scent on the air the unpleasant pong that often indicates the hoary holy presence of the Teeth-Mother. The whiff that tells us that something is decaying and dying in order for something new to arise. However, my sense that something transformational was underway didn't solve the very real problem of what was going to happen to our dog.

The night after receiving Violet's message, I lay awake in the motorhome, listening to Peter's peaceful breathing at my side. I opened myself up to the experience of terror flooding my system, just as I'd formerly done with the migraine attacks. I observed what was happening inside me. I observed it kindly. I laid it out before my gaze as reverently and diligently as if I were laying up the altar in an empty, silent, expectant church early on a Sunday morning.

I eye-balled the familiar pattern of response unfolding inside me in the face of harsh criticism, and refused to look away. I recognised it all so well: the unpleasant sinking feeling in the stomach, which is how I feel guilt and shame; the sickening sense of 'being-found-out' in wrong-doing; the internal self-flagellation, the *beating-myself-up* which tracks so tidily back to my teenage years when I'd repeatedly witnessed domestic violence; the panicky breathless feeling of being overwhelmed by too much emotion; and, finally, the emotional collapse into a deadening numbness.

The predictable next step, which I could feel looming on the horizon of my awareness, was to back off - to withdraw from an unsafe situation in order to protect myself and in order to seek refuge somewhere else safer. Or, to put it more succinctly, to cut and run.

However, this time, I chose differently. Supported by my eldest daughter and by Peter, instead of running, I stood my ground. I turned to face the Teeth-Mother inside me. She was terrifying. Medusa-like and haloed with snakes, she hissed and snapped at me venomously. Holding my daughter's hand (metaphorically, as it was 3 a.m., we were on the phone and she was three-hundred miles away, staying with her grandmother – my mother), I braced myself to face my fears.

I stopped running and turned around to look into the eyes of the Teeth-Mother, the Owl-witch, Cailleach, Shadow-dancer. She is the personification of my deepest, darkest fears. She is the one who whispers to me in the night-time quiet that the *truth* about Melanie, the truth Melanie keeps well hidden, is that I am a liar and a fake and untrustworthy.

My daughter gently reminded me yet again of the truth which we both knew - that our family dog had never been neglected or unloved. *We remembered together what I, in my distress and panic, could not remember on my own.* I followed the breadcrumbs of my daughter's love for me, and her deeply wise knowing of me, back through the dark forest and allowed them to guide me home. I settled back into my own skin. I came back home to myself. Looking in the mirror of my daughter's strong, unfaltering love, I remembered the truth of who I am. Like mother - like daughter – like grandmother.

The spiral spins and holds us pinned to the centre of the flaming Catherine Wheel of our very own story. The phone call with my daughter didn't last long, barely fifteen minutes – and when it was done, we both knew it was done. I fell into a deep, restful sleep.

Chapter Twenty-Five

SITTING ON THE CHARGE

The next morning I awoke feeling my strength as never before – my ROAR as never before. I knew what I had to do. To Peter's surprise and indeed consternation, I announced that we needed to drive to Wales that very day to collect Black-beauty. The situation with Violet had become intolerable and I needed to sort it out. While Violet retained the dog, it felt to me that she was in some way holding me hostage to her agenda. I needed to change gear, put myself back in the driving seat and reclaim my right to steer my own vessel. I needed to go and get my dog.

I texted Violet to let her know that we were on our way to collect the dog. She immediately forbade me to come to her house. I suggested that either she or her husband bring the dog to a nearby café. She refused. She insisted that there were still "issues" in my relationship with the dog and that she wouldn't hand the animal back to me until those were resolved to her satisfaction. I then asked her again whether she wanted to take legal responsibility for Black-beauty. And I pointed out that if she didn't, the dog was therefore still legally mine, and I had a right to come and collect her. By then Peter and I were clear that Violet had to jump one way or the other. As he so eloquently phrased it, "She needs either to piss or get off the pot".

Peter was indeed seriously pissed-off.

"If needs be", he growled, "I'll pick the bloody dog up by the scruff of her neck and carry her out of their house!"

I soothingly suggested that before it came to that, it'd perhaps be best if we popped into the police station in Aberystwyth, explain the situation, and ask for their advice about how to retrieve our dog in a non-violent and non-confrontational manner. Always easy to calm, he agreed that was the way to go.

We cancelled the property viewings we'd arranged, and set off on the thousand-mile roundtrip to Wales. Violet had fallen silent, but we kept going anyway. After eight hours driving, we parked up near Lake Vrnwy in north Wales, close to one of my Deepening sisters. I arranged to see her the next day but I told her nothing about what was going on. Even the next morning over coffee and lunch, I didn't reveal the reason we were there. I said there was a sensitive crisis which needed our immediate attention and that I'd prefer not to go into the details. It was partly that I didn't want to muddy her relationship with Violet, and partly that I was determinedly 'sitting on the charge' of the situation. I'll describe what I mean by that in detail in a moment. First let me finish telling you the story about my dog and falling out of friendship with my wise and much-loved horse-sister.

After lunch at our friends' house in Machynlleth, we planned to head to Aberystwyth and to take it from there. Finally back in signal, the phone pinged and a text arrived from Violet saying that she and her husband had decided they would take legal responsibility for the dog. It was a huge relief. Neither Peter nor I had any doubt that this was the best solution. In spite of the awfulness of the previous couple of months, and the breakdown of my personal relationship with Violet, I still felt Violet was best placed to sort out Black-beauty's need for a permanent home.

About a week later, back in Scotland, I wrote Violet a letter. I spoke about my sense that we were dancing together in the Shadow-lands. I asserted my sovereign freedom to be the queen of my own soul-story and invited her to share more of her soul-story with me. Sadly, she never replied and we haven't spoken since. For someone used to being liked (and why not, I've worked hard at it for most my adult life), that took some serious getting used to. However, it strengthened my 'tough-love muscle' for sure, and that's no bad thing.

Most days, before I eat lunch, I practise the plank – balancing on toes, elbows and forearms, with my legs and torso suspended straight-as-a-plank above the ground. I'm aiming for a five-minute plank and the most I've managed to date is about three-and-a-half minutes. The plank is the opposite energy to the psoas muscle rest I mentioned in chapter fifteen. The plank requires that I hold my central core steady and strong, whereas the psoas-muscle rest is about releasing and letting go of the core. Both are important and both are needed.

I've 'held' a lot hidden deep inside, so letting go of that holding has been my main practise for many years. However, strengthening the core and learning how to hold it is necessary too. As we get older, especially, if we've delivered a baby (or babies) vaginally, our entire pelvic hammock of muscles can become stretched and loose – hence the risk of leaking wee into your panties if you sneeze violently. Our body – wise as ever – reminds the mid-life woman how important it is to keep her core strong. That doesn't mean over-strong (most of us don't need a six-pack in our fifties or sixties) – softly strong, I like to say.

So, let's explore the spiritual practise which I call 'sitting on the charge'. It's a sort of spiritual pelvic floor exercise, not that dissimilar to planking. At the most superficial level it could be described as keeping your own counsel. It's that and much more. It involves holding the energy of a situation close to your chest or in your heart in a conscious manner. It means resisting the urge to contact all and sundry (scatter-gun conversations) to collect views and opinions. It means holding your tongue. Like planking, it's not an easy practise. It shouldn't be confused with seeking appropriate support during a crisis, or with keeping inappropriate secrets. It does not preclude taking appropriate action to stay safe. Far from it. Sitting on the charge is about deciding not to let the energy of a particularly highly-charged (and therefore potent and potentially transformative) situation leak out of your system.

The temptation to have scatter-gun conversations about a crisis is huge – and the bigger the crisis, the bigger the temptation. The back-brain, or reptilian brain (a term used by Robert Bly) fires up, and rushes to muster support and rally self-serving opinions. It's the oldest part of the brain and houses the amygdala which is where our fear-based responses reside. I'm intimately familiar with the functioning of my amygdala – the two almond shaped structures in the brain closely associated with PTSD. I've found, however, that when I resist the urges of the amygdala and *pause*, something interesting starts to unfold. Other parts of me have time to catch up – the so-called higher brain, where I make conscious choices, and the deep wisdom of my whole body, which so often knows more than I 'think' I know.

I'm fascinated by the recent research into the role of neuropeptides, the protein-like molecules which signal and communicate with each other throughout the nervous system. Our entire body is a complex web of internal information highways.

This recent research talks about the brain, i.e. communicating intelligence, being as much in the cells of the stomach, or heart, as in the actual physical brain. Scientists talk about 'thinking cells' throughout the body. I suspect this is what we're tuning into when we speak of intuition or 'gut feelings'. It's something which women, traditionally, are said to be very good at.

My gut feeling is that all humans, like all wild animals, are good at it and have the same capacity for it – huntsman exercise this sort of whole-body intelligence when out stalking or tracking or fishing. It's just that 'western' culture has, through its educational system, predominantly encouraged and lauded males who do most of their thinking in their heads. Head knowledge is easily verbalised - body knowledge less so. Most of us are familiar with the experience of knowing something to be true because we 'feel' it, but we're unable to express it or communicate it in words.

I've learned that in a crisis, when I 'do nothing' and pause long enough to let the dust settle, my perception of the crisis shifts all on its own and begins to change its shape. I'd also discovered that when I resisted the urge to grab my phone and immediately talk to someone about the situation (that quick release of uncomfortable emotional energy), something unexpected happened. The energy changes and somehow it becomes potentised. It calls to me to pay attention to it.

And the more I pay attention to it, the more lucid, diffuse and transparent it becomes. It ceases to feel so dense, or so sticky, or so disturbing. The pause allows space. It allows space for both the situation and me to breathe and to expand, to soften and open up (I'm deliberately using female descriptors). Within that space, there's a better chance of remembering how to be kind, how to be whole-hearted, how to be brave.

I've found that quietly and gently sitting on the charge allows the situation the time and the space (and the grace) it needs if it's to take off the masks, come out of hiding and reveal its true face. I've discovered that underneath the performance and the panic, my deeply hidden, wounded self is actually incredibly shy. She's very young, very vulnerable, and very easily frightened. She needs to feel safe, really safe, before she'll make an appearance. Otherwise, she'll dress herself up in one of those gorgeous costumes taken from her ballet-dancing days, and pretend to be someone else. Magical princess, ugly duckling or the dying swan are amongst her favourite roles to play. These days I know how best to lure her out of hiding. The quieter and more transparent I am around her, the more she can be encouraged to come, sit on my knee and tell me where she's hurting. Getting close to the frightened, deeply hidden Melanie, I find is actually not that much different from trying to catch a nervous horse. Patience pays off.

When the amygdala fire up and I experience fear, I try to remain consciously, kindly and honestly aware of what is happening inside me. If I'm really panicking, I may need to reach out and hold someone's hand (literally or figuratively) to help me pause, breathe deeply and reconnect with my inner equilibrium. My intention is to choose not to close down, not to run off in the opposite direction into distraction, and not to armour-up and seek allies.

In this way, the roller-coaster of the crisis can slow down sufficiently for me to disembark safely, stand back, see it in a more accurate perspective and decide what needs to be done – if anything. Then, if an action needs to be taken, it's pretty straightforward. There's less circular thinking, less angst and less energy leakage. There's also less shame and less blame.

This seeming to do nothing, I sometimes call 'sacred passivity'. It's yet another pause. A really important pause. It's a waiting, a listening; a careful tracking that needs my single-pointed attention. It's impossible to do if my concentration is dissipated by too much superficial external input (scatter-gun talking, screen-time, scurrying or noise). I need to shut-up, slow down, and be still. And, more than anything else, I need to listen – to listen to my own soul. This is the work. While I'm busy with the work, I'm not actually doing nothing, of course. I'm doing something and something rather valuable. I'm quietly engaged in deeply interior, invisible, transformational soul-work. To my way of thinking, it's the preliminary work that needs to be done before taking any serious action in the world.

If I haven't worked my own 'shit' internally, composted it down, way down deep below the conscious mind, then it's harder to act consciously and creatively in the world. If I haven't composted it into something nourishing and fecund, then, more than likely, I'll just end up shovelling more toxic waste out there into the world – and the world really, really doesn't need any more untreated human crap.

In actuality composting isn't something we do ourselves, it happens naturally. It's a passive unfolding. All we have to do is put the ingredients in a suitable container within a suitable environment. Life/energy does the rest. This is sacred passivity in action. It's what monasteries and ashrams are for, or a prayer stool or a meditation cushion. It's also what toilets are for.

I love the story that the contemporary spiritual teacher Adyashanti tells of his moment of awakening. Duality falls away and he sees only 'Oneness'. It was an experience which occurred while he was sitting on his meditation cushion one morning in his home in North America. It changed him (and everything else) once-and-for-all. He says he tested the experience by looking at his toilet bowl. "Does Reality/emptiness include this? Is this too *it*?" he asks. The answer, of course, was an unshakeable yes.

My erstwhile friend Violet knows this just as well as does Adya or me or whoever else knows it. After all, Violet and her husband are amongst the rare few who literally and deliberately compost their own human manure. I've not included the episode about finding a permanent home for my dog in order to set me up as right and Violet as wrong. I include it because it belongs in the story about my journey of home-coming. To that home-coming I now turn.

Chapter Twenty-Six

HOMECOMING I – WE'RE ALMOST THERE

On the way back from Wales after sorting out the difficult situation with our dog Black-beauty, we stopped at Loch Lomond. It had been a long hard drive and we were tired. While we'd been at my friend's house near Machynlleth, enjoying the warmth of friendship, wonderful food and the opportunity to avail ourselves of the internet - we'd arranged to view a property for sale. It was a ruin but had land and loch frontage. Access was by boat only, or on foot. We got out the car to have a look at it from the opposite side of Loch Lomond. Our hearts sank.

"Impossible," Peter said glumly. "The cost of getting building materials there by boat would be off the scale. There's no way you'd get a twenty-seven ton lorry along that track. It can't be done."

Peter's realistic assessment cut through the mist of my hazy dreams with his usual clarity.

"I'd better phone to cancel tomorrow's viewing," I said equally glumly.

"Have you got signal?"

"Yeah, actually I've got 4G so you can trawl the internet, if you like, to see if you can find something else out there for us to view." I cancelled our viewing and handed him the phone. "I'll make us some lunch."

I brewed a pot of tea and cooked an egg-and-bacon sandwich for us while quietly wondering, what next? The drive back to Wales to sort the dog had left me feeling hollowed out and empty.

"That property on Loch Rannoch is still listed," Peter said between mouthfuls.

"Really?" I looked over his shoulder at the tiny screen on the phone. "But I thought it was under offer."

Peter shrugged.

"Dunno. It's still listed here like."

"Shall I give them a call?"

"Can do." He grinned at me. "Nothing else pressing on our time, eh?"

I phoned the estate agent in Pitlochry and was told that the house had just come back onto the market that very day. We booked a viewing for two days time on the Saturday, and headed the seventy miles back towards Loch Rannoch.

We parked up on the north side of the Loch and cooked supper looking eastwards towards the mountain Shiehallion – the so-called fairy mountain of Caledonia. It was still snowy and the surrounding scenery looked stunning. We'd deliberately arrived a day early to scout out the area, and the next morning soon got chatting with a friendly couple who lived close by. Over tea and cake we were given a fount of useful local information, and began to feel quietly hopeful about the next day's viewing.

We arrived bang on time at the bungalow, and the owner showed us around outside. It was only about one-and-a-half acres of land – a fraction of what we'd originally thought we'd wanted. But it had an additional fully appointed one-bedroom cottage which I could see would be great for guests. There was a little cove and a beach – I could just picture our boat out there bobbing happily on the water. With the mysterious and alluring backdrop of seven miles of ancient Caledonian forest hugging the shoreline, the bungalow looked snug – held safe by the boundaries of deep water and quiet woodland. It felt both impressive and comforting.

We went indoors and she introduced her husband to us as "a fisherman and a hunter". I introduced my husband likewise and we all laughed. The two men fell into an easy rapport, sitting side by side on the sofa, sharing fishing and hunting stories. The view from that sofa across the loch was simply magical and Peter, usually shy with strangers, was totally at-ease, relaxed and chuckling – he even had his stockinged-feet up resting on the coffee table. Talk about making yourself at home.

Peter looked at me and a glance passed between us that had my heart racing. *This was it!* This was home. I knew it and he knew it. How the hell had that happened? It was totally unexpected and totally unlike everything we thought we were looking for. The couple selling the bungalow were as taken with us as we were with them, and we quickly came to an understanding that we'd make an offer and they'd accept it. The next day, with snow coming in yet again, we parked up in the nearby town of Pitlochry, settled in for a few days and instructed our solicitor to put in a verbal offer on the property on Loch Rannoch.

The next day was our wedding anniversary and when the offer was accepted, it was the perfect anniversary gift. A few days later, our solicitor phoned to say that the vendors wanted to complete the sale very quickly. We were living in a motorhome, so as far as we were concerned, the quicker the better and we agreed a date just a week-and-a-half away. It seemed nothing short of a miracle. We had waited so long and worked so hard to find somewhere, and now it was all happening unbelievably fast – we would be moving into our new home in just a fortnight.

The next two nights we parked up just outside the village of Kinloch Rannoch near Dunalastair Water. During the Saturday night we heard four or five different owls calling as they flew up and down the river. It was a beautiful and haunting sound. On Sunday morning Peter awoke to the sound of an ambulance going past and soon we both heard the helicopter. I sent out a prayer that no-one was badly hurt. We had breakfast and headed off towards Glen Lyon and the Bridge of Balgie. We couldn't get terribly far up the steep glen because of the snowy driving conditions, but it was beautiful and we enjoyed a peaceful, pleasant day.

On Monday morning we visited the five-thousand year-old yew tree in Fortingall churchyard – purportedly the oldest living being in the world and a very special place for us – at one point in our wedding planning, we'd hoped to be married in Fortingall church. We then walked the river Lyon, revisiting salmon pools where we'd fished in our early years in Scotland. While we were sitting in a fisherman's hut happily reminiscing, the phone rang. It was our solicitor calling to give us some very sad and shocking news. She said that the husband of the couple who were selling the bungalow had died suddenly on Sunday morning. We were devastated. We realised that the ambulance and helicopter we'd heard had been for that lovely man. How very, very sad. As a result, our solicitor informed us, the sale of the property could not therefore proceed as planned.

We had been so sure that this was *it*. This was home. What now? Well – yes, you've guessed it – we paused. We sat by the magnificent river Lyon holding hands as we wept for John, for his family, and for ourselves. We'd believed that the dream was within our grasp only to see it vanish into the Sunday morning mist. We knew that on the deepest level everything was unfolding just exactly as it needed to. Knowing that though didn't remove the sadness and the uncertainty. Clearly, there was more cooking needing to be done. I used to think myself an impatient person. I am no longer. Entering the Majesteria ironed out that particular crease.

The next day we phoned our solicitor so she could explain the situation to us clearly. On hearing the news of John's death, my mind had gone blank and I'd been unable to relate to Peter the details of what had been said. Our solicitor explained that the sale could not proceed until the widow had been 'confirmed' by the High Sheriff as the executor of the estate. She suggested we pause for a few days to consider our options. I smiled softly to myself as I heard her use the word "pause". The sacred pause of menopause: a pause within a pause within a pause... on and on it went. How much deeper did life want us to go?

We headed off to Glen Affric - one of the few well-known places we hadn't yet visited, to take stock. It lived up to its reputation for being one of the most beautiful lochs in Scotland. It's also the place where the charity, *Trees for Life*, have planted a wonderful native forest. The snow was still heavy on the ground and the loch was partly frozen. We parked up for four nights and walked each day. We felt at peace and knew that somehow, despite appearances and the awful shock of an unexpected death, a deeper magic was at work. This far into our journey, we'd learned to trust it. In my journal of our Scottish Adventure, that word: TRUST, appears again and again and again.

We phoned our solicitor to say that we didn't want to pull out of the sale and we asked how best to proceed. The widow, from whom we were buying the house, was relieved to hear that we still wanted to continue with the purchase, and she instructed her solicitor to find a way to ensure that we were protected during the lengthy legal process that inevitably now had to take place. A mutually acceptable contract was drawn up. We were told once again that until the High Sheriff granted 'confirmation' of the widow as executor of her husband's estate, it remained uncertain whether the sale of the house could proceed. It was a sticky position to be in. Our solicitor was clear that if we wanted to pull out and begin looking for a new property, we were free to do so and no-one would be surprised. We chose to hang on in there. This was *it*. We were sure of it. This was our dream home. Surely it was worth the uncertainty and risk? Peter and I decided to move forward and to carry on as if that bungalow would one day be ours. We kept an eye on new properties coming onto the market even so, but nothing could match it.

"I've lived all my life as 'a woman of faith'," I said to Peter, "and I'm not going to stop now."

After Affric we headed to Mull, our sanctuary in times of difficulty. We parked up in a lay-by overlooking the Sound of Mull not far from the fishing village of Tobermory. On the first day while out walking we saw the rare Scottish Crossbill for the first time – a breeding pair were sitting at the top of one of the fir trees. It has a distinctive song and we were thrilled to have stumbled across them.

The next day we set off following a deer track through some ancient oak woods. The track cut close to the cliff edge so that we were looking down on the tops of the trees below us. Suddenly, directly below us we spotted a huge bird perched in one of the trees. It was a white-tailed sea-eagle, which is bigger than the golden eagle, with a wing-span of eight or nine foot. Just sitting, it was over three feet tall. It was absolutely stunning. We hunkered down and watched it through our binoculars.

Then, from behind us, came the cry of another eagle. In response, the perched bird dropped like a bullet from the branch before unfolding its huge wings and soaring out into the Sound of Mull. It was breathtaking. We continued to follow the deer track further into the wood, clinging to the cliff edge, scrabbling on our hands and knees through the undergrowth in the hope of another sighting. Then below us, only about forty-feet away, soared the female whom we'd heard calling. Much larger than the male, she was magnificent.

We wove our way back home through the trees talking in hushed ecstatic whispers; hoping beyond hope for yet another glimpse. From a tree below us, the male flew out once more. This time we spotted the two green tracking tags on his wings. Back at the motorhome I googled 'white-tailed eagles on Mull' on my phone. It turned out that the island was famous for the birds. Mull attracted visitors from all over the world in the hope of seeing one. We'd no idea. It felt like pure gift. That evening we sat outside the motorhome eating our supper and watching the porpoises swim by; humbled and awed by this wondrous miracle that is life.

The next day after breakfast, Peter was sitting in the driver's seat looking at the map. Suddenly he called out my name. I dashed to the front of the motorhome and there she was: the female sea-eagle. She flew directly towards the motorhome, very low and unhurried, only about thirty feet above us. As she flew over us her wingspan filled the windscreen. It was like seeing a pterodactyl and my heart-rate shot up as if with some prehistoric memory. Peter and I both had tears in our eyes. Our hearts were simply full to bursting. She was a sovereign queen: *Majesteria Incarnate*.

Chapter Twenty-Seven

HOMECOMING II – IT'S NOT HAPPENING

We needed the inspiration of seeing Majesteria incarnate because, on leaving Mull, another challenge loomed. The dry-mooring at the marina in Southampton for our boat was about to come to an end and we knew we had to move her. We were given permission to moor her in the cove by the bungalow and we began to organise how to get her from Southampton and onto Loch Rannoch. We hired a boat haulage firm to bring her up. However, the problem was she was too big to launch on the loch. There are very few boats on the loch and the only other boat of similar size was a RIB (rubber inflatable boat) and therefore nowhere near as heavy or with as deep a keel as our boat. *Star of Avalon* weighs in at over two-and-a-half tons.

We consulted with the Loch Rannoch Conservation Association, which has oversight of the loch, and they were helpful but not hopeful. Everyone we spoke to said that it would be impossible to get a boat of her size onto the water. The loch is very shallow at the edges and then plummets to over a hundred and fifty metres. We were stumped. Were we a couple of complete fools? We'd bought the boat before the house and now we were seeking to moor her somewhere we couldn't be certain we'd end up living. There wasn't even a mooring ready for her – we'd have to sink one ourselves. The whole venture seemed foolish and overwhelming.

In typical fashion, we went ahead and booked the boat haulage company anyway. We knew that *Star of Avalon* needed to leave Southampton (if only in fairness to her ever-patient, long-suffering, previous owners), and we wanted her with us in Scotland. We booked an appointment with Loch Tay Marina to discuss a possible mooring for her there. That was expensive but doable, so we knew we had that option in our back pocket. We then met the guy in charge of the moorings and boats at the head of Loch Tay. He too could accommodate us if required. He was a fount of useful information and put us in touch with a company near Edinburgh who could fit out a deep-water mooring for us.

We drove there and discussed options with them. The challenge wasn't just making a deep-water swivel mooring (ground chain, rising chain, mooring and pick-up buoys etc,) – that, they could do easily – but how to get the mooring sunk and fixed securely at the bottom of the loch? They couldn't help with that. It would need a specialist diver. Nor did this solve the problem of how to get *Star of Avalon* actually onto the water. She was coming up from Southampton on a boat trailer so we needed to find somewhere on the loch shallow enough to reverse the trailer into the water safely, but deep enough to get her afloat. So many questions needing an answer – our heads were buzzing. I went everywhere with a little blue notebook in which I jotted down all ideas and suggestions.

Everyone around the loch was interested in our dilemma and eager to help – though it was clear that they all considered the task we'd set ourselves doomed to failure. Peter was lent some chest-waders and we began wading out to find the right depth at the various possible launch sites to which we'd been signposted. We then – in the midst of all this – realised that we needed a tender – a small boat to get us from the shore to the *Star of Avalon,* if and when she was finally launched.

We hunkered down in a little café in the village of Kinloch Rannoch with internet and began to hunt for tenders for sale. There was a suitable one at a sensible price near Macclesfield: an eight-foot fibreglass rowing dingy. Time was running out and these little tenders were selling like hot-cakes. If we wanted her, we couldn't hang around. I messaged the vendors and asked them to hold her for us. I explained that we were going to have to drive five or six hours to reach them, and we didn't want to find she'd been sold before we got there. I reassured them that she seemed exactly what we were looking for, and, although we were buying her unseen, they could be pretty sure of the sale. They kindly agreed and we set off early the next morning.

The boat was perfect. Peter handed over the cash and I named the boat *Puck.* Now, how to get it back to Scotland? The couple from whom we'd bought *Puck* looked at Peter in disbelief.

"You're going to take the boat back *inside* the motorhome?"

Peter had done the measurements and he knew that, in theory, if the rowlocks were removable, the boat should go in through the motorhome's narrow door. I knew Peter. If he said it was possible, then it was possible. They didn't know him. They clearly thought he was mad. The two guys lifted the boat up and turned it onto its side while we two women watched from their front lawn. I have to admit my heart was racing a little. We had no back-up plan if the boat wouldn't fit through the door. We didn't have a trailer and nor would it be possible to fix the boat to the back or on top of the roof. We'd looked.

With a couple of millimetres – literally - to spare, she glided in. Laughing, we shook their hands and headed back towards Scotland. We stopped overnight en route, relieved and exhausted. I've some terrific photos of Peter making breakfast the next morning alongside Puck who *fills* the motorhome's living space. Peter looks very pleased with himself – in fact he looks pretty smug.

Well, that was one piece of the jigsaw puzzle in place. We still needed to have a swivel mooring made, get the mooring fixed onto the loch bottom, and get *Star of Avalon* launched onto the water. We took Puck out in the cove near the bungalow to see what sort of depth was there. Although the depth of Loch Rannoch rises and falls because of the nearby Hydro Power Station, we were hopeful that it might be possible to launch *Star* from the beach by the bungalow. That would be the best spot for us. That way we could avoid having to skipper her from a launch site somewhere along the twelve mile loch to bring her to the bungalow where her mooring would be – we who had never sailed a boat before.

We explained these various challenges to the guy who was collecting her from Southampton and he was blessedly relaxed and unfazed.

"It'll all work out fine," he said in a broad West Country accent. "I'll be out of touch now for the next three weeks while I sail a yacht to her new mooring in France and then I'll be back to collect your boat. Give me a call then with the details of where you want me to bring her. And, don't worry I can skipper her wherever you need her to go. Yeah, and if you can get hold of that telescopic handler you mentioned, that could work. Speak soon."

Golly, I thought, he makes it all sound so easy.

Peter had noticed a telescopic handler near the Hydro Power Station and so he went to have a chat with the guys there. The machine could pick up three tons, so could easily lift *Star of Avalon* off the boat trailer. Moreover, because of its high wheel base, once it had lifted the boat, it could go quite far out into the water without damage – hopefully far enough and deep enough for us to launch.

The idea of seeing *Star* swinging mid-air terrified me, but Peter reassured me that she'd be properly strapped, and if the driver was competent and knew what he was doing, there'd be no problem. If! More ifs! Still, it didn't look as if there was any other way. The guys at the energy station, however, although friendly, were clear that the machine wasn't available for public hire.

Deflated, we began to think that maybe we'd best accept that we'd have to book a mooring on Loch Tay. We drove over to speak again with the guy there. He only had two moorings left for the season, so if we wanted one, we shouldn't leave it too late to let him know. He lent us a depth-spyglass and a couple of life-jackets so we could continue sounding out possible launch sites along Loch Rannoch.

One of our favourite places to park up the motorhome overnight was near Loch Tummel and Peter had noticed a farm plus caravan site nearby with a lot of agricultural machinery. He rightly guessed they'd have a telescopic handler. We walked over and met a couple of members of the family who owned the farm and holiday park. To our delight, they were eager to help and said they had a telescopic handler available we could use. Chatting to the two of them, both so up-beat and positive, we began to think that maybe a launch on Loch Rannoch was going to be do-able after all.

We still needed a mooring made and a way of fixing it to the loch bottom, so I phoned a company in Dundee who specialised in deep-water moorings. They suggested two five-ton concrete blocks to be sunk to ensure the mooring stayed secure. As I've said, Loch Rannoch drops to over a hundred and fifty meters off a steep ledge and we didn't want *Star of Avalon* disappearing into the murky depths. She wouldn't be the first boat to have sunk in the loch. All the locals delighted to share with us their tales of the ship-wreck *Gitania* and the many hidden hazards in the loch – which did nothing to alleviate our anxiety.

The company in Dundee, however, were confident they could sink a secure mooring that wouldn't shift in the high winds that can sweep in from the west coast. They also said that they'd be able to come and fix it *and* they could do it in the time-scale we required. The price was steep but, by now, we were willing to pay whatever it cost. Time was running out, before long *Star* would be on her way from Southampton. I asked them to send me a priced up, scaled drawing of the proposed mooring.

To my horror what landed in my inbox was a hastily hand-drawn sketch of a mooring using two steel wheels filled with concrete to secure it.

"That's rubbish. I could make that myself", Peter spluttered.

There was no way we were going to pay several thousand pounds for something we could make ourselves for a fraction of the cost. When I phoned the guy who had sent the drawing to ask what had become of the two five-ton concrete blocks; it became clear that he also had no idea how we were to get the 'concrete wheels' out and sunk into the water. After I had fired a list of questions at him, to which he had no answers, we never heard back from him.

We were bitterly disappointed. We seemed to be going round and round the houses (or the loch) and getting nowhere. We'd made an appointment that evening with the guy from Loch Tummel to view possible launch sites using his telescopic handler, and we ploughed on with that. Peter had been impressed with him and I sat with fingers (and toes) crossed while they hopped into the guy's van to view possible launch sites.

They were gone a couple of hours while I waited expectantly. Peter came back despondent. The shore line around the loch is mostly soft sand and the guy said it was too dangerous. The weight of the boat on such soft ground would destabilise the telescopic handler and it could tip over. It's a huge machine and that was an accident we didn't want to witness. He shook hands with Peter and said he was sorry he couldn't be any help.

The next day a member of the Loch Rannoch Conservation Association stopped by in the lay-by where we were parked up. He suggested we phone the guy with the RIB who ran the boat tours on the loch. Perhaps he could help?

What a god-send. We met the boat-tour operator a couple of days later and he was straightforward, hopeful and matter-of-fact. He took us to a beach on the north-west shore of the loch.

"This is where I launch my boat from," he said. "Although she's a RIB with no keel, the water's deep enough here for you to launch. I've no doubt about it whatsoever. You'll be fine."

Moreover, he was having a diver coming over from Ireland to check out his own deep-water mooring and he suggested we contact him to see if he would sort ours. He said that he'd known the guy for years and we'd be in safe hands. He then gave us the contact details of the company he'd used to make his own mooring.

"You can check out with the Macdonald resort and see if they'll let you moor your boat temporarily in the marina there, while the deep-water mooring is being sorted. My RIB is usually berthed there, but she's out the water having maintenance, so there'd be room there for yours until your mooring's done. How does that sound?"

It sounded fantastic. I was straight on the phone and made all the arrangements. The boat-tour operator apologised that he'd be working away on the day of the launch, but suggested we speak to a local farmer to ask if he could be available with a tractor - just in case rain made it impossible for our boat haulier to reverse the trailer down to the launch site over the soft ground. The farmer was willing to help but on the day of the launch he was going to be away in Inverness. It looked like we'd have to do it on our own. Nothing new there.

"Where are you launching from?" he asked.

We told him.

"Oh you'll never get three foot of water from that beach," he said.

Our hearts sank.

"It's fine to get the RIB afloat, but you'd never manage it with something bigger. Have you tried the LRCA place near the Power Station? That's where they launch their fishing boats."

We explained that, yes, we'd looked at the Loch Rannoch Conservation Association launch site, and at about a dozen others, and this was our only hope.

"Well, I wish all the best for ye," he concluded. "We'll be back from Inverness around tea-time and if I see a great lumbering boat capsized on the shore-line, I'll be straight down with the tractor to give ye a hand."

His eyes twinkled and he gave Peter a firm handshake.

"Well, one thing's for sure," I said to Peter as we walked back down the farm track towards the motorhome.

"What's that?"

"That quiet, discreet entrance into our new life on Loch Rannoch ain't gonna happen."

He guffawed.

"Yup," he concurred. "Everyone hereabouts has heard of us now and we haven't even moved in."

"The good thing is that everyone we've met so far has been really kind and helpful. We wouldn't have found that out if we hadn't had to struggle like this to bring the *Star of Avalon* here."

"Well, that's one way of looking at it, I guess," he said. "They must think we're crazy."

I smiled.

"Probably a good thing. Otherwise, we'd be a terrible disappointment to them."

He laughed again and squeezed my hand. The nightmare which had kept us awake at night seemed to be drawing to a close. Everything was lining up nicely. The mooring was being made to our exact specification; the diver was booked; the RIB would carry the mooring out; and until then, *Star of Avalon* would be moored at the decommissioned marina at the Macdonalds resort. The pieces of the impossible jigsaw were falling finally into place.

Chapter Twenty-Eight

HOMECOMING III – IT IS DONE

The day before the launch we parked the motorhome near the Power Station so we had phone signal, and were relieved when a message pinged through from her previous owners to say the boat was safely loaded and had left the boat-yard in Southampton. She should arrive by lunchtime the following day. We couldn't believe it. The *Star of Avalon* was on her way. Six months after we'd bought her, she was at last coming to join us in – what we hoped and trusted would eventually be - our new home.

The day of the launch arrived and we awoke early full of the jitters. Over breakfast Peter began to list all the things that could go wrong. I held up my hand to stop him.

"We've kept faith with her, this far," I said. "Whatever happens today, at some point she's going to be bobbing happily in the cove outside the bungalow. That's been our dream, and it's going to happen."

"And so it is," he replied with a wink.

The boat haulier, William, had kept in touch as he drove her up through England and across the Scottish border. The route north of Glasgow was straightforward following the A9. We'd checked out the various routes once he left the A9 because the roads became narrow and, around Loch Tummel, busy with coach loads of tourists. We'd decided the best way was to avoid that and follow the quieter road from Pitlochry towards Blair Atholl, which involved going under a narrow bridge in the hamlet of Struan. The boat plus trailer was slightly wider than the motorhome, but Peter judged they'd just squeeze through. William, in his customary relaxed fashion, agreed also.

We were mightily relieved, however, when he phoned to confirm he had safely arrived at the east end of the loch in Kinloch Rannoch and had stopped for a quick cuppa in the village. We said we'd meet him by the Power Station, seven miles further on, and would guide him to the launch site. It was a terrific feeling seeing the boat come round the corner and William pulling up. I had tears in my eyes. So much had happened since we'd left Wales, driven to the south of England and bought her. She'd been the guiding star on our journey, and now she was here. Here, but not yet launched on the water. The biggest challenge was yet to come.

We jumped into William's car and drove to the beach where we hoped to launch. The day was fine with no sign of rain. All boded well. William kept up a breezy chatter and was consummately relaxed and confident. He'd been launching boats for thirty years and although this was the remotest place from which he'd launched one, he said, it wasn't the worst by far. He reversed the trailer down the beach and into the water.

Once he was ready, I put on my life-jacket and climbed aboard. I was needed to direct William along the loch to the marina. Peter stood on the beach and held onto the mooring rope. William put on his chest-waders and heaved at the boat to loosen her off the trailer. There were no rollers, so brute force was called for.

"Peter," William shouted, "Whatever you do, don't let go of the rope."

He shoved again. Alone on the boat, I watched the two men at work. One more heave and the boat would float clear.

"Peter," I shouted, "Whatever you do, don't let go of the rope!"

"Yup. I heard it the first time," he shouted back, strong hands clenched tightly around the thick rope.

The boat broke free and, caught by the water, pulled away sharply. Peter was yanked forward into the water up to his thighs, muscles straining, as he clung to the end of the rope.

William got quickly out of his waders and into his deck shoes, and climbed aboard.

"I can't hold her!" Peter yelled.

"Okay. Let her go," William commanded as he started up the engines.

And we pulled away from the shore.

As Peter turned away to walk the two miles back to the Bessacar, an osprey hurtled down from the sky into the loch. It appeared a few moments later with a huge silver fish in its talons. The sign could not have been more propitious. We'd done it.

"Right, you can take her from here, Melanie."

I opened my mouth in astonishment, but since William had already let go of the wheel and was proceeding to get himself comfortable at the front of the boat, I had no choice but to comply.

"It'll do you good to get the feel of the boat," William said. "I'm just going to give my wife a call."

I gulped. There was quite a high wind and it was choppy. I'd never sailed a motor cruiser before. I reminded myself that she was our boat and this was what all the stress and effort had been for – to sail her here on Loch Rannoch.

I lifted my chin and set course with the lovely mountain, Shiehallion, up ahead, dead centre of the prow where William perched chatting on the phone. Within a few minutes, I was loving it. Absolutely loving it. I grinned from ear to ear. *Star of Avalon* held a steady course up the loch and rode the waves with ease. Now, I understood why Peter had chosen us a substantial and sturdy sea-going vessel. She was safe. An hour later William took over just before we entered the harbour. Peter pulled up in the motorhome and came running down to meet us. We'd managed to arrive before him.

Star of Avalon remained at the Macdonalds marina for the next two weeks. We took her out a couple of times but didn't venture too far. We then heard the good news that we had permission to move into the bungalow as tenants while the legal process continued to move slowly towards completion. It was time.

On May 13th 2018 we collected the keys and parked the motorhome on the driveway. It would be a couple more weeks before the removal firm could deliver our furniture from Wales, but we were content to continue to sleep in the Bess. She'd been our comfortable home for nine months, and we felt no rush to leave her.

A week after we'd moved into the bungalow (or, at least into the garden), the mooring specialist arrived from Ireland. With the RIB carrying the hefty gear, the deep-water mooring was set in the cove by the house. We were almost there. It was time for us to bring *Star of Avalon* home from the marina. I skippered her the seven miles across the loch. Approaching the mooring for the first time was nail-bitingly nerve-wracking. Peter's job was to grab the pick-up buoy from the water and secure the boat to the mooring while I held her steady. We managed it without a hitch. I then changed into my wet suit, swam to the shore, collected Puck and rowed her back to *Star of Avalon* where Peter was waiting ready to come ashore. That evening we sat in our living-room and watched our boat bobbing on her mooring, in the cove, outside our new home. We'd done it. We'd flipping well done it. We had kept faith. We were HOME.

Two weeks after we'd moved into the bungalow, the removal lorry arrived from Aberystwyth with all our furniture and worldly belongings. It was nice to see them again. It had been a long time. Twelve weeks after we'd moved in as tenants, we received the good news that the High Sherriff had confirmed that the widow was the executor of her husband's estate and therefore the sale could proceed.

On the 15th August 2018 – six months after the original date – our home became legally ours. Our move from Wales to Scotland had taken a year. We had ended up in the perfect place – and it looked nothing like the idea of the dream-place with which we had set out on our Scottish Adventure. God/Goddess/Life had had some fun with us, for sure, along the way.

Before I conclude this story and step off the roller-coaster that carried me across the threshold into my Majesteria years, I want to take you on one final ride. Make sure you're strapped in tightly because this ride defies gravity and shoots upwards high enough to reach right into the heavens. Let me tell you about my StarChild vision.

Chapter Twenty-Nine

THE STARCHILD VISION

One night, about half way through the menopausal journey of entering the Majesteria, I awoke with a migraine. It was bad but not severe and I lay quietly while the pain flowed through. I began to hear the beautiful singing which sometimes accompanies a numinous experience. I opened my eyes and in the centre of the blind spot, I could see the outline of a figure moving towards me. Around it an aura of rainbow-coloured light flickered and pulsed.

At first I thought it was an angel but as it got closer, I recognised it was me. This wasn't me at one particular age, however, this was all the ages of Melanie somehow held within a single form. Thirty, or forty, or fifty images flickered simultaneously before my eyes like an incandescent transparent Babushka doll.

I was filled with a deep love for her and an overwhelming sense of peace. She hovered close to the bed and spoke to me.

"I'm your soul," she said. "I'm StarChild."

She settled as the image of a very old Melanie – in her nineties perhaps - and then transmitted to me a very detailed body of work that I was to undertake during the remainder of my lifetime: website, online offerings, retreat programmes, this book, a children's story series, it went on and on. She finished the transmission by giving me a vision of our true destiny as Earthlings.

Everything she told me confirmed the deep truths I already knew - some of which I'd gleaned through my love of the Christian Mysteries (not to be confused with the out-dated doctrines of the church) - and which are shared by, and known to, mystics of every spiritual lineage and in every age.

What I hadn't known, and what surprised me, was her revelation about planet Earth. It contradicted the popular notion (which I'd sort of half-accepted) that conscious pseudo-human life occurs elsewhere – and is possibly replicated in other galaxies and sun-star systems. StarChild told me that this planet is unique. This recollection is based upon words I recorded in my dream-diary.

"Everything shares one true nature. This one true nature is the source, the expression and the end-point of all being - and all beings, including the human-being. This one true nature is most easily experienced and described by the human-being in the word 'love'. On planet Earth, and only on this planet, the great mystery which is life has chosen a very particular way to express its true nature. For this and for this alone, the human-being evolved."

StarChild paused and I waited expectantly. Her words echoed familiar words I knew from St Paul's letter to the people of Philippi in the Bible.

"Love," she said, "emptied itself of its true nature as love, in order to experience what it's like to *find* or to *become* love. The gift which was given to allow this unfolding to occur is human free-will: the freedom to *choose* love."

"And its corollary, the freedom to choose not to love", I added.
StarChild slowly nodded.

"All creation waits with bated breath to see whether the human-being will, in the end, choose to become love," she said. "Time is running out for planet Earth because of the damage that's been done to her. And that's why so many in the unseen realms have now come to our aid."

She held out her hand and in her palm I saw a tiny Earth rotating slowly.

"Her true name," StarChild told me, "is the Blue Jewel. She is precious and loved within all the realms of being because she is *free*. This Blue Jewel is intended to be set within the crown of creation: the place where love freely *chose* to be love."

I was suddenly afraid.

"What if humanity fails?" I asked. "What if we carry on as we are, choosing to do harm to the planet rather than choosing to protect her?"

"Then this dance will come to an end," StarChild said sadly. "This will truly become the Age of Extinction. Humanity will have chosen to become extinct rather than choosing to become love. And there will be no Blue Jewel in the crown of creation.

All the dimensions and aeons of time, and all the realms of manifest being, from which this planet has been so intricately and carefully woven and spun into orbit, *everything*, will fall into silence. The Deep-water-Dreaming that is planet Earth, will be over."

"But love cannot die," I whispered.

StarChild paused. I waited for her reassurance and when none came, I said again, though a little more emphatically,

"Love cannot die. That's the truth upon which I've based my entire life. It's the hope I've held out at every funeral. It's what I *know*, deep inside me – love is the unbreakable diamond at the centre of existence."

StarChild smiled softly and I felt myself grow hot and uncomfortable.

"Am I wrong?" I asked, "Is this just me wanting a happy-ever-after ending?

"In this great unfolding that is planet Earth, and in her unique expression, the human-being, we cannot know the outcome. This is the mystery. Will love choose the beloved? Will the beloved choose love? If we knew the ending, then where would be the freedom? It'd be a farce, wouldn't it? It'd be just pretence, a show - a mere performance - that's all. It wouldn't be *love*. For it to be love – true love – it must risk everything."

"Everything?"

"Everything. In being true to its nature, how could love offer less than true love? There is no other way."

I nodded. I felt I wanted to weep.

"But how could love risk everything like this? It's complete folly. If the human-being fails to choose to become love then all is lost. What a waste. What a total and utter waste."

She tilted her head to one side.

"Ah, I think you've answered your own question, Melanie. If the human-being fails to choose to become love then all is lost," she said, echoing my words, "so if the human-being ..."

"Of course!" I exploded. "If the human-being chooses love, all is saved!"

She grinned at me.

"But surely, StarChild, it can't be enough for just one person to choose love? Surely it requires each and every one of us to choose love?"

She shrugged her shoulders.

"I don't know. I'm your soul – just one tiny soul, Melanie - I didn't create the story. And, as I said, it's a story that's never been told before, so how can we know the ending?"

I smiled back at her.

"That feels right, though doesn't it?" I said. "That feels right. And it's actually what all human spiritual traditions say – that when one person is 'enlightened' or 'saved' or whatever, then everyone is. And, of course, it's what the Christian Mysteries point towards too. The church proclaims it too, though admittedly in an old-fashioned clunky way, when it preaches about one man dying on the Cross in an act of love to 'redeem' the sins of the world. Yeshua's story is trying to show us that one person's act of love is equivalent to the whole of humanity enacting, becoming, choosing - love."

"Could be," she smiled. "It's a lovely thought, for sure - that one human heart contains all love."

"My head hurts," I said and we both burst out laughing.

We yawned loudly and I could feel her fading, fading back into me.

"Good night, StarChild," I said sleepily. "And thank you."

"You're welcome. Sleep well."

And I did.

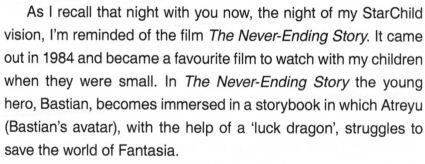

As I recall that night with you now, the night of my StarChild vision, I'm reminded of the film *The Never-Ending Story*. It came out in 1984 and became a favourite film to watch with my children when they were small. In *The Never-Ending Story* the young hero, Bastian, becomes immersed in a storybook in which Atreyu (Bastian's avatar), with the help of a 'luck dragon', struggles to save the world of Fantasia.

Towards the end of the story it becomes clear that the only person who can save Fantasia is Bastian himself. He must believe in the power he has within himself to save an entire world. In order to believe in himself and to tap that latent source of power, he must let go of all the ideas he has about himself: that he is a powerless, helpless, little boy who is *outside* the story as merely an impotent observer. In reality, he is utterly intertwined with the story and its outcome is dependent upon his acceptance of that. He doesn't want the responsibility - who does? To make or break an entire world is a weighty destiny to shoulder. But shoulder it he must if Fantasia is not to fall into eternal darkness and silence and be consumed by 'the Nothing'.

It seems to me that our journey across the threshold into our majesterial years is not that dissimilar. We have to unlearn who we think we are. We have to demonstrate tremendous fortitude and bravery and love. We have to move from the place of outside observer into the place of co-creator. We have to shoulder the co-responsibility for making or breaking our world. And we have to tap into a source of tremendous power within ourselves and offer it in the service of our planet. It's a big ask.

It's an especially big ask when the world around you is telling you that as a middle-aged woman, you're 'past your best', and that you're 'dried out and washed up'. It's tough to believe in the best, biggest, boldest, version of yourself when you're facing divorce, or redundancy, or an empty nest, after you've devoted your (so-called) best years to the rearing of youngsters. Mid-life women are surrounded by messages that tell us that 'it's all downhill from now' - saggy breasts, shrivelled skin, parched vaginas. No wonder so many mid-life women feel depressed and passed their best.

My hope is that my menopausal story will be an encouragement to you not to listen to those siren voices. I'm utterly convinced that the best is yet to come. And so, I invite you, if it appeals and if you feel drawn, to come with me across the threshold and enter the Majesteria. I've no idea what that will mean for you. I've no idea what you will look like or sound like. What clothes you will wear, or how you'll choose to name yourself, or whether your hair will turn grey or blue or red or purple. I simple know I'd very much welcome your company.

My menopausal story draws to a close. From our living room window I can see our boat, *Star of Avalon*, bobbing on the loch. Like my facial tattoo, she symbolises so much. For me and Peter, *Star of Avalon* is the dream towards which we were reaching, and which will carry us into an as yet unseen future. She's been our anchor and our compass. If we hadn't bought the boat before we bought the house, goodness only knows where we would have ended up. We knew we needed somewhere for our boat first and foremost. This is what we kept coming back to as we looked at property after property.

Several times during the nine month 'pause' between homes, while we were travelling on the road in the Bessacar, I checked out with Peter if he was still clear that having the boat was necessary. He never faltered. In spite of his great fear of deep water, he knew that the boat represented something *new*, something he hadn't even known he wanted, until he found her.

It's early days. We've only been in our new home a few months and we're still very much novices when it comes to sailing. My hunch, however, is that this boat will do for Peter what the horses do for me – make him 'work' his fear. I think that's why she's here. He thinks so too – but that's a story for another book. Suffice to say here, our boat, *Star of Avalon*, like our very own north star, guided us all the way through our travels until we safely arrived home. We owe her a deep bow of gratitude.

I cannot remember ever feeling as free as I do now – except perhaps as a small child. Interestingly, during the nine months we spent travelling in the Bessacar, I got back in touch with many childhood memories that I'd forgotten – happy memories of times spent with my older sisters and with my parents. Somehow in remembering those lost times – before my parents' divorce and before witnessing domestic violence – my 'lost' teenage years have been returned to me as well.

I see Melanie, the teenager, and I know she's at peace. She's enjoying having two baby sisters to delight in, and she's enjoying the friendship of a young step-mother. My older sisters are here too – and my beautiful Mummy. We're all home. This isn't a fantasy – it's my Deep-water Dreaming. This is sacred space, holy space – where soul-medicine has worked her magic. I feel I've done a full circle. I've returned to an inner place which I thought I'd lost forever. I've returned home after a long, long journey. And I am changed.

I look behind me towards the glitzy roller-coaster ride called 'The Change of Life'. Gaudy music blares in the background as the wurlitzers spin. I hear the laughter, the shouts and the squealing screams. I smell the popcorn and the candy floss. I can still taste the hot dog with onions. I look back. I remember. But I belong there no longer. The gate has closed. The journey is done. I face forward into a new future. I stand in a new country and breathe in the sweetly fragrant, softly musky air. I am a sovereign Autumn Queen. The high priestess of my own soul: Swimming Forest Seer. I am Melanie Santorini - Wild Woman Walking.

Afterword

I hope that the story of my menopausal journey through the seven years it took me to enter the Majesteria, has energised and inspired you to view 'The Change' differently. If this book has encouraged you to regard menopause more positively than before, then I'll have achieved what I set out to do. If you cease to tolerate disparaging comments about 'senior moments' and dismissive comments such as 'I'm just being menopausal', I'll be pleased. If you share with other women, including your daughters and grandmothers, your thrill at finding yourself entering your own majesterial years, I'll be over-the-moon.

I'm creating a workbook-journal to accompany this volume. It'll be a way to record and reflect upon your own menopausal journey. It'll also offer guidelines for setting up your own *Majesteria* circle of elder-women in your local community. I'm all in favour of on-line circles of women (and belong to several), but nothing is as powerful as sitting in circle with your sisters in the flesh – smelling her fear, smelling her perfume, smelling her sweat. I find it's harder to hide and easier to detect bullshit when physically face-to-face. I hope you find both the volumes useful. If you don't, please pass them on to someone else who might. We're all very different in how we approach and navigate

The Change of Life, which is exactly as it should be. The forest floor is littered with many, many different sorts of leaves. The *Majesteria* workbook-journal will be available in the autumn of 2019, and you'll be able to order a copy from my website www.melaniesantorini.org.

> With love and
> in remembrance of Her,
> Melanie x

Appendix 1

MELANIE'S
MENOPAUSAL PORRIDGE

I made this porridge daily for breakfast during the last year of menopause. It's exactly what my body needed and I wish I'd started earlier.

Adapt it to create your own tasty power-start to the day.

If you want to cut down the preparation time, plus bump up the nutritional potential even further, get your ingredients ready the night before because the benefits hidden in seeds and berries are enhanced by soaking.

- 1 tsp each of quinoa, chia seeds, pumpkin/sunflower/ sesame seeds, goji berries, ground flaxseed, shelled hemp seed, coconut oil, honey
- ½ tsp each ground turmeric, cardamom, cinnamon, ginger
- Ground black pepper to taste

Mix together all the above in a saucepan, cover with water and cook until quinoa is ready (10-15 minutes), stirring occasionally.

While the porridge is cooking mix together in your favourite bowl:

- 1 tsp maca powder
- 1 tsp ashwaganda powder
- 1 tsp desiccated coconut
- Fresh organic berries if you can get them

Mix together all the ingredients, pour over some hemp milk, add a generous dollop of live yoghurt or home-made kefir, take a couple of deep breaths, remember to soften and relax your belly, give thanks, smile and enjoy.

May your day abound with blessing for our world.

Appendix 2

MELANIE'S MAJESTERIA PRACTISE: A YONI STEAM BATH

In the workbook-journal that accompanies this book, there are several suggestions to help you create your own *Majesteria* ceremonies. Here, however, I want to share with you just one – my favourite.

- Clean your toilet. Make sure the bowl, with the seat raised is thoroughly clean – sufficiently clean to sit naked upon; or ensure your bidet is sparkling clean (a simple solution of vinegar and/or baking powder is better than harsh chemical cleaning products).
- Find a basin that will sit snugly inside your toilet bowl or you can use the bidet as it is.
- Grab a clean bath towel and leave ready near the toilet or bidet.
- Go into your garden and gather favourite fragrant herbs: mine include, rosemary, sage, thyme, bay and mint.
- Feel them, smell them, be *aware* of them (wee little silent light-beings)

- If you don't have fresh herbs, you can use dried herbs, but the freshly picked are best
- In a saucepan gently place bunches of your herbs. Bruise the leaves to release the oils and cover with water
- Add your favourite petals: mine include, rose, lavender, marigold, nasturtium
- 1 drop of tea-tree oil
- If you have no fresh or dried herbs, you can use essential oils – but be careful, they are potent. 1 drop of each will suffice and check for skin sensitivity beforehand
- Boil and allow the fragrance to fill the space
- Meanwhile, prepare yourself: undress and cover yourself with a bathrobe; light a candle, sit quietly and meditate, or lie flat on your back on the floor, or listen to Peruqois and sound an emotion that's calling to you, or chant, or boogie to music, or drum, or shriek, shrill and shake - whatever gets you inside your own skin
- When you're ready, pour the contents of the saucepan into the basin and carry through to your bathroom
- Disrobe and wait until some of the steam from the bowl has evaporated sufficiently to cool a little
- It wants to be hot enough but not too hot (your yoni is very delicate skin so be careful not to scald her)
- Lower yourself carefully over the bowl with your legs straddled either side of the toilet bowl or bidet and sit
- Wrap the towel around your middle to keep in the steam
- Talk to her, if you wish, and listen to her reply. Your yoni carries a lot of your herstory: menstruation, sex, childbirth etc.
- Be aware of the different parts that make up your yoni: labia, clitoris, vagina, cervix, womb-space, ovaries (and

include awareness of your anus – honouring our own 'shit' is important)

- Take your time
- When you're finished, wrap yourself back up in your bathrobe.
- Empty the contents of the bowl onto the earth (if possible) and relax, or journal, or get dressed, and get on with your day.

Acknowledging and honouring our essentially female body-parts in this way can be very healing. It also super-charges them so be aware of how you feel (in your ovaries, cervix, womb, vagina, genitalia, anus) as your day unfolds. Record the experience, if you wish, in your *Majesteria* journal.

May this practise bring you blessing and the deepest well-being.

Bibliography

I'm an avid reader so rather than an exhaustive list, I've included here only the books that travelled with me on my journey through the menopausal gateway, and which I've carried across over the threshold into my majesterial years. There are some wonderful thinkers and writers here, all of whom have nourished and energised me along the way. I'm deeply grateful to them all. Enjoy.

Aron, Elaine, *The Highly Sensitive Person* (London, 1999).

Atwood, M & Robert Weaver eds. *The Oxford Book of Canadian Short Stories in English* (Toronto, 1984).

Adyashanti, *Resurrecting Jesus: Embodying the Spirit of a Revolutionary Mystic* (Boulder, 2014).

Ash, Steven, *Sacred Drumming*, (Hampshire, 2001).

Berryman, Jerome, *Teaching Godly Play: How to mentor the spiritual development of children* (Denver, 2009).

Blackie, Sharon, *If Women Rose Rooted: The Journey to Authenticity and Belonging* (London, 2016).

Borax, Mark and Elias Lonsdale, *Cosmic Weather Report: Notes from the edge of the Universe* (Berkeley, 2010).

Bourgeault, Cynthia, *The Meaning of Mary Magdalene: Discovering the Woman at the Heart of Christianity* (Boston, 2011).

Brown, Brené, *Braving the Wilderness: the quest for true belonging and the courage to stand alone* (London, 2017).

Calder F. ed. *Nisga'a: People of the Naas River* (Toronto, 1993).

Catton, William, *Overshoot* (Illinois, 1982).

Eardley, Laura, *The Jade Egg: Dynamic pelvic floor exercises and vaginal weight lifting* (Boston, 2014).

Edwards, Gill, *Conscious Medicine: Creating health and well-being in a conscious universe* (London, 2012).

Feinstein, David, Donna Eden and Gary Craig, *The Healing Power of EFT & Energy Psychology* (London, 2005).

Fenwick, Elizabeth and Peter, *The Art of Dying* (London, 2008)

Griffiths, Jay, *Wild: An Elemental Journey* (London, 2007).

Harding, Esther, *Woman's Mysteries: Ancient and Modern* (New York, 1976).

Hay, Louise, *The Bone Broth Secret* (London, 2016).

Horrigan, Bonnie, *Red Moon Passage: The Power and Wisdom of Menopause* (London, 1996).

Hyman, Mark, *The Ten-day Blood Sugar De-tox* (London, 2014).

Jenkins, J. *The Human Manure Handbook* (Toronto, 1999).

Klein, Naomi, *This Changes Everything: Capitalism vs the Climate* (London, 2017).

Knight, Peter, *Stolen Images: Pagan Symbolism and Christianity* (Wiltshire, 2015).

Kolanov, Linda, *The Tao of Equus* (New York, 2001).

Krystal, Phyllis, *Cutting the ties that bind: growing up and moving on* (New York, 1986).

Lonsdale, Elias, *The Christ Letters: An Evolutionary Guide Home* (Berkeley, 2012).

Mason Dodd, Kerry, *Sunlight in the Shadows; the landscape of Emily Carr* (Toronto, 1984).

McCartney, Margaret, *Living with Dying: finding care and compassion at the end of life* (London, 2014).

Meisenbach Boylan, Kristi, *The Seven Sacred Rites of Menopause: The Spiritual Journey to the Wise-Woman Years* (Santa Monica, 2000).

Meyer, Marvin and James Robinson, *The Complete Nag Hammadi Scriptures* (New York 2008).

-----, *The Gospels of Mary* (New.York, 2012).

Monbiot, George, *Feral: rewilding the land, sea and human life* (London, 2014).

Myss, Caroline, *Anatomy of the Spirit* (London, 1997).

-----, *Why People Don't Heal and How They Can* (London, 1998).

----- and Norman Shealy, *The Creation of Health* (London, 1999).

-----, *Sacred Contracts* (London, 2001).

Normandin, C. ed. *Echoes of the Elders: The Stories and Paintings of Chief Lelooska* (New York, 1996).

Northrup, Christiane, *Women's Bodies, Women's Wisdom* (London, 1998)

-----, *The Wisdom of Menopause: Creating Physical and Emotional Health during the Change* (New York, 2012).

Penn, W.S. ed. *The Telling of the World: Native American Stories and Art* (New York, 1984).

Richardson, Diana, *The Heart of Tantric Sex* (Hants, 2008).

-----, *Tantric Orgasm for Women* (Rochester, 2004).

Roberts, Bernadette, *The Path to No-self: Life at the Center* (New York, 1991).

-----, *The Experience of No-Self: A Contemplative Journey* (New York, 1993).

-----, *What is Self?: A Study of the Spiritual Journey in terms of Consciousness* (Boulder, 2005).

-----, *The Real Christ* (unpublished manuscript, 2011).

Rosas, Debbie and Carlos, *The NIA Technique* (New York, 2004).

Sharkey, John, *Celtic Mysteries* (London, 1975).

Shinoda Bolen, Jean, *Goddesses in Older Women: Archetypes in Women over Fifty* (N ewYearr, 2001).

Sierra, Claire, *The Magdalene Path* (Bloomington, 2014).

Stauguard-Jones, Jo Ann, *The Vital Psoas Muscle: Connecting physical, emotional and spiritual well-being* (Chichester, 2012).

Stone, Merlin, *When God Was A Woman* (New York, 1978).

Tolle, Eckhart, *The Power of Now: A Guide to Spiritual Enlightenment* (London, 2005).

Walker, Barbara, *The Woman's Encyclopaedia of Myths and Secrets* (London, 1983).

-----, *The Woman's Dictionary of Symbols and Sacred Objects* (London, 1988).

-----, *The Crone: Woman of Age, Wisdom and Power* (New York, 1985).

Warner, Felicity, *A Safe Journey Home: A simple guide to achieving a peaceful death* (London, 2008).

-----, *The Soul Midwives' Handbook: The Holistic and Spiritual Care of the Dying* (London, 2013).

Weed, Susan, *New Menopausal Years: the wise woman's way* (New York, 2002).

Wienrich, Stephanie and Josefine Speyer, *The Natural Death Handbook* (London, 2003).